The Global Master Bakers Cookbook

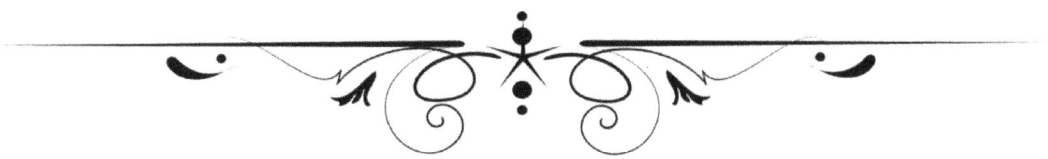

An Outstanding Collection of Recipes from Master Bakers Around

the World Including Jimmy's World-Famous Conger Loaf

Jimmy Griffin Jury President – Coupe du Monde de la Boulangerie 2016

The Global Master Bakers Cookbook

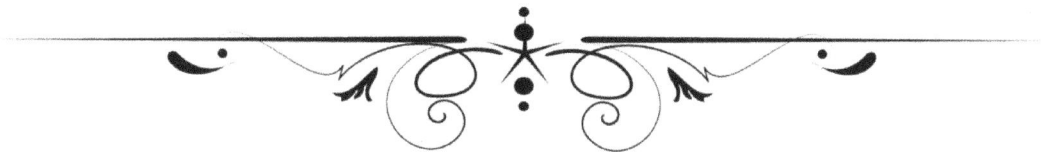

An Outstanding Collection of Recipes from Master Bakers Around

the World Including Jimmy's World-Famous Conger Loaf

Jimmy Griffin

Barna Caf Publications

Copyright © 2021 by Jimmy Griffin All rights reserved. No part of this book may be reproduced, transmitted, or stored digitally or otherwise, in any manner, including photocopying, recording, and imaging without written permission of Jimmy Griffin Publications. For permission to reprint material, contact Jimmy Griffin at griffjimmy@gmail.com.

When quoting material under Fair Use exemptions, please use the following citation:

Griffin, J. (2021). *The global master bakers cookbook. An Outstanding collection of recipes from master bakers around the world, including Jimmy's world-famous conger loaf* (1st ed.). Jimmy Griffin Publications.

Published by
Barna Caf Publications
Wild Winds, Forramoyle West
Barna, Co Galway
Ireland. H91 XHY7

Website: http://jimmyg.ie
YouTube: http://www.youtube.com/c/JimmyGriffinbaking/
Instagram: @jimmyg51

Editor
Susan Hueck
Cook International
Document Development Services
1418 Diamond Lane
El Cajon, CA 92021, USA
susan@cook-int.com

First edition May 2021

ISBN - 978-1-8381082-5-0

Dedication

I dedicate this book to my beloved wife Bogna, who has been unfaltering always in her encouragement and belief in me to pursue my goals, dreams, and wishes; to my son Dillon and daughters Janice and Sophie, who are always there to support me and make me laugh (and sometimes cry); and my brother Mark for supporting me and always having my back.

I salute and thank all the wonderful people who have contributed to this publication and made it possible. Without my friends' contributions from the global bakery world, this book wouldn't have been possible. In particular, I also want to mention my wonderful editor Susan Hueck for her unfaltering help, guidance, attention to detail and encouragement these past 6 months.

Remembering Patricia Carrick, who sadly lost her battle with cancer in 2020 and left this world all too soon. She is survived by her loving husband Damien and young family. In her honour, 10% of the profits from the sale of this book, for the life of its publication, will be divided and contributed to two local cancer care organizations: Galway Hospice and Cancer Care West, both of which provide amazing services to cancer patients in the West of Ireland and which provided expert care to Patricia during her illness.

Acknowledgements

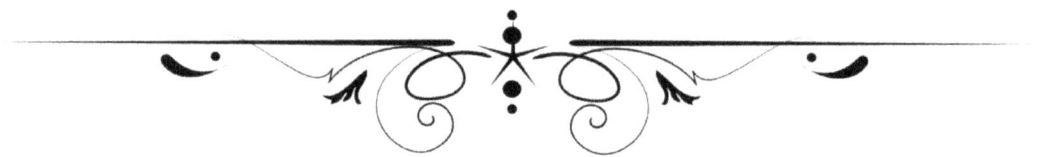

A book not only reflects an author's interests and passions, but it also provides a glimpse into the circumstances and experiences that have influenced their life. Often, and certainly the case for me, a critical component of those experiences is people. Many people have played an integral role in influencing me to write this book in my professional life. Apart from the masters who have generously given their time, energy, and recipes to this project, there are others to acknowledge.

I'm eternally grateful to Christian Vabret and Nathalie Bruiel from CDM de la Boulangerie for selecting me as a jury member for mostly all of the most important bakery competitions throughout the world in 2002. Christian's vision for the CDM de la Boulangerie competition has elevated the standards of baking globally beyond anything ever imagined. As a juror, I had a grandstand view of the master bakers and pastry chefs, which made me one of the very few people ever to get to so closely watch and learn from the world's best bakers. Through these experiences, I educated myself in their ways and methods. I truly have been inspired by each and every one of them.

I also must acknowledge Corinne Lesaffre and Nadine Debail of the Lesaffre Group, without whom none of the CDM de la Boulangerie competitions would ever have taken place. Their decades-long sponsorship and support of bakers worldwide have been generous, thorough, and without compromise. Their heavy investment in people has enabled many aspiring bakers and pastry chefs to pursue excellence and achieve greatness. I'm fortunate and will forever be thankful to have been chosen to participate in this amazing journey of world-class baking.

Table of Contents

Dedication v
Acknowledgements vi
Table of Contents vii
Preface 1
Forward 3
Introduction 5

Section 1 First Things First 6
    Scales 6
    Flour 7
        Milling Flour 7
        Extraction Rates, Ash Content, and Protein Content 7
        Common Flour Types 8
    Yeast 11
    Desired Dough Temperature 11
    Bread Making 13
        Stage 1. Scaling the Ingredients 13
        Stage 2. Mixing/Combining Ingredients 13
        Stage 3. Bulk Fermentation/First Resting 14
        Stage 4. Stretching and Folding/Degassing 14
        Stage 5. Scaling/Weighing the Dough 15
        Stage 6. Preshaping 15
        Stage 7. Intermediate Proofing 16

    Stage 8. Final Shaping...16
    Stage 9. Final Proofing...17
    Stage 10. Scoring...17
    Stage 11. Baking the Bread...18
    Stage 12. Adding Steam 19
    Stage 13. Purging the Steam 19
    Stage 14. Removing the Bread from the Oven...19
    Stage 15. Cooling...20

Section 2 Recipes from Master Bakers 21
  Bread & Buns 21
    Fernando de Oliveira (Brazil)...22
    Alan Dumonceaux (Canada)..27
    Mario Fortin (Canada)...33
    Marcus Mariathas (Canada)...36
    Wang Li (China) 40
    Ibrahim Mohamed Ghoush (Egypt)..45
    David Bedu (France)..48
    Jean Claude Choquet, Meilleur Ouvrier De France (France) 52
    Sébastien Lagrue, World Champion Chocolatine 2019 (France)..................56
    Déborah Ott-Libs, World Champion Viennoiserie 2018 (France)...............59
    Christian Vabret, Meilleur Ouvrier de France (France) 62
    Pierre Zimmermann, World Champion 1996 (France & United States) 64
    Tobias Exner (Germany) 67
    Max Kugel (Germany)..71
    Bernd Kütscher (Germany)...75
    Daníel Kjartan Ármannsson (Iceland) 78
    Robert Humphries, World Champion 2006 IBA Cup (Ireland) 81
    JP McMahon, Michelin Star Chef (Ireland) 84
    Jimmy Griffin, World Silver Medallist Chocolatine 2019 (Ireland) 86
    Derek O'Brien (Ireland) 100
    Dario Bertarini (Italy) 103
    Piergiorgio Giorilli (Italy) 105
    Japan Home Baking School (Japan)..108
    Antonio Arias Ordóñez (México) 110
    Peter Bienefelt, World Champion 2018 (Netherlands) 114
    Anna Gribanova (Russia) 117
    Haif Hakim (Senegal) 120
    Judy Koh (Singapore) 122
    William Woo (Singapore) 127
    Ricky Ellis (South Africa) 131

- Arturo Blanco (Spain) 133
- Vicente Sancho Colomer (Spain) 136
- Josep Pascual (Spain) 138
- Beesham Soogrim (Sweden) 141
- Ellen Yin (Taiwan) 143
- Gülten Yağmur (Turkey) 148
- Wayne Caddy (United Kingdom) 150
- Jacob Baggenstos (United States) 155
- Jeffrey de Leon (United States) 157
- Alan Negrete (United States) 163
- Mike Zakowski, World Silver Medallist (United States) 168
- Hector Facal (Uruguay) 171
- Kao Sieu Luc (Vietnam) 175

Cakes 179
- Jack Hazan (Israel) 179
- Günther Koerffer (Sweden) 181

Tarts 187
- Benny Swinnen (Belgium) 187
- Erica Roessing Almeida (Portugal) 190
- Olivier Hofmann, European Gold Medallist (Switzerland) 193
- John Slattery (United Kingdom) 196

Other Pastries 200
- Sergio González (Argentina) 200
- Brett Noy (Australia) 203
- Christophe Debersée, World Champion 2008 (France) 206
- Ludovic Richard, Meilleur Ouvrier De France (France) 209
- Marios Papadopoulos (Greece) 211
- Paul Kelly (Ireland) 213
- François Wolfisberg, European Gold Medallist (Switzerland) 216
- Lulu Lee (Taiwan) 220
- Kathryn Gordon (United States) 221
- Peter Yuen (United States) 225

Bibliography 231

Appendix A: Glossary of Abbreviations 232

Appendix B: Resources from Jimmy Griffin's YouTube Channel 233

Appendix C: Characteristics of Wheat Flours 236

Appendix D: Characteristics of Rye Flours 237

Index 238

It's all about a balancing act between time, temperature, and ingredients: That's the art of baking.

~Peter Reinhart

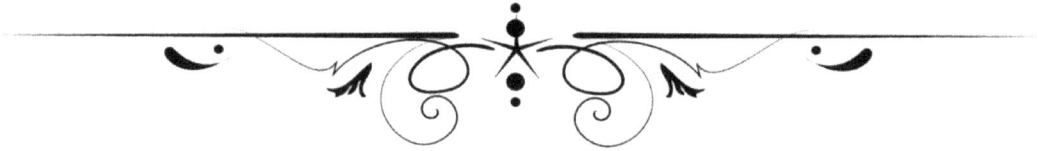

Preface

In November of 2016, I served as president of the jury for the CDM de la Boulangerie in Paris, France and completed my master of science degree. As part of the requirements for my degree, I completed a brief (i.e., thesis) on the influence of August Zang's Viennese style baking legacy on the artisans of the CDM de la Boulangerie, 2016. As I conducted interviews to collect data, I realised I was not only among 10 of the most talented master bakers on the planet but among friends and colleagues as well. Each of them had the most interesting backgrounds—both personal and professional—and I somehow connected with each of them. It was then that I began to think how interesting it would be to write a book to share the stories of my connections with these superstars throughout my baking journey and, better yet, to include recipes from each of them.

Although the response to my invitation to submit recipes was immediate, encouraging, and exciting, the journey to this book was long and not without challenges. Most notably, in 2019, I made the difficult decision to close my family bakery after 143 years. Having to let workers go and, at the same time, let go of such a rich family history and tradition was painful. I'm grateful for all the support I received from family, friends, and colleagues during this time.

The finished work is a unique collection of 61 exclusive recipes from 59 international top-class specialist bakers from 31 countries. The information for each master baker has been provided to me by the masters themselves, and each has received and approved a proof to verify content and the recipes before publication. The recipes in this book are suitable for all levels and tastes, so whether you're an experienced baker ready to tackle the royal wedding cake my dear friend Gunther

Koerffer made for the Princess of Sweden or a novice baker looking to master a simple sourdough starter, I'm confident you'll find something that suits you. I hope you'll enjoy your baking adventures and wish you much baking success.

This book details the world of the master bakers—their stories, diverse cultures, symbolism, and background—and how each one has touched my life in such a positive way. It contains a stunning collection of breads, cakes, tarts, and pastries. It highlights the skills of the art and craft of baking, which provides bread worldwide, in differing forms, shapes, and ingredients. Bread is the backbone of many of our daily foods worldwide. It also encompasses the love of treating ourselves to life's little luxuries and sharing those things with others. Bread and baking brings family, friends, and communities together. This book is a celebration of that unique human facet of sharing, togetherness, and global community.

Forward

I first met Jimmy Griffin more than 38 years ago when he enrolled in the Baking Technology and Management Diploma course at the National Bakery School, Dublin Institute of Technology (DIT), where I was lecturing at that time. I remember I was immediately struck by his agreeable personality and infectious enthusiasm for his chosen career. Jimmy is the 6th generation of his family to have baked bread, cakes, and pastries for eager customers in the city of Galway. Over the past 38 years, he's proven himself to be a specialist baker who has a remarkable knowledge of his craft and, most importantly, baking technology. In this field, Jimmy is both passionate and knowledgeable. He holds a master's degree in food product development and culinary innovation. He's a lecturer in the School of Culinary Arts and Food Technology at Technological University Dublin.

Over the years, Jimmy has been successfully involved in various European baking competitions, both as a competitor and as a team coach. He also has been a member of the international bakery jury for the CDM de la Boulangerie since 2002. He's judged at most of the World Baking Championships and World Baking Masters' Competitions since then. In 2016, he was appointed as president of the jury at the CDM de la Boulangerie in Paris, a significant recognition of his status in the world of baking. Jimmy speaks four languages and is widely acknowledged as Ireland's specialist communicator and bakery ambassador. Without a doubt, Jimmy Griffin is highly regarded by his contemporaries throughout the baking world.

Jimmy also is the 2019 world silver medallist CDM Chocolatine and an active competitor in world competitions. He's a highly regarded tutor and specialist demonstrator. He's given many masterclasses in Europe, China, Taiwan, Brazil, Japan, Russia, and the USA. I was privileged to accompany him to a number of these events and, particularly, to Stavropol, Russia, in 2015, where he was conferred with an Honorary Professorship of Bakery and Pastry Arts by the University of Stavropol. I am delighted to have been asked to write the preface to this work. It's important to understand that this is not just another baking book—it's much more than that. In this book, Jimmy Griffin has compiled an incredibly interesting selection of recipes, all of which have been willingly supplied by his worldwide group of colleagues and friends, each one a highly regarded specialist baker in their own country. As a bonus, he's shared the recipe and method for his world-famous conger loaf. Don't miss the backstory to that recipe—it reads like an action movie!

This book is written and compiled by a baker for bakers. It represents artisan baking at its very best. The recipes don't contain improvers, additives, or dough conditioners. I have no doubt it will prove to be of huge interest to both professional and home bakers alike. As the reader navigates through this wonderful book, they are introduced to a worldwide range of interesting bread, cakes, and pastry products, each with easy to follow and proven recipes and methods. I am confident you'll be as impressed and please with the book as I am.

Derek O' Brien

Head, National Bakery School, DIT, Dublin (retired)
Head, Diploma in German Baking, IBA, Weinheim, Germany (retired)
Director, Baking Academy of Ireland (retired)

Introduction

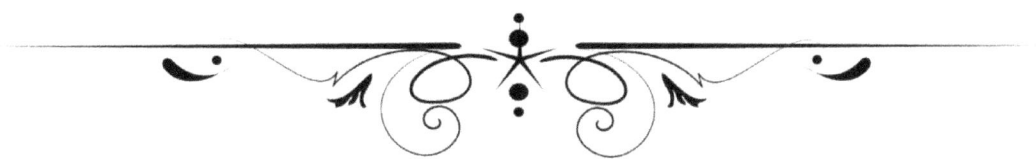

This book is organized into two sections. Section 1 includes some basic information about baking that likely will help less experienced bakers successfully navigate the recipes in this book. Some of the master bakers have provided pictures of the processes and links to tutorials. Those should help you as well. Additionally, a short list of abbreviations common in the baking industry is included for you as Appendix A. Section 2 is made up of recipes shared by master bakers. The recipes are presented in alphabetical order, first by country of origin and then by the contributor. I took the time to scale down the recipes so they could be made both at home and in commercial bakeries and kitchens as desired.

I use only metric measures in this book—all the recipe ingredients are listed in grams—because they are most exact, and using metric measures also allows recipes to easily be made smaller or be scaled-up for mass production. All baking temperatures in the book are given in degrees Celsius (°C). In some recipes, the contributors have provided the equivalent temperature in degrees Fahrenheit (°F). (You can easily find temperature conversion calculators online.) Additionally, many of the recipes include optimal temperatures need for making consistent dough.

Each recipe is accompanied by a short story about the master baker who created it. You'll note that each story includes mention of how our paths crossed. In most instances, I met the master bakers through my work, teaching, travel, and experiences at the Coupe d' Europe de la Boulangerie 1995–2005, CDM de la Boulangerie 2002–2021, and my involvement in the UIBC. A list of online resources from my YouTube channel is presented in Appendix B.

Section 1
First Things First

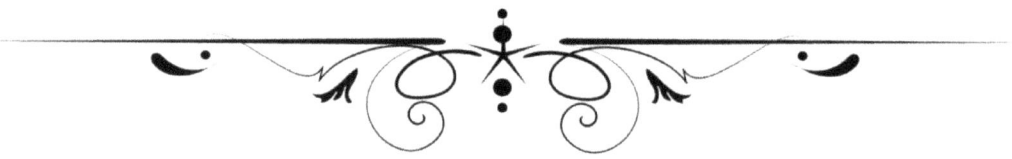

They say that cooking is an art and baking is a science. Because I'm very much a believer in that philosophy, I can't stress enough how important it is to use exact measurements for every ingredient in a recipe, to ensure ideal dough temperature, and to use the correct flour for a particular recipe. The discussions in this section are intended to help you succeed in these areas. Sprinkled throughout the discussions, I've included a few definitions and hints for less experienced bakers.

Scales

Because baking recipes require a perfect balance of ingredients, a good scale is fundamental for great baking. If you don't already have one, go get one. It'll be one of the best investments you make in your baking. I recommend a digital scale as they eliminate measurement errors and provide accurate ingredient measurements every time. Digital scales are inexpensive and durable, and easily accessible in the marketplace. Any brand will do. Many also offer conversions at the touch of a button so they can be used to weigh in grams, imperial measures, or US pounds and ounces.

Flour

The many wheat types used to make flour are grown in different climates and soils and during different seasons. The differences in how and where the wheat is grown give flours their distinct qualities and applications in the food industry. The process of milling flour is a specialized and complex science and beyond the scope of this book. My intent here is to give a brief introduction to how flour is made, the types of flour that are used globally, and how those different flours can be used worldwide to produce the recipes in this book.

Milling Flour

Flour for most bakery applications is made by grinding seeds or cereal grains such as wheat, rye, spelt into a powder by a process called milling. In the baking industry, flour is extracted from various grains. Because wheat is the most widely used grain in baking applications globally, here I briefly explain the milling process as it applies to wheat. However, the milling of other grains is similar.

The extraction process consists of a series of steps; sorting, grinding, sifting, and regrinding the wheat grain to produce various types of flours bakers use to make bread. The sorting step is used to remove unwanted materials such as stones, sticks, oats, and barley from the wheat berry supply. The grinding step, which can be done with stone or steel rollers, breaks apart the wheat berries. The ground flour is then sifted through a mesh screen. The finer the miller wants to make the flour, the more times the flour will be ground and the finer the mesh screens that are used for each subsequent round of sifting.

Using this process, millers separate the wheat berry's endosperm from the outside bran and wheat germ layers. Although the bran and wheat germ may be sold as separate ingredients from the flour extracted from the endosperm, a miller also can use the entire wheat berry.

Extraction Rates, Ash Content, and Protein Content

The higher a flour's extraction rate, the greater the number of components extracted from the grain. The higher the extraction rate, the darker the flour will be because more of the darker bran is extracted along with the lighter endosperm. Conversely, the lower the extraction rate, the fewer the number of components extracted from the grain and the lighter the flour will be because less of the darker bran is extracted along with the lighter endosperm. Flours with the lowest extraction rates will include no bran and be completely white.

Flours with different extraction rates also will have different ash and protein contents. As the name implies, protein content refers to the amount of protein present in the flour. Knowing the flour's protein content is important because it determines whether the flour is suitable for bread, pastry, or cake making. There are two types of protein present in flour, glutenin, which is water-insoluble, and gliadin, which dissolves in water. When flour is hydrated with water and the two are mixed, the water, glutenin, and gliadin bond to form an elastic gluten matrix that acts as a superstructure for the bread, cake, or pastry. It's this gluten matrix that helps dough hold its shape after being formed. The gluten matrix also traps the CO_2 gas bubbles produced by the yeast as a by-product of fermentation, which gives lightness and a crumb texture to the bread.

The higher the extraction rate, the higher the ash and protein content of the flour and vice versa. To determine ash content, a sample of the flour is burnt. The residual ash is then weighed to determine the ash content of the specific flour. Ash content is a measure of the flour or of particular flour's mineral content and is important to know because the ash helps the baker determine how pure or refined a flour is and how much volume it will produce.

Most flours for making bread, cakes, and confectionery are made from wheat, rye, spelt, buckwheat, and other cereal grains. I've provided a little information here about the most common types of flours you'll use in your baking projects. In the text you may notice that many of the flours are distinguished by numbers and the letter *T*. In these instances, T stands for type. However, some countries use W for wheat, *R* for rye, and D for Dinkel or spelt.

Common Flour Types
Wheat
Worldwide, wheat flour is the most commonly used grain for making bread, pastry, and cakes. Extraction rates and ash and protein content for wheat flours from 17 countries are provided in Appendix C. Because of the many variables involved in milling flour, the provided extraction rates are approximate.

Generally, wheat grains are classified as being either hard or soft wheat. Hard wheat produces strong flour with higher protein contents and is generally most suitable for making products like bread, pizza dough, laminated pastry, hard rolls, or noodles. On the other hand, soft wheat generally has lower protein contents and is more suitable for baking biscuits, cakes, cookies, crackers, or flatbreads. To further complicate matters, grains that are sown in the fall are known as hard winter or soft winter wheat, and those sown in spring are known as hard spring or soft spring wheat. Millers often blend several hard and soft kinds of wheat to get what is known as a grist. The blending of flours results in flour with specific dough making characteristics, such as extensibility or a specific protein content or percentage.

Wheat grains are generally categorised by colour, so you may have red winter wheat or white spring wheat. The colour referred to in the name describes the appearance of the colour of either the outside of the wheat berry, called the bran, or the inside of the wheat berry, called the endosperm. The bran of red wheat has a reddish/brown tint. The white wheat is an albino relative of red wheat. Wheat berries also come in other rarer colours, such as purple and blue. The colours in the berries come from anthocyanins, which are water-soluble vacuolar pigments. The pH of the anthocyanins dictates the colour of the berries. Finally, flours are categorised by their extraction rates. Flours with the lowest extraction rates are mostly used for making cakes, biscuits, and pastry type foods, whereas flours with higher extraction rates are typically used for making bread. Flours milled from soft wheat and with the lowest extraction rates are mostly used for making cakes, biscuits, and shortcrust pastry type foods. Flours milled from hard winter wheat, and low extraction rates will produce strong, pure white flour suitable for making a range of bread type products such as brioche and laminated pastry. Flours with higher extraction rates are typically used for making bread, such as whole meal bread.

Unfortunately, there isn't a universal system for naming flours according to their extraction rates. This means that the names of flours vary from country to country. For example, in English, flour with an extraction rate between approximately 90%–98% may be called whole meal or whole wheat flour. Flours with an extraction rate between approximately 67%–70% may be called cake, pastry, biscuit, or patent flour. In some countries, including France, Germany, and Portugal, flours are identified by number according to a classification system unique to that particular country. For example, in France, flour with an extraction rate between approximately 82%–85% is identified as Flour Type 80, and in Germany, it's identified as Flour Type 812.

Because the minerals in the wheat berry are found mainly in the bran and wheat germ, the more refined a flour is, the less bran and wheat germ it contains and, therefore, the fewer minerals it'll have. Conversely, the less refined flour is, the more bran and wheat germ it'll have and the more minerals it'll have. Because bran, by its nature, has sharp shards or edges that act like tiny razors, they cut the gluten matrix as it tries to develop and penetrates the gas bubbles in the dough, which reduces the volume of the dough. Therefore, the higher the bran content in a flour, the higher the ash content and the lower the volume of the baked product. Conversely, the lower the bran content in a flour, the lower the ash content and the baked product's volume. This means that whole meal bread will have a lower volume when compared to white bread.

Rye

There are many different types of rye flour available in the marketplace. Because many recipes in this book are made with rye flour, I've provided, in Appendix D, a table of extraction rates and ash and protein content for rye flours from 6 countries. Because of the many variables involved in milling flour, the provided extraction rates are approximate.

In the table, you'll notice that in Ireland, the UK, and the USA, the description of the colours of the different rye flours are used to describe how much of the grain is milled into the flour. Typical terms used in these countries are *white, light, medium, whole grain,* and *dark*. In Germany, rye flours are named according to their ash content. Rye flour grading numbers in Germany begin with 700 and end at 1740. The higher the number is in this range, the darker the rye flour. For example, Type 1150 is classified as a medium to dark rye flour. Numbers above 1740 refer to rye meal or crushed grain and are not flours.

The darker the rye flour, the stronger the rye flavour will be in the bread. Also, because there is far less gluten in rye grains, there is subsequently less elasticity in the dough and less gas is trapped leading to less bread volume. This means that rye bread will have a much denser texture than wheat-based bread, for example.

Spelt

Spelt flour is available in just two forms: white spelt and whole meal spelt. Having only two options makes selecting the right spelt flour much simpler than choosing wheat or rye flour. White spelt flour is typically indicated with the label Dinkel 630, and brown or whole meal spelt flour is typically indicated with the label Dinkel 1050. Some Nordic and Eastern European countries use the German term *Dinkelvollkorn,* translated as dark whole meal.

Yeast

Yeasted bread dough can be made successfully from fresh, instant dry, osmotolerant, or active dry yeast. Osmotolerant yeast is a type of instant dry yeast available worldwide but most notably in Europe. This type of yeast is used particularly for sweet dough varieties where the recipe's sugar content is in excess of 5% of the total flour weight. A popular brand of osmotolerant yeast is called SAF-Instant Gold (made by the Lesaffre Yeast Corporation). The yeast is specifically designed for high sugar/fat recipes such as brioche and laminated croissant pastry and provides outstanding fermentation action when baking highly enriched fermented products.

Active dry yeast needs to be hydrated (have water added to it) to kick off the fermentation process. Both fresh yeast and instant dry yeasts can be mixed directly into the dough, saving you time when baking. My preference, however, is to always mix the yeast in the water before adding it to the dough. Using a hand whisk will help ensure the yeast has been completely dissolved. If a recipe calls for fresh yeast, but you only have dry yeast or vice versa, you can generally calculate the weight of dry yeast to be half the fresh yeast's weight. If the recipe calls for 30 g of fresh yeast, you should use 15 g of dry yeast.

When you're using any type of dry yeast, you must read the instructions. Yeast is a living organism and requires food, warmth, and hydration to thrive. The starch in the flour provides food, and the water provides warmth and hydration. If the yeast gets too cold, it will ferment much slower, prolonging the process, possibly by hours. If the yeast gets too hot, it will act too quickly, and the dough will fail to take on colour and will have a very sour, overpowering, yeasty taste. In other words, the dough will perish. This is why a baker needs to control the fermentation process by making dough at a specific temperature.

Desired Dough Temperature

Bakers and pastry chefs make bread and pastry worldwide, from tropical areas to colder locations in the Northern and Southern Hemispheres. This means that daily working temperatures won't be the same for every baker. A baker in Ireland or the UK may come to work to meet flour, sugar, and equipment at 10 °C, whereas a baker in the Bahamas or Namibia may be working with ingredients and equipment at 22 °C. These temperature differences are important because to kick start the gassing process and achieve consistent dough fermentation, it's crucial to ensure the final dough temperature is between 24 °C and 26 °C. This temperature range is referred to as the DDT. The baker in Ireland may need to warm their ingredients (e.g., flour, water). The bakers in Namibia may need to chill their ingredients in a refrigerator overnight before using them.

Luckily, there's a good rule of thumb you can use to roughly calculate the dough temp so that when the dough is finished mixing, it'll be at the desired or optimum temperature to promote fermentation. Generally, when using flour at room temperature, you'll need to adjust the water temperature to achieve the DDT. Every baker should commit this calculation to memory and employ it as part of their daily decision-making processes.

Calculating the Desired Dough Temperature

When calculating DDT, *twice the required dough temperature minus the flour temperature gives you the required water temperature.* Considered as a formula, the rule looks like this:

$$(DDT \times 2) - \text{Flour Temperature} = \text{Water Temperature}$$

or

$$(DDT \times 2) - FT = WT$$

The formula generally considers the friction factor (i.e., the temperature increase due to the heat generated by a mixer) when mixing the dough. A couple examples may be helpful. Let's use the temperature examples given earlier in this section.

Example 1. Cold climate (10 °C)

The DDT for a particular recipe is 26 °C. Therefore, the bakery temperature, and therefore everything else in the bakery, including your flour, is 10 °C.

$$(DDT \times 2) - FT = WT$$

$$(26\ °C \times 2) - FT = WT$$

$$52\ °C - FT = WT$$

$$52\ °C - 10\ °C = WT$$

$$42\ °C = WT$$

Twice the DDT of 26 °C is 52 °C minus the temperature of the flour (10 °C) gives you the needed temperature of the water (42 °C).

Example 2. Warm climate **(22 °C)**

The DDT for a particular recipe is 26 °C. Therefore, the bakery temperature, and therefore everything else in the bakery, including your flour, is 22 °C.

$$(DDT \times 2) - FT = WT$$

$$(26\ °C \times 2) - 22\ °C = WT$$

$$52\ °C - 22\ °C = 30\ °C$$

Twice the DDT of 26 °C is 52 °C minus the temperature of the flour (22 °C) gives you the needed temperature of the water (30 °C).

Bread Making

Bread making occurs in stages, and most bread is made the same way. Here, I explain the most common process for making bread. Keep in mind that this process may need to be varied for a particular recipe. Always follow the directions for the recipe you're using.

Stage 1. Scaling the Ingredients

Scaling a recipe refers to either increasing or decreasing the number of ingredients you use so that you get the batch size you're looking for. If you don't work in a bakery, you probably aren't interested in baking 20 loaves of bread at a time. In this case, you'd scale down a recipe so you can make 2 or 4 loaves. The same idea works in the other direction to scale up recipes. No matter which way you're scaling, be sure to scale the wet and dry ingredients separately or as advised in your specific recipe.

Stage 2. Mixing/Combining Ingredients

Ingredients can be mixed either by hand or using a dough mixer/stand mixer with a dough hook. When water is mixed with flour, the water activates the natural enzymes present in the flour. These enzymes stimulate the proteins in the flour to begin gluten development. Additionally, the enzymes begin to break down starch and convert them into simple sugars on which the yeast feed during the bulk fermentation and final proofing stages. The idea is to allow the gluten matrix to become as elastic as possible. That elasticity enables the developing dough to trap carbon dioxide gas produced as a by-product of fermentation. The trapping of the gas is what gives the bread its light crumb structure.

Some bread recipes are straight doughs, where all the ingredients are combined at once and then mixed. Other breads, including sourdough, are made using a process called autolysis. This process simply means that you blend the flour, starter, and water together and let it rest for a specified time before adding the other ingredients. Autolysis enables the natural enzymes present in the flour to activate. The resting period, however, also allows the starch to fully absorb the available water. The technique was championed by Professor Raymond Calvel to enable the maximum hydration of the dough, bring about gluten alignment, reduce mixing times, and give the bread a nice open crumb.

Stage 3. Bulk Fermentation/First Resting

Bulk fermentation is the time given for bread dough to ferment, produce gas, rise, and relax following the mixing process. The resting period, which happens before the dough is scaled and shaped, can last anywhere from a few minutes to hours, depending on the type of dough being made. When the dough is resting for any reason, it's critical that it's covered to prevent it from skinning (i.e., forming a hard skin or crust), which will cause the bread to become misshaped as it proofs and bakes and ultimately leaves you with hard lumps in your bread. The easiest way to cover your bread is to use plastic wrap. It's flexible and can be easily moulded over the dough.

Stage 4. Stretching and Folding/Degassing

Depending on the type of bread you're making, all dough must either be stretched and folded or degassed after bulk fermentation. In both cases, the processes are necessary because fermentation generates heat. After the dough rests, the dough mass centre will be at a higher temperature than the outside. By stretching and folding the dough or degassing it, you equalize the dough mass temperature and help develop the dough's elasticity and increase the dough strength.

Doughs that require stretching and folding after resting are highly hydrated doughs that generally have a very irregular open honeycomb texture with large holes in the crumb. Examples of these types of bread are Ciabatta, baguettes, pizza dough, and sourdoughs.

Doughs that require you to degas or knock back, the dough to reduce the amount of trapped gas in the dough are breads that require a closed structure/crumb and even texture. Examples of these types of breads are sandwich bread, Challah, and batch bread. To release the gas, simply press the dough firmly on your work table with your hands and shape it tightly.

Stage 5. Scaling/Weighing the Dough

Once your dough has completed its bulk fermentation stage, it's ready to be scaled for individual loaves. Check your recipe for the required dough weight (in grams) of the particular bread you're making, then, using a bench scraper, divide your dough by chopping it into pieces of the desired weight. Using a digital scale will help you ensure each of the loaves in your batch is the same and correct weight to obtain the correct yield from the recipe and achieve consistent bake times for each loaf.

Stage 6. Preshaping

After the individual dough pieces are scaled to their required weights, they're formed/shaped/moulded into an intermediate shape before final shaping. This first shaping, called *preshaping*, can take the form of a ball of dough for a bread roll or boule, a batard for a pan loaf, or a cylinder for a baguette. The first shaping realigns the gluten matrix, giving the loaves a basic structure or shape, building strength into the dough for final shaping.

Stage 7. Intermediate Proofing

Once the dough is preshaped, it's given a second resting or recovery period before final shaping. When preshaped fermenting dough is allowed to rest, the process is called *intermediate proofing*.

The gluten structure in dough only has a certain tolerance for handling and manipulation. If the dough is worked too much, too soon, or too forcibly, it will tear, and the appearance and volume of the bread will suffer. Proofing preshaped dough gives the gluten structure time to recover from the handling it underwent in Stages 4 through 6. Simultaneously, it enhances the dough's extensibility, elasticity, and strength so it can hold its form during the final shaping, and you can complete that step without damaging the dough. Don't forget to cover your dough!

Stage 8. Final Shaping

In the final shaping stage, the individual dough pieces are folded and elongated to make baguettes, folded and shaped into boules or batards to make sourdough bread, or folded and coiled to make sandwich bread.

Stage 9. Final Proofing

During the final proofing stage, the fermenting dough is allowed to rise to its maximum volume before baking, roughly double in size. Boules and batards are proofed on trays. Sandwich breads are proofed in the pans in which they'll be baked. Hearth breads (i.e., breads baked on a pizza stone or directly on the oven floor), such as sourdough, pizza, baguettes, and other artisan breads are proofed in wicker baskets called *bannetons* or on linen cloths called *couche cloths*. Tea towels dusted with flour also work.

When the dough is proofed in a banneton, prepare the bannetons in advance of shaping by lightly dusting them using a sieve with either rye or potato flour. The thin coating of flour on the basket's inner surfaces prevents the dough from sticking to the shape, assists the dough's release following proofing, and imprints a pleasant pattern of lines around the dough. The dough is generally placed in a banneton with the closure seam facing up or on the top and the smooth, shaped top of the dough resting on the banneton's bottom. This way, when the dough is flipped upside down to release it from the banneton after proofing, the seam will remain hidden at the bottom of the loaf.

The final proofing stage can be done in a proofer if you have access to one, or you can simply leave the dough in a warm place. If you're letting the dough sit out to proof, be sure you cover it with plastic and keep it out of any draft so it doesn't develop a skin. In the case of sourdough, the dough-filled bannetons are generally placed into a refrigerator at 3 °C overnight or as specified in the individual recipe. Like all the other doughs, the dough in the bannetons should be covered with plastic to prevent the dough's skinning.

Stage 10. Scoring

After the dough has risen, it's scored with a sharp blade to encourage the loaf to expand further along the cut lines to achieve its maximum volume and open crumb structure. Scoring is also a decorative process and can give your bread a unique look—think about the cuts along the baguette. (Also see Fernando's genipapo bread, Recipe #2, and Marcus's maple cherry nut loaf, Recipe # 5.)

Dough that has been proofed in bannetons must be removed from the banneton before scoring. To remove dough from a banneton, gently tip it out of the banneton and place it on an oven peel. (Think spatula-type tool for pulling pizzas from ovens. Also, see the profile picture for Robert Humphries.)

Stage 11. Baking the Bread

Whether you're baking in a professional bakery or at home, you need to get your proofed bread into the oven and baked according to the recipe directions. Some bread will be baked in tins, some will be baked on trays, and some will be baked on the oven floor. Handling trays and tins of bread is straight forward—you just lift the trays and place them in the oven. Transferring hearth or oven bottom bread such as sourdough to the oven can be a little tricky, though. Professional bakers often use parchment paper sheets cut to the oven floor's size, or pieces of parchment paper cut approximately 4 cm larger than the baskets or bannetons the dough was in to slide the dough into the oven. You can do this too. When you tip your dough out of the bannetons, just tip it directly onto the parchment. Then you can slide the parchment with the dough on it and position it expertly wherever you desire. If you just want to use a peel without the parchment paper, just be sure the peel is well-floured, so the bread won't stick to it. When you transfer your hearth bread from the oven peel to the oven floor, be careful you don't let the dough slide off of the peel and onto the floor.

Most professional bakers already have commercial ovens with stone bases for baking hearth bread. This won't likely be the case for home bakers. However, Dutch ovens, which are generally made of cast iron and have a lid, or pizza stones, will give you the same baking conditions professionals enjoy. If you're going to use a Dutch oven, you'll need to preheat it in the oven before putting the proofed dough in it. Then you can score the dough, put the lid on the pot, and return the pot to the oven to bake.

Stage 12. Adding Steam

Most professional bakery ovens have a steam button. By pre-setting a timer or pushing a button, water is atomised and sprayed into the oven, creating a moist environment in the oven chamber. The dough's surface in the oven becomes covered with a thin film of water which delays the formation of a crust and enables the dough to rise to its maximum volume. If you bake at home, you can use a garden sprayer to spray atomised water into the oven to generate steam or you can place a small tray in the bottom and to one side of the oven and add ice cubes after loading the bread. Another method is to use barbeque lava rocks in a small tray in the bottom of the oven and, just like in a sauna, pour a half glass of water onto the lava rocks after the bread is loaded into the oven. Take care not to scald yourself if using this method.

Stage 13. Purging the Steam

As bread bakes, it gives off steam. This naturally occurring steam and the steam you added in the last step must be removed about halfway through the baking process to enable a dry, crispy crust to form on the bread. Commercial ovens have a damper or flue, which can be opened to drain off the steam. When baking in home ovens that don't have a flue, you can purge the steam by opening the oven door or propping it open ever so slightly with a small tin. It's okay to leave the tin you used for the ice cubes or lava rocks on the bottom of the oven in place since any moisture you added to it will have evaporated by this point. When baking bread in a Dutch oven, the lid is generally removed after 20 minutes of baking to purge the steam, and the bread is baked for the remaining bake time without the lid. In all cases, great care must be taken to prevent scalding by the steam.

Stage 14. Removing the Bread from the Oven

The bread is removed from the oven when it's baked to the required time, turns a satisfactory colour, or a combination of both.

Stage 15. Cooling

Baked bread is taken from the tins or shapes it was baked in/on and placed on a wire rack in an area with a light airflow to assist in cooling the bread and prevent the loaves' bottoms from getting wet or sweating as they cool. Wrap and package bread only after it's fully cooled.

Section 2
Recipes from Master Bakers

The recipes in this section were contributed by some of the most amazing people I've had the pleasure of encountering along my journey as a baker, competitor, jury member, and teacher. Each master baker is highly skilled and recognised internationally as a specialist and leader in their respective fields of baking, cooking, business, or academia. Yet, if you were to meet any one of them, you would straight away spot their down-to-earth demeanour, one of the many characteristics that make them pillars of their respective communities.

Each recipe represents a personal favourite of the contributor. In some cases, the master baker especially enjoyed the baking process. In other cases, they most enjoyed the outcome. Whichever becomes true for you, I anticipate one or more of these recipes will become your favourites as well.

Bread & Buns

The recipes in this section are a mix of daily bread, the type one would consume daily, and speciality breads, the type with added ingredients such as seeds, nuts, dried fruits, and even potatoes. Although the recipes were chosen personally by the masters, I think you'll find the recipes are well-varied and offer something for everyone. Like things on the hot and spicy side? Try Daníel's Icelandic fiery sourdough (Recipe #17). Prefer sweet and exotic? Then Déborah's chocolate raspberry brioche (Recipe #11) and Alan's chocolate caramel sticky buns (Recipe #3) are likely to suit your fancy. Regardless of your preferences, I invite you not only to try recipes within your comfort zone but to branch out as well. You just may be surprised!

Fernando de Oliveira (Brazil)

Fernando de Oliveira was born in Vinhedo, São Paulo. He's a respected confectioner, chocolatier, and baker who started his professional journey at just 13 years old as a baker and assistant confectioner at a bakery near his home. Sometime later, he fell in love with the art of confectionery and quickly decided that he wanted to pursue the profession.

Fernando took many courses with reputed chefs in São Paulo's interior, spending hours hunched over books searching for knowledge. He worked in other companies as both a confectioner and a baker. After working outside the field for almost a decade, Fernando travelled to Paris in search of inspiration at Europain, one of the biggest baking exhibitions in the world. He also took a croissant and baguette course at the INBP à Rouen, a macaron course at Le Cordon Blue, and an artistic pieces of chocolate course at Ècole Gastronomique Bellouet Conseil.

For the respect that Fernando has earned in the industry, he often is invited to be a jury member at many global professional championships, such as the Louis Lesaffre Cup, which took place in October 2014 in Rio de Janeiro. He was selected to participate in the World Chocolate Masters in Brazil, where he won 2nd place in the general competition and best in South American Bonbon for his bee bonbon made with camu camu honey and cipó uva honey.

Nowadays, Fernando is involved in many diverse bakery and food-related projects in Brazil, one involving the use of more than 30 tons of chocolate. He also teaches classes, trains baking teams, and does consulting work. Fernando was chosen to represent Brazil's flavours and culture at the 2021 SIGEP, an international trade show of artisan gelato, pastry, bakery, and the coffee world. At the time of publication, it was anticipated that the event, which was to be hosted in Rimini, Italy, would be cancelled due to the COVID-19 pandemic.

In 2014, his work using Brazilian ingredients was showcased in Dulcypas, a Spanish confectionery magazine. Additionally, Fernando has written two books: *Classic, Basic and Sophisticated Confectionery* and *Macarons for all Occasions*. His next confectionery book will consist of products made with mostly Brazilian ingredients. Fernando also recorded several DVDs about the baking, confectionery, and chocolate industries. Other achievements include 3rd place World Chocolate Master, South America; coach of the Brazilian Bakery Team, South America 2015; coach of the Brazilian Bakery Selection at the World Cup, France 2016; candidate, CDM de la Patisserie, 2017; Masters de la Boulangerie coach, France 2018; winner, Mondial du Pain, Brazil 2018; and World Final du Pain, France 2019.

Fernando first met Jimmy back in 2008 at the CDM and again later in 2016 when Jimmy was president of the Jury and Fernando was coach to the Brazilian bakery team. The two spent time together during the competition and at the gala dinners following the competitions. They have remained friends ever since. For Fernando, similar to a painter with his paintings, candies, sugars, and chocolates are his tools of the trade. He truly is a superstar baker. Check out his Instagram page and his legion of 84k fans: @cheffernandodeoliveria

Follow Fernando: Instagram, https://www.instagram.com/cheffernandodeoliveira/

~Fernando de Oliveira

1. Fernando's Babassu Bread

Before making this bread, make the sprouted wheat and lentils, both of which are added at the end of the mixing cycle so they don't break down too much in the dough. The wheat and lentils give this bread a full and meaty bite with each slice. Making sprouted grains is not difficult, and the procedure is outlined for you after the directions for making the bread.

Ingredients: Bread Dough

1,000 g	Wheat flour T65
890 g	Water
110 g	Babassu flour (Indian seed flour)
440 g	Hard levain (See Recipe #42)
85 g	Wheat germ
22 g	Salt
2 g	Fresh yeast
110 g	Sprouted wheat
110 g	Sprouted lentils

Making the Bread Dough

1. Initiate autolysis by combining the wheat and Babassu flours with 700 g of the total water and mixing in a stand mixer with a dough hook. (You also can mix the autolyse by hand.) Mix on slow speed until the dough just comes together, and no un-hydrated flour is visible in the dough. There is no need to knead the dough at this stage. Remove the bowl from the mixer, cover with plastic wrap, and place the autolyse mixture in the refrigerator for 1 hour at 3 °C.

2. After the resting time has finished, place the autolyse back in the stand mixer and combine it with the hard levain, wheat germ, and salt. Dissolve the yeast in the remaining water using a balloon whisk. Using 1st speed, begin mixing the dough and adding the remaining 190 g of water little by little until all the water is fully incorporated. Mix for 8–10 minutes on 1st speed and another 3 minutes on 2nd speed. Finally, add the sprouted wheat and sprouted lentils (see directions for Making the Sprouted Wheat/Lentils).

3. Remove the mixed dough from the mixer, place it in an oiled container, do a stretch and fold, and allow the dough to rest for 30 minutes.

4. Do another stretch and fold and allow the dough to rest another 30 minutes.

5. Divide the dough into pieces of 400 g each. Preshape the dough pieces into ball shapes, cover, and allow them to ferment for 20 minutes.

6. Gently final shape the dough into oblong loaves. Place the dough into dusted bannetons with the seam facing up and cover the bannetons. Place the covered bannetons inside a refrigerator for approximately 12 hours at 5 °C to allow the dough to proof.

7. After the fermentation is complete, tip the proofed dough out of the bannetons and onto baking parchment. Make cuts on the surface with a very sharp blade or scalpel and bake in a deck oven with steam at 255 °C for approximately 40 minutes.

Making the Sprouted Wheat/Lentils

1. Soak the wheat grain and lentils in filtered water for at least 24 hours. Change the water at least every 6–8 hours.

2. When a small white tip is visible on the grains, transfer them to a sieve. Rinse the grains. Cover the sieve to protect the sprouting grains. Rinse at least 3 times a day for 2 days.

3. After approximately 40 hours, the wheat is ready to use. Ideally, the wheat sprouts will have grown to approximately 2 cm. Until used, store the sprouts in a dry, ventilated place and out of direct sunlight.

Nutritional Value

This bread was developed by the Brazilian team in partnership with a nutritionist using typical ingredients from Brazil. Our intent was to make it healthy and nutritious. The main highlight of the bread is the use of Babassu flour, which is produced by indigenous people of the Xingu Indigenous Park region in the Midwest of Brazil, where the Xingu River passes through the Amazonian Forest. The Babassu palm tree grows naturally in the forest without receiving agro-toxics or fertilizers, and the fruit used to make the flour is harvested in the woods when it falls naturally when it's ripe. Thus, besides contributing to the sustainability of indigenous communities, Babassu is a nutritious source of food. It's rich in iron and soluble fibres and has a high concentration of starch and minerals. It helps improve cholesterol levels, balances blood sugar, and increases energy. For these reasons, Babassu flour is being used as a partial replacement for wheat flour to enrich bread and cakes to meet Brazilian communities and schools' nutritional needs. Another highlight of this bread is the use of sprouted grains such as wheat and lentil. A sprouted grain is a live food, so it's nutritionally much richer than food that has been harvested for days. Sprouted grains contribute to a healthy diet because they are easy to digest, have high nutrient concentrations, and are rich in proteins, fibres, and antioxidants.

2. Fernando's Genipapo Bread

Your eyes are not deceiving you. This bread is blue! The colour comes from milk made with genipapo (also spelled jenipapo), a fruit native to Brazil. The recipe used to make the genipapo blue milk for this bread is provided for you.

Ingredients: Genipapo Dough

1,000 g	Wheat flour T65
630 g	Water
150 g	Genipap (Indian fruit), blue milk (directions provided)
22 g	Salt
400 g	Hard levain
3 g	Fresh yeast
8 g	Amburana (aromatic seed)
50 g	Tapioca flakes (from manioc flour)
150 g	Licuri (Indian nuts)

Making the Bread Dough

1. Initiate autolysis by combining the wheat flour, water, and genipap milk. The autolyse can be mixed by hand or on a stand mixer with a dough hook. Mix on slow speed until the dough just comes together, and no un-hydrated flour is visible in the dough. There is no need to knead the dough at this stage. Remove the bowl from the mixer, cover with plastic wrap, and place this autolyse mixture in the refrigerator for 1 hour at 3 °C. Then, add all the remaining ingredients except the Licuri nuts and mix for 8 minutes on 1st speed and 2 minutes on 2nd speed.

2. Add the Licuri nuts and mix to clear at a slow speed.

3. Place the mixed dough in a sealed, greased container and allow it rest for 45 minutes. Then do a stretch and fold and allow it to rest for another 45 minutes.

4. Divide the dough into pieces of 500 g each, preshape, and let it ferment for 20 minutes.

1. Prepare a couche cloth or banneton baskets by dusting them well with rye, potato, or rice flour. Then shape the dough into cylinders and place the shaped dough cylinders onto the couche cloth or into the bannetons. Allow the dough to proof for 40 minutes.

2. When proofed, tip the bread out of the couche cloth or baskets and place the bread on baking parchment paper. Score using a sharp razor blade.

3. Bake at 250 °C with steam for 15 minutes. Then drain the steam.

4. Continue to bake for another 15–20 minutes or until achieving a satisfactory colour.

5. Remove bread from the oven and cool on wire racks.

Ingredients: Genipap Blue Milk

  50 g   Green genipap (skinned)
150 g   Milk

Making the Genipap Blue Milk

1. Beat the skinless genipap (retain seeds) in a food blender with the milk until well ground.

2. Strain the mixture and bring it to a boil. It should turn blue. Allow the milk to cool before using it to make the distinctly blue dough.

Alan Dumonceaux (Canada)

Alan Dumonceaux has been involved in the baking community for the past 35 years. For the last 17 years, he's been an instructor and the academic chair at the Northern Alberta Institute of Technology for the Baking and Pastry Arts Programme. He's been a great supporter of Skills Canada for our young bakers for the last 19 years, and he's been the manager for Baking Team Canada since 2009.

Alan has competed for Baking Team Canada in viennoiserie in two Louis Lesaffre Cups: Las Vegas, USA in 2010 and Buenos Aires, Argentina in 2015. In 2016, Alan represented Canada as the viennoiserie candidate at the CDM de la Boulangerie. Alan next competed in the World Bakery Master's Competition in 2018 as the Canadian viennoiserie specialist, where he made a great impression on all who sampled his wonderful creations.

Alan met Jimmy in 2016 at the CDM de la Boulangerie when Jimmy was that year's president of the jury. Alan and Jimmy have remained friends ever since and regularly call each other to discuss their teaching endeavours at their respective Universities.

Follow Alan: Instagram, https://www.instagram.com/allcanadianbaker/

~Alan Dumonceaux

3. Alans' Chocolate Caramel Sticky Buns

This recipe takes 2 days to prepare. This recipe has five components: poolish, sweet dough, sticky pan glaze, caramel, and the chocolate ganache filling. Because the poolish needs to be made 6–8 hours before mixing the sweet dough, this recipe could take 2 or 3 days to complete. If completing in 1 day, most of the components' preparation will be completed on Day 1. Day 2 will be made up primarily of the assembly and baking of the buns. These buns are nutty, sticky, and delicious to eat at any time of the day!

Day 1. Preparing the Components

Ingredients: Poolish

237 g	Water at 20 °C
1 g	Instant yeast
237 g	Bread flour

Making the Poolish

1. Place the water in a 2-litre glass or plastic container. Sprinkle the yeast into the water and swirl around with a rubber spatula/small balloon whisk.

2. Add the flour and mix until a smooth paste is formed—no more than 60 seconds.

3. Preferment at room temperature, preferably 21 °C, for 6–8 hours or overnight. If the ambient room temperature is warmer, lower the water temperature by a few degrees. Conversely, if the room temperature is cooler, raise the water temperature a few degrees. The ripened dough should have bubbles visible throughout.

Ingredients: Hand-Mixed/No-Knead Sweet Dough

16 g	Water at 27 °C
158 g	Room temperature eggs
11 g	Instant yeast
475 g	Poolish
237 g	Bread flour
158 g	Pastry flour
95 g	Room temperature unsalted butter
63 g	Sugar
9 g	Salt

Making the Hand-Mixed/No-Knead Sweet Dough

1. Place water and eggs in a medium bowl. Sprinkle the yeast into the water and eggs. Whisk together with your hand.

2. Add the poolish and blend together with your hand for 10 seconds.

3. Add the remaining ingredients and knead together with your hand only until all the ingredients look well combined. (The dough will look very coarse, and that's okay. There is no need to develop the protein.) Cover and place it in the refrigerator overnight.

Recipes: Breads & Buns

Ingredients: Sticky Pan Glaze

- 220 g   Brown sugar
- 100 g   Unsalted room temperature butter
- 55 g   Golden corn syrup
- 32.g   Whipping cream

Making the Sticky Pan Glaze

1. In a stand mixer with a paddle attachment, mix the brown sugar, unsalted butter, and corn syrup together on medium speed for 1 minute.

2. Increase the speed to high and mix for 3 minutes.

3. Stop the mixer and scrape down the bowl's sides, ensuring the consistency of the mix and that all ingredients have been incorporated effectively.

4. Restart the mixer on low speed and slowly stream in the whipping cream until it has been fully incorporated into the mix. Then return the mixer to high speed and cream for 10 minutes, with 1 bowl scrape to ensure a homogenous mix.

5. Scrape the glaze into a small bowl, cover, and store in the refrigerator overnight at 3 °C.

Ingredients: The Caramel

- 85 g   White corn syrup
- 125 g   Sugar
- 20 g   Unsalted butter
- 160 g   Whipping cream, warmed

Making the Caramel

1. Bring corn syrup to a boil in a small saucepan.

2. Divide sugar into four equal parts: approximately 31 g each.

3. Slowly sprinkle ¼ of the sugar into the boiling corn syrup and stir with a high heat rubber spatula.

4. Continue to add the three remaining portions of sugar in increments until it's all incorporated. Be sure to fully incorporate each portion before adding another.

5. With a sugar thermometer, boil the mixture over low to medium heat until the caramel reaches 182 °C. It should be caramel in colour. Stir the mixture as it's boiling.

6. Add the butter and stir until it's fully melted.

7. Quickly warm the whipping cream to 45 °C–50 °C (easily done in a microwave) and slowly add it to the mixture while stirring continuously. The temperature will drop when the whipping cream is added.

8. Continue to cook on low to medium heat while stirring until the mixture reaches 120 °C.

9. Remove from heat, pour the cooked mixture into a bowl, and cool for 30 minutes. Then cover and place in the refrigerator overnight at 3 °C.

Ingredients: Chocolate Ganache Filling

200 g   Dark couverture chocolate
200 g   Whipping cream

Making the Chocolate Ganache Filling

1. Choose your couverture chocolate of choice between 55%–70% dark chocolate. Cocoa Barry, Lindt, and Valrhona are a few premium brands to consider.

2. If you have a block of chocolate, chop it into pea-size portions. Place chopped chocolate or chocolate callets/pistoles into a bowl.

3. Bring whipping cream to boil in a saucepan over high heat. Ensure that the saucepan is large enough to allow the whipping cream to rise as it comes to a full boil.

4. Pour the whipping cream over the chocolate and allow it to sit for 1 minute. Then, slowly combine with a rubber spatula, stirring until a smooth consistency is achieved.

5. Allow to cool for 30 minutes, then cover and place in the refrigerator overnight at 3 °C.

Day 2. Assembling and Baking the Buns

Between 30 minutes and 1 hour before preparing the baking pans, remove the sticky pan glaze, chocolate ganache, and caramel from the refrigerator to warm.

Preparing the Baking Pans

1. Smear the sticky glaze into any available pans (e.g., cake tins of any size, muffin tins, a loaf pan, or shallow baking dish). There should be a healthy coating of glaze in the pan.

2. Pour a thin layer of whipping cream on top of the glaze, and then sprinkle pecan pieces on top of the sticky glaze and whipping cream. If you're using muffin tins, use 1 tablespoon of cream in each muffin cup. Set the pans to the side.

Preparing the Chocolate Caramel Ganache

Using a rubber spatula, mix together 200 g of caramel and 400 g of chocolate ganache until well combined. Set the mixture to the side.

Preparing and Baking the Sweet Dough

1. On a floured surface, with a rolling pin, roll out the dough into a rectangular sheet. For larger sticky buns baked in 10 cm pans, you'll want a dough thickness of about 4 mm. For smaller sticky buns baked in 20 cm pans, you'll want a dough thickness of 3 mm.

2. Blend the chocolate caramel ganache with a rubber spatula to soften slightly and then spread all of the caramel/ganache mixtures across the top of the dough with a spatula or pallet knife. Sprinkle chopped pecans on top of the ganache.

3. Roll up the dough into a spiral cylinder and cut into the desired size based on the pan you use. If you use a muffin tin, you'll portion 25 g of the cylinder per muffin cup. If you use a 10 cm (4") cake pan, you'll cut 1 portion of 120 g from the cylinder. If you use a 20 cm (8") cake pan, you'll cut six portions of 80 g each from the cylinder.

4. Place the cut portions into the prepared pans, cover them, and allow them to rise for 1–1 1/2 hours at room temperature.

5. Place the pans into an oven preheated to 190 °C and bake for at least 20 minutes or until the top of the dough turns a light golden brown. The caramelised mix will be bubbling in the bottom of the tin.

6. After removing the buns from the oven, allow them to cool for 20–30 seconds. Then cover with another pan lined with silicone or parchment paper and invert the buns so the pastry's bottom becomes the top and the caramelised mixture flows over the pastry. Take special care not to splash any of the glaze on your skin while inverting the pan.

7. Allow the melted glaze to drain for 5 seconds, then remove the top pan.

8. Some of the pecan pieces may have fallen off the sticky bun. If that happens, scoop up the pecans, and any extra glaze, with a teaspoon and place them back on top of the bun.

9. Allow the buns to cool slightly. Pipe or spoon the remaining caramel on top of sticky buns.

10. For storage, wrap individually and freeze (-18 °C) for later use.

Mario Fortin (Canada)

Mario Fortin is president of FORMA–LAB, an international bakery consultancy founded in 1998. Mario is the third generation of bakers in his family and jokes he was born between two flour bags. Mario competed in the first edition of the Louis Lesaffre Cup in 2004, representing Team Canada. Mario met Jimmy 4 years later when they were jury members at the 2008 CDM de la Boulangerie. Mario was president of the jury for the first edition of the master's, held in Paris in 2010. He's also a member of the Elite de la Boulangerie International. For the last 10 years, Mario's been involved with the Japan Home Baking School. It was through Mario's influence and connections that Jimmy became involved with the Japan Home Baking School.

In Japan, Mario's famous hot dog guédille has been recognised as the number 1 product since 2000.

The school has sold over 25,000 of these pans for making his famous buns. Mario is scheduled to give the Olympic Baking Seminar in Japan in 2021.

Contact Mario: 1400 Richelieu Street, Beloeil, Québec, Canada, J3G 4R7. Tel: 514-984-1355, mariofortin@forma-lab.com, www.forma-lab.com

~Mario Fortin

4. Mario's Hot Dog Guédilles (with Salad Filling)

This recipe makes 21 hot dog rolls.

Ingredients: Hot Dog Guédilles

800 g Hard wheat flour (13% protein, extra-strong/high protein)
480 g Cold water
100 g Sugar
 40 g Vegetable oil
 16 g Salt
 40 g Fresh yeast

Making the Hot Dog Guédilles

The DDT is 27 °C.

1. In a stand mixer with a dough hook, mix all the ingredients together for 3 minutes on 1st speed and 5–6 minutes on 2nd speed to form a dough at full development.

2. Allow the dough to rest for 10 minutes in a covered bowl.

3. Scale the dough at 70 g per unit to get a yield of 21 pieces. Preshape, cover, and allow to rest for 10 minutes.

Recipes: Breads & Buns

4. Final shape into long cigar-shaped pieces of dough and place into a low rectangular oven tin. This type of tin will force the rolls to batch.

5. Proof the shaped dough for 50–60 minutes at 40 °C and 70% humidity.

6. Bake in a convection oven at 175 °C for 13 minutes.

7. Remove the trays from the oven. Remove the buns from the trays and allow them to cool fully on wire racks/trays before slicing down the centre and ¾ of the way down through the bun, making sure not to cut entirely through to the bottom.

8. Spread soft butter on both sides and toast the outsides.

9. Fill with the rolls with the salad mix and serve.

Ingredients: Dressing

- 50 g Mayonnaise
- 2 g   Table salt
- 1 g   Black pepper

Ingredients: Salad Mix

- 200 g Fresh chopped lettuce
- 200 g Italian tomatoes
- 120 g Fresh onion

Preparing the Dressing and Salad Filling

1. Mix all the dressing ingredients together. Set aside.
2. Cut all the salad filling ingredients into small pieces and mix them together.
3. Add the dressing to the salad filling and mix again.

Filling the Hot Dog Rolls

Spoon the salad mix into the cut and toasted rolls.

Variations

For a luxury version of this recipe, top the salad-filled rolls with lobster, crab, or chicken.

Marcus Mariathas (Canada)

Marcus is from a small island off the coast of Sri Lanka. During the Civil War there, he left for Canada, arriving in Toronto in the middle of winter. It was freezing (−10 °C), and Marcus was wearing only a T-shirt! In 1995, while studying finance and accounting at the University of Toronto, Marcus took a part-time job working as a night-time baker at ACE Bakery. As the months passed, he began developing a fascination with the baking process—the numbers, the formulations, the recipes, and the products all fascinated him. Eventually, he worked his way up to head baker.

In his 24 years in the bakery business, Marcus has embraced the Canadian culture and been fortunate enough to work alongside and be taught by incredibly talented and inspirational master bakers from various countries. He learned about baking and the bakery business, including operations and sales.

Marcus still works at ACE Bakery in Toronto, which has grown from one small bakery to one of North America's largest artisan bakeries (now part of Weston Foods). He also makes artisan bread using the same authentic processes without shortcuts and only uses natural ingredients and no preservatives. Currently, he's a master baker and the senior director of food product development for the company, a position he enjoys because he teaches others the tips and tricks he's learned throughout his career. Marcus appreciates the opportunities he's had to travel worldwide, connect with other members of the same industry, and speak to customers and media throughout his career. He also is proud to have been with the same organization since the beginning of his career, delivering authentic artisan bread to consumers across the continent. Marcus gets great joy from seeing someone enjoy and appreciate true authentic bread, and from knowing it's achievable and accessible for them.

Marcus's greatest personal achievement is his participation in the Louis Lesaffre competition for more than 8 years. At his first competition, as part of Team Canada in 2010, his team didn't advance to the next level; however, Marcus admits that gave him a taste for competition and the drive to work hard to get another opportunity. As part of Team Canada in 2015, Marcus competed in the Baguettes and Bread of the World category, which won the Coupe Louis Lesaffre Americas and qualified for the CDM de la Boulangerie—a first-ever for Canada! The following year, Marcus participated in the CDM de la Boulangerie in Paris alongside his Team Canada teammates. Marcus is as proud of that honour today as he was in 2016. Given his performance there, in 2018, Marcus competed in the Masters de la Boulangerie.

Marcus met Jimmy in 2016 at the CDM de la Boulangerie in Paris. Marcus was a competitor representing Canada, and Jimmy was the president of the jury at that time. Marcus says his first conversation exemplified Jimmy's hard work and dedication to the craft, which he describes as inspirational. The two were amused to learn that one of Team Canada's new members was Jimmy's former students. Since the two first met, they have met at multiple baking exhibitions and competitions worldwide, including the most recent (January 2020) CDM de la Boulangerie in Paris, where they worked together to assist the teams and the jury and supporting the event host to ensure the event ran smoothly. Marcus and Jimmy share a passion for baking and very much enjoy each other's company.

Follow Marcus: Instagram, https://www.instagram.com/marreg157/

~Marcus Mariathas

5. Marcus's Maple Cherry Nut Loaf

This recipe takes 2 days to prepare. The poolish and soaked nut mix are prepared on Day 1 to kick start the flavours that will infuse this bread with beautiful aromas. The dough is made and baked on Day 2. This recipe will make six loaves (980 g each).

Day 1. Preparing the Components
Ingredients: Poolish

796 g   White strong baker's flour/AP flour, T −55
817 g   Water (22 °C)
  1 g   Dry yeast

Making the Poolish

1. Add all the ingredients together and mix for 4 minutes at 1st speed. Then mix for 2 minutes at 2nd speed.
2. Cover the poolish (in a bowl) and leave it in a cool place for 8–12 hours.

Ingredients: Soaked Nut Mix

66 g	Maple syrup
166 g	Ice wine or sweet white wine
364 g	Dried sweetened cherries
287 g	Toasted pine nuts, walnuts, or pecans
364 g	Chocolate chips
4 g	Cinnamon

Making the Soaked Nut Mix

Excluding the chocolate chips and cinnamon (save for making nut mix on Day 2), gently blend all the remaining nut mix ingredients. Soak the nut mix overnight for a minimum of 8 hours.

Day 2. Mixing the Components

Finalizing the Nut Mix

Add the chocolate chips and cinnamon (see ingredients list for Soaked Nut Mix) to the soaked nut mix and mix on slow speed for 1 ½ minutes. Set aside.

Ingredients: Dough

1,538 g	White flour
265 g	Malted wheat flakes or large oat flakes
9 g	Malted barley flour (diastatic)
265 g	Maple syrup
53 g	Brown sugar
138 g	Whole eggs
707 g	Water (+/- 10% depending on the flour quality)
1,614 g	Poolish
10 g	Dry yeast
48 g	Salt
Entire	Soaked nut mix

Making the Dough

The DDT is 24 °C.

1. Excluding the poolish, dry yeast, and salt, add the remaining ingredients together and blend them in a bowl.

2. Mix for 4 minutes at slow speed in a mixer with a dough hook.

3. Rest for 15 minutes to autolyse.

4. Add the poolish, dry yeast, salt. Mix for 3 minutes on slow speed and 4–7 minutes on 2nd speed.

5. When the dough is fully developed, add the finalized soaked nut mix. Don't over mix the finalized soaked nut mix through the dough.

6. Once the dough is mixed, divide it into six pieces (980 g each) and preshape them round.

7. Cover and allow 20–25 minutes to rest in intermediate proof.

8. Final, shape the dough into a pear shape, place on couche cloths, cover, and proof for about 60 minutes at room temperature or at 22 °C–23 °C in a proofer with 80% relative humidity.

9. Once the loaves are ready to be baked, place them on parchment paper. Cut the dough's thick end through completely 1/3 of the way down and spread the dough out to form a heart shape.

10. Dust the dough pieces with flour or top them with your favourite seeds or crushed nuts before scoring the loaves and baking them for about 30–35 minutes at 215 °C–230 °C with a dash of steam. Drain off the steam and bake dry for the last 10 minutes of baking.

11. After removing the loaves from the oven, cool them on wire racks.

Wang Li (China)

Wang Li began her professional career by studying at the Shanghai Young Bakers' School, a programme sponsored by Lesaffre, China. She completed her programme in 2011 and travelled to L'École Christian Vabret Boulangerie Pâtisserie Cuisine (formerly L'École Française de Boulangerie, Pâtisserie d'Aurillac) in France where she obtained her CAP later that year. After obtaining her baker's certificate, she returned to Shanghai to give back what she learned in France by teaching at the Shanghai Young Bakers' School. In 2014, she was awarded the Trophy of Food Contributor (Jeune Espoir) by the French Ministry of Agriculture. After leaving school in 2015, Wang sought to perfect her skills. With the support of Lesaffre, she enrolled at INBP and graduated in 2016. Wang again returned to Shanghai, where she became the senior trainer at the Hirondelle Academy, the Lesaffre China Group's technical school. Wang has been very active in the Chinese bakery industry since then.

Wang is an official jury member in the Chinese national competitions and was a jury member at the Shanghai bread festival (2017–2019). She was the technical manager in the Asia selections for the Louis Lesaffre Cup, and in 2020 was the coach of Team China during the CDM de la Boulangerie in Paris, where they won the gold medal. During the same year, Wang received the prestigious award from founder Christian Vabret for her exceptional contributions to the Chinese Association of Bakery and Confectionery Industry. Wang also is a member of the Elite de la Boulangerie International. Wang was responsible for organising the international jury members' travel to the Louis Lesaffre Cup, Shanghai (2019). Through the many emails she exchanged with Jimmy in preparation for this travel to China, they became acquainted. Wang and Jimmy got to know each other better during the week of competitions as Wang worked to organise dinners and meetings.

Follow Wang Li: Facebook, https://www.Facebook.com/li.wang.7739814

~Wang Li

6. Wang Li's Red Date & Pomelo Brioche

This viennoiserie requires three dough types: brioche for the centre and white and black doughs for the sides. You can make the viennoiserie in two different sizes of triangular moulds. Using 1 kg of flour, the yield is 30 large brioches, 70 small brioches, or 20 sets of brioches (20 large and 20 small). You can easily make smaller quantities by halving the recipe.

Large: 13 cm (L) × 13 cm (W) × 5 cm (H)
Small: 9 cm (L) × 9 cm (W) × 3.5 cm (H)

Stage 1. Making the Three Doughs and Preparing the Pans

Ingredients: Brioche Dough

1,000 g	High protein flour (Chinese flour or equivalent)
160 g	Sugar
18 g	Salt
15 g	Fresh yeast
350 g	Water
300 g	Egg
100 g	Liquid sourdough (33.3 g sourdough; 33.4 g water; 33.3 g flour)
400 g	Butter (add once dough development has taken place).

Making the Brioche Dough

The DDT is 24 °C.

1. Mix all the ingredients, except for the butter, in a mixer with a dough hook for 5 minutes on 1st speed. Then mix for 5 minutes on 2nd speed until the dough is smooth and soft.

2. When a windowpane develops, add 1/3 of the butter at a time on 1st sped. Be sure that you mix to clear each time before adding more butter. (For ease of incorporation, you can prepare the butter by cutting it into small cubes of approximately 1 cm.) You mustn't start adding the butter until the windowpane is developed.

3. Mould the dough to a round shape and place it in a container with a lid. Ferment the dough for 60 minutes at room temperature.

Recipes: Breads & Buns

4. After the first fermentation is complete, degas the dough and ferment the dough a second time for 16 hours at 5 °C.

5. Scale the large pieces at 75 g and the small pieces at 30 g each.

6. Allow the pieces to rest for 30 minutes at −18 °C in a freezer.

Ingredients: White Dough

450 g	Low protein flour
180 g	Icing sugar
45 g	Butter
180 g	Milk

Ingredients: Black Dough

450 g	Low protein flour
180 g	Icing sugar
45 g	Butter
5 g	Dark cocoa powder
180 g	Milk

Making the White and Back Dough

1. Mix the white dough ingredients very well using a dough hook on a stand mixer. Remove the dough from the mixing bowl. Repeat this process for the black dough.

2. Separately, roll out pieces of the white and black dough (100 g each) into baguettes approximately 20 cm long.

3. Cut each piece in half and randomly plait (braid) the dough. Then roll out the dough using a rolling pin until the dough is 1 mm thick. (You should now have sheets of merged and marbled dough.) Refrigerate the dough for 1 hour.

Preparing the Pans

When the dough sheets are chilled, cut them into strips the size of the height and length of the pan(s) you're using and use the strips to line the inner sides of the moulds. As needed, carefully retrim the dough with a very sharp knife or blade so it's the exact height of the tin and looks neat. Set the prepared pans aside. Make the brioche filling and fill the dough. A tutorial for this process is available: https://www.youtube.com/watch?v=uRKfVOb6bGU

Stage 2: Filling the Brioche and Baking the Viennoiserie

Ingredients: Red Date Financier

- 80 g   Almond powder (ground almonds)
- 160 g Red dates chopped very fine or blended to a paste
- 350 g Icing sugar
- 125 g Low protein flour (biscuit or cake flour)
- 335 g Egg white
- 180 g Butter
- 30 g   Glucose syrup (trimoline, honey, or golden syrup)
- 3 g   Baking powder

Making the Red Date Financier

1. Melt the butter. Then blend all ingredients evenly.
2. Pour the batter into the silicone mould.
3. Bake in a convection oven at 180 °C for 15 minutes.
4. Remove from the oven and cool.

Ingredients: Pomelo Sauce

- 400g Pomelo purée
- 100g Sugar
- 30g   Water
- 10g   Corn starch

Making the Pomelo Sauce

1. Melt the pomelo purée in a pot. Add the sugar and melt.
2. Mix the water and corn starch into a batter.
3. Blend all ingredients and stir until it gets thick and blended fully. Set aside.

Filling the Brioche

1. Using a teaspoon or scoop, pack the date financier and pomelo sauce into the dough. For the 75 g pieces, use 30 g of date financier and 15 g of pomelo sauce. For the 30 g pieces, use 12 g of date financier and 10 g pomelo sauce.

Recipes: Breads & Buns

2. Place the filled brioche in the centre of the triangular moulds and gently press down well with the seam to the bottom of the shapes ensuring each corner angle is filled.

3. Final proof the prepared pans with filled brioche for 60 minutes at 28 °C.

Baking the Assembled Brioche

Bake the assembled brioche with a tray on top of the pans and several weights on top of the tray to ensure that it doesn't rise in the oven during baking. Set the oven to 225 °C. When it reaches the temperature, load the pastries, close the oven door, reset the oven to bake at 195 °C. Bake the large pans for 15 minutes, and bake the small pans for 11 minutes.

Stage 3: Decorating the Viennoiserie

Ingredients: Decorative Wings

- 450 g Low protein flour/cake flour/biscuit flour
- 180 g Icing sugar
- 45 g   Butter
- 160 g Milk

Making the Decorative Wings

1. Mix all the ingredients together very well using a dough hook.

2. Put the dough into the wings mould and trim any rough edges.

3. Bake in a warm oven at 150 °C until it takes some colour. Remove from the oven.

4. While warm, stand one end of the wing up on the side of a tin and bent it until it cools and sets. This will give the wing a curved or teaspoon shape into which you'll place the garnish of raspberry and ground pistachio nuts as your finishing touch.

Applying the Finishing Touches

You'll need fresh raspberries, apricot glaze, and chopped pistachio nuts to finish the viennoiserie. The viennoiserie can be stacked with a small one on top of a large one or finished individually.

Recipes: Breads & Buns

1. Using a bench scraper, mask the centre of the triangle and dust each corner equally with icing sugar, leaving the centre clear for the top's decorative wing.

2. Dip the open side of a raspberry in a boiled apricot glaze and then in chopped pistachio nuts.

3. Garnish the wing's bottom with the prepared raspberry and fix the decorative wing to the pastry's centre top in the undusted area.

Ibrahim Mohamed Ghoush (Egypt)

Ghoush is an Egyptian artisan baker/pastry chef of note. He's been at the forefront of the Egyptian national bakery team for many years and is a viennoiserie specialist. He's a very kind and generous man and passionate about baking. In 2017, Ghoush competed in the African Bakery Cup in Casablanca, Morocco, as part of the Egyptian team. He and his team competed again in 2019 and won. The team participated in the CDM de la Boulangerie in Paris, France in 2020. They didn't win, but they did Egypt proud by being the first Egyptian team to qualify for the CDM.

Ghoush first met Jimmy at the 2017 African Bakery Cup in Morocco when Ghoush was competing and Jimmy was president of the jury. The two have been friends ever since and are in regular contact with each other online.

Follow Ghoush: Instagram, https://www.instagram.com/chefghoushofficial/

~Ibrahim Mohamed Ghoush

7. Ghoush's Forgiveness Tablet Bread

The history of Egyptian tablet bread extends back thousands of years to Ghoush's ancestors, the Pharaohs. The bread was made and distributed in temples and tombs as an offering to the gods. After the Islamic conquests, Egyptian authorities distributed this bread to the poor and needy at cemeteries as acts of kindness and asking for God's forgiveness. The bread is made with hummus, yeast, sesame seeds, ghee, and dates—all typical Egyptian ingredients used by the forefathers of all bread making. This recipe takes 2 days to prepare. The hummus yeast and date paste are made on Day 1. The dough is made on Day 2.

Day 1: Preparing the Components

Ingredients: Hummus Yeast Preparation

100 g	Crushed hummus
300 g	Warm milk

Making the Hummus Yeast Preparation

1. Mix hummus and warm milk together.

2. Cover and ferment in a warm place for 24 hours.

Ingredients: Date Paste

1,000 g	Seedless dates
200 g	Ghee
100 g	Sesame seeds

Making the Date Paste

1. Mix the dates in a stand mixer with a cake beater until it becomes a paste.
2. Add the ghee and sesame seeds. Mix to clear on slow. Cover and set aside.

Ingredients: Dough

2,000 g	Strong flour/bakers flour/AP flour
200 g	Sugar
2 g	Salt
5 g	Fresh yeast
60 g	Hummus yeast
800 g	Ghee (softened)
800 g	Buttermilk
50 g	Water

Making the Dough

The DDT is 26 °C.

1. Mix the ghee with warmed buttermilk and 180 g of the sugar in a mixer with a dough hook on low speed. After the buttermilk and sugar are creamed, add the flour and salt.
2. Slowly add and mix the 20 g of the remaining sugar, the 50 g water, and the fresh yeast.
3. Add the hummus yeast and mix at 1st speed for 2–3 minutes until incorporated.
4. Mix on 2nd speed for another 6–7 minutes to form a smooth dough. Check for windowpane development. The dough should be 26 °C.
5. Leave the dough to rest for 1 hour in bulk fermentation.
6. Scale the dough into small balls of 100 g each.
7. Allow the dough to rest for 15 minutes. Using a rolling pin, roll out the dough to 15 cm.
8. Fill the centre of the dough with 70 g of the date paste and seal.
9. Using a rolling pin, roll out the dough to a flat circle measuring approximately 15 cm.
10. Pierce/dock the dough to create a vent for the date filling as it cooks.
11. Moisten with egg wash and dip into sesame seeds. Then place on trays lined with parchment paper.

12. Proof for 1 hour at 28 °C.
13. Bake at 200 °C for 25 minutes.
14. Cool on wire racks after baking, and enjoy a taste of Egypt!

David Bedu (France)

Baker, pastry chef, chocolatier, and cook-caterer David Bedu, was born in Sancerre, France, on a hill by the banks of the Loire known for its Sauvignon Blanc wine. David became a baker and a pastry chef by chance. Avant-garde and non-conformist, David is recognized for his innovative techniques in artistic baking and pastry making. This characteristic has gotten him in hot water with the traditional style village baker for more than 35 years. One of his unique creations is the famous two-tone croissant bicolour, which has become an international classic for more than a decade.

Winning the title of one of the best young bakers in France (1988–1989) introduced David to the world of baking excellence that motivated him throughout his professional career and led him to participate in the CDM de la Boulangerie in Paris in 2005, where he won the silver medal for France. David also worked as a pastry chef in Agadir, Morocco, in an international luxury restaurant alongside a French chef. It was there that he developed a taste for the effervescence of Moroccan cuisine, which he brought back with him to France when he returned. Soon after, he joined the Relais Châteaux in Montfavet, near Avignon, as the pastry chef for the 1 Michelin star restaurant at the Hôtellerie les Frênes, before moving to Montpellier as an artisan baker where he remained for more than 15 years.

In 2008, he decided to try a new adventure. He travelled to Piacenza, Italy, near Milan, where he took a job as chef baker in a complex bar, pastry shop, bakery, and luxury restaurant. In 2010, he became director of the gastronomic school Gustar in Pistoia, Tuscany. The school is dedicated to baking, pastry making, cooking, and bartending. In 2014, he opened his bakery, Pank la Bulangeria, in Florence's historic halls, a stone's throw from the Duomom, the famous marble cathedral in the city's tourism heart. Through Pank la Bulangeria, David has received many distinctions from Italian gastronomic guides. He also has collaborated with the magazine *Il Panificatore Italiano* to take charge of a column in which he shares his vision of the artisanal and artistic bakery with his Italian colleagues.

David and Jimmy had met virtually for many years over various social media platforms. The two finally met each other face-to-face in 2019 at the Cremai exhibition held in Casablanca, Morocco. The show's organiser, Kamal Rahal Essoulami, invited David to be a jury member for the African selection of the World Bakery Cup organized by Christian Vabret. Jimmy was also a jury member at the event. From that time, the two formed a great friendship. Their love of all things in bread and pastry has collectively united them in their baking journeys.

Follow David: Instagram, https://www.instagram.com/pank_bulangeria/

~David Bedu

8. David's Flowerpot Tomato Bread

This recipe takes 2 days to prepare. The flowerpots (you'll need seven small flowerpots measuring 9 cm in diameter × 10 cm high) are partially prepped and the poolish is made on Day 1. The flowerpots are prepared for baking (you'll need soft butter and black poppy seeds) and the dough is made and baked on Day 2.

Day 1: Preparing the Flowerpots and Poolish

Initial Preparation of the Flowerpots

Place the terracotta pots in cold water overnight for about 12 hours.

Ingredients: Poolish

- 63 g   Italian flour Type 0 (W200/220)
- 37 g   Water
- 32 g   Tomato pulp
- 0.25 g   Yeast, fresh

Making the Poolish

Mix ingredients together to form a dough. Allow to ferment 23 °C–25 °C for 15–18 hours.

Day 2: Making and Baking the Dough

Preparing the Flowerpots Moulds for Baking

1. Remove the pots from the water (after soaking for 12 hours) and let them dry well.

2. Using soft but not melted butter, grease the inside of the mould up to the edge of the flowerpot. Cover the bottom and sides with the poppy seeds so that the seeds adhere evenly in the pots.

3. Leave the prepared moulds on a baking tray in the refrigerator for about 1 hour to let the butter and seeds skin and firm up before putting the dough in the flower pots.

Ingredients: Dough

275 g	Bakers flour or Italian flour Type 0 (W200/220)
38 g	Rye flour
188 g	Water
7 g	Fresh yeast
15 g	Salt
3 g	Wheat germ
132 g	Poolish
19 g	Dried tomatoes in oil
1. 25 g	Dried oregano
1. 25 g	Fresh basil (ground with a knife)
25 g	Fresh garlic (crushed and chopped garlic)

Making the Dough

The DDT is 24 °C.

1. Using a spiral mixer, or stand mixer with a dough hook, mix together the two flours, water, yeast, salt, wheat germ, and poolish. When these ingredients are well-mixed, incorporate the dried tomatoes in oil, oregano, fresh basil, and garlic.

2. Mix the dough for 10 minutes on 1st speed and 3 minutes on 2nd speed. Then let the dough rest for 1 hour of bulk fermentation.

3. Scale the dough at 100 g. Preshape into round balls, cover, and let rest for 30 minutes.

4. After the dough has rested, flatten the balls and then roll them up again. Then put them in the ready moulds. Let the dough rise for 1½ hours at 25 °C. (You'll add the Margherita decoration on top of the dough 45 minutes into this proofing process. See directions for Making the Hard Dough for the Margherita Decoration on the Bread.)

5. Dust the bread with wheat flour and place a half-cut cherry tomato in the centre of the Margherita flower.

6. Bake for 25 minutes in a convection oven at 170 °C with steam.

7. Remove from oven and cool on wire racks.

Ingredients: Hard Dough for Margherita Decoration on the Bread

150 g	Bakers flour or Italian flour Type 0 (W200/220)
93 g	Water
2.5 g	Salt
1.25 g	Yeast
38 g	Rye flour

Making the Hard Dough for Margherita Decoration on the Bread

1. Mix all the ingredients to make a smooth dough.

2. Roll out the dough by hand or with a sheeter to a thickness of approximately 2 mm. Place between two plastic sheets and refrigerate for at least 1 hour.

3. Using a pastry cutter, cut the daisy to place on top of the bread, lightly brush the flower's edges with oil, and place the decoration on the loaves 45 minutes into the proofing stage.

Jean Claude Choquet, Meilleur Ouvrier De France (France)

Jean Claude Choquet entered the baking profession in 1963. In 1967, he earned a master's degree, and by 1977, he had taken over the family business with his wife, Marie Madeleine. By 1995, Jean Claude was working for a company with his son Jérôme.

Passionate about his job, he earned the title of "The Best Worker in France" in 1986 and created the French bakery team, holding the vice president's position. He served as the French jury during the first World Cups created by the French teams. Jean Claude created and founded the European Bakery Cup at the Serbotel Fair in Nantes, 1993, under the Loire-Atlantique Baker's Federation's umbrella. It was during this event that Jean Claude met Jimmy, and a friendship was born. In 2019, Jean Claude and his wife visited Jimmy at his family bakery in Galway. They share a passion for the profession and are in constant search for excellence. They both work at passing on their know-how,

combining tradition and modernity as the common thread of their professional careers.

After almost 20 years in the industry, Jean Claude became involved in the defence of the Baker's Federation of Loire-Atlantique profession. In 1988, 6 years later, he became its president, and then a few years later, the president of the 4th region, which includes 12 departments. Jean Claude was deputy president of the confederation for 6 years while overseeing the INBP. He also is president of the chamber of trades and crafts of Loire Atlantique of the Pays de la Loire region. He was vice president of the permanent assembly chambers of trades and crafts (APCMA) for 10 years and then treasurer for 5 years.

Passionate about training, Jean Claude's worked in Poland, Germany, Russia, Korea, and Africa. Solicited by the Ivorian State in 2015, he created with three partners a bakery/training centre in Abidjan. He signed an agreement with the state and La Chambre de Métiers et de L'Artisanat (CRMA) of Pays de la Loire to include BAC + 3 students and make them trainers or business managers. Jean Claude's son Jérôme currently manages the centre. Ivorians appreciate the baguette, of which more than 4,000 units are produced daily.

~Jean Claude Choquet

9. Jean Claude's Millet Bread with Tamarind Juice

Ingredients: Tamarind Syrup

2,000 g	Water
250 g	Tamarind
200 g	Sugar
2 g	Juice from 2 lemons

Preparing the Tamarind Syrup

1. Boil the water, sugar, and tamarind.
2. Let infuse then filter.
3. Add the lemon juice.
4. Keep cold for use in the dough.

Ingredients: Millet Bread Dough

2,600 g	Flour T–65
400 g	Millet flour
60 g	Salt
5 g	Yeast (dry)
1,200 g	Tamarind syrup
500 g	Water
1,800 g	Liquid leaven (See Judy Koh's starter: Recipe #29)

Making the Millet Bread Dough

1. Mix all the ingredients together and knead using a stand mixer for 5 minutes on 1st speed and then for 8 minutes on 2nd speed.
2. Let the dough proof for 1 hour in the bowl or container, covered.
3. Divide the dough into 12 pieces of 530 g each.

Recipes: Breads & Buns

4. To make the flowers' parts, divide each 530 g piece into five dough pieces of 90 g each, 5 dough pieces of 10 g each, and 1 dough piece of 30 g.

5. Shape the 90 g and 10 g dough pieces into rolls, pointed and tapered at one end.

6. Flatten the 10 g dough pieces only into a leaf/petal shape using a small rolling pin.

7. Apply some oil to one side of each leaf/petal along the outside edges so they'll lift during the bake and give the bread its 3-dimensional flower shape.

8. Roll the 30 g dough piece into a tight, round ball for the centre of the flower.

9. Arrange the 10 g flattened, oiled dough pieces (oil side down) on the 90 g pieces.

10. Take the five assembled pieces and arrange them on a tray in the shape of a flower, with the pointed ends facing out. Be sure to arrange the pieces, so the 10 g petals of the flower are facing upwards. Then place the 30 g ball in the centre of the flower, pressing it down firmly to finish the shape.

11. Proof for 1–2 hours at 24 °C–26 °C.

12. Using a sieve, dust each flower with white wheat flour.

13. Score under each petal using a sharp razor blade to create a flap. Then, using both scissors and a blade, gently incise and score the leaves to make a pretty floral shape.

14. Bake at 240 °C with steam for 30–40 minutes, venting the steam for the final 10 minutes.

15. Remove from the oven and cool on wire racks.

Stages of Dough Showing Scaling, Shaping, and Assembly

Step 4. Subdivided dough (90/10/30 g)

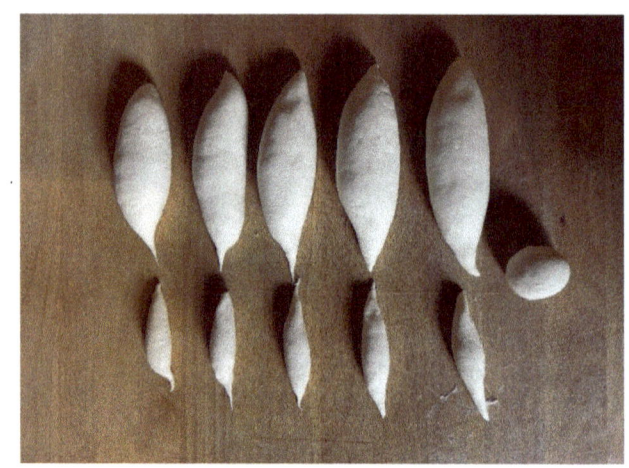

Step 6. Rolled dough pointed at one end

Step 7. Small (10 g) pieces rolled out thin

Step 8. Edges brushed with oil

Step 11. Assembled flower

Step 14. Dusted flower (before cutting)

Nutritional Value and Benefits of the Bread

This bread is not only beautiful with a little nutty taste, it's also nutritionally sound, and its ingredients have a variety of health benefits. Millet contains significant amounts of essential amino acids and proteins. It's rich in phosphorus, magnesium, calcium, zinc, and manganese, as well as vitamins B1 and B6. Its zinc content effectively boosts the immune system, and magnesium and calcium contribute to good mineralization. It doesn't contain gluten, so it's very digestible and recommended for people with gluten intolerance. Its consumption promotes good cholesterol and helps decrease the symptoms of diabetes. It even has antioxidants that fight against the ageing of the skin.

Tamarind, also called turkey date palm, was introduced to Europe by the Arabs. Tamarind contains calcium, phosphorus, iron, sodium, and potassium and is rich in vitamins B1, B2, B11, PP (B-3), and C. Tamarind's healing and antiseptic virtues are well-known in Chinese and Arabic medicines.

Tamarind is known to aid digestion and combat the effects of cellular ageing. It's used for the symptomatic treatment of constipation and is recommended for its antiseptic benefits, especially for urinary (cystitis), skin, and respiratory problems. The laxative and anti-infective properties of tamarind have been studied in association with certain anticancer treatments. Laboratory studies seek to demonstrate the effects of geraniol present in tamarind in the fight against pancreatic cancer. Tamarind pulp has a European Pharmacopoeia registration number and a control signature.

Sébastien Lagrue, World Champion Chocolatine 2019 (France)

Originally from Rouen in Upper Normandy, in 1990, Sébastien Lagrue entered the vocational high school of bakery and pastry Herbouville, a neighbour of the famous INBP Rouen, where he studied for 3 years. In 1992, he obtained the baker's CAP, and in 1993 the pastry chef, chocolate maker, ice-cream maker, and confectioner CAP. In 1994, after a year spent serving the national service, he joined his wife Sophie Boulangère, a pastry chef he met 3 years earlier in high school, at his family bakery/pastry shop in the Hautes Pyrénées (Arras en Lavedan). The shop was founded by his grandfather in May 1949 and had been taken over by his parents. Sébastien heads the bakery as the baker, and Sophie is the pastry chef. Since 2013, they've taken over the family business as managers, and together, they have two shops—one in Arras in Lavedan and another in Argelès-Gazost. In 2019, the 4th generation joined their bakery team. Son Anthony, the eldest, studied pastry/chocolate, and Elian studies bakery/pastry.

For several years, Sébastien has been vice president of the Pastry Chefs of the World, which is committed to valuing these fine craftsmen and allowing them a global exchange with, among others, a Facebook group with more than 28,000 members. This association's focus is to highlight the profession's expertise through competitions, workshops, and meetings.

Sébastien met Jimmy at the CDM Chocolatine 2019 in Toulouse, France. Sébastien, like

Jimmy, particularly enjoys lamination. He's studied under master bakers such as Peter Yuen, Gaëtan Paris, Eric Chevallereau, and Michael Chesnouard. He credits their guidance, flair, and talent for his 1st place world champion win at the CDM Chocolatine in 2019. (Jimmy came in 2nd place!) Today, Sébastien works in his company and provides training to share his bakery know-how worldwide with his world-class viennoiserie. His product, called the Tordeau, has been made in Sebastien's business since 1949.

Contact Sébastien Lagrue: www.auxdelicesdesophie65.com
Aux Delices de Sophie / 21, route du Val d'Azun 65400 Arras en Lavedan- FRANCE
Tel: +33 6 33 27 06 98, e-mail: formaseb65@gmail.com

~Sébastien Lagrue

10. Le Tordu (Ou Torsadé)

This recipe makes three 620 g pieces. The process for making the dough in this recipe requires bassinage, a French term for holding off a portion of the total water until the end of mixing. This process enables the dough to mix better at lower hydration levels as the dough is stiffer. As the dough develops, the starch absorbs more liquids, enabling extra water to be incorporated into the dough at the end of the mixing process.

Ingredients: Dough

850 g	Wheat flour/traditional Française T-65/AP flour
150 g	Rye flour T-170
650 g	Water
20 g	Salt
5 g	Fresh yeast
125 g	Liquid levain (See Judy Koh's starter: Recipe #29)
125 g	Water (for bassinage)

Making the Dough

DDT is 24 °C–26 °C.

1. Using a spiral mixer, place all ingredients together into a bowl.
2. Blend together for 3 minutes on 1st speed. Then mix for 8 minutes on 1st speed and then for 2 minutes on 2nd speed.

3. Incorporate the bassinage. Adjust the bassinage according to the dough mix to clear.
4. Dough consistency should be soft and wet.
5. Ferment for 2 hours. Stretch and fold dough after 1 hour.
6. Scale three pieces of dough at 620 g each. Roll into a ball shape.
7. Rest for 20 minutes of intermediate proofing.
8. Shape and form into a batard shape (tight shape). Rest for 15 minutes.

9. Using a thin rolling pin, dust the dough with flour. Flatten in the centre.
10. Twist the dusted side from the outside towards the centre to form a cone.
11. Continue twisting until the dough piece is all twisted.
12. Place on well-dusted couche cloths with rye flour. Proof for 1 hour.
13. Bake for 45 minutes at 240 °C on the sole of the oven.
14. Add steam to the oven. Drain the steam after 15 minutes.
15. Bake at a falling temperature for the remainder of the bake dropping to >225 °C
16. Place the bread on a wire rack to cool.

Stages of Dough Twisting

Step 9. Dust and flatten centre of dough

Step 10a. Twist the dough to form a cone.

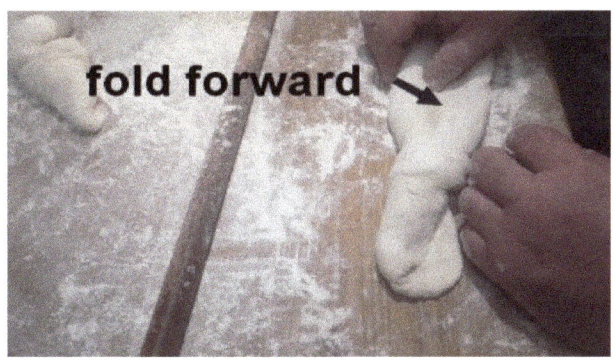
Step 10b. Fold dough forward.

Step 10c. Form initial twist.

Step 11. Finish twisting the dough.

Déborah Ott-Libs, World Champion Viennoiserie 2018 (France)

Déborah Ott-Libs is a master baker from Alsace, France. Since Déborah was 15 years old, she lived in the exciting world of bakery and bakery competitions on a local, national, and international level. Always competitive, she won the gold medal in 2009 at the IBA European Cup. Her innovative viennoiserie earned her a place on the French bakery team at the CDM de la Boulangerie 2016 in Paris, France. Deborah and Jimmy met when Jimmy was president of the jury at the competition. The French team won bronze at this event. In 2018 Déborah was selected on the strength of her innovative and exciting viennoiserie as a candidate in the world masters. She became world champion at the

competition, wowing the jury with her dainty creations. She visited Galway in 2018 with her then-fiancée Chris Libs and worked with Jimmy in his bakery, where they made laminated pastry and Conger bread together. Jimmy attended her wedding as a guest in June 2019, in Alsace, France, where she married her sweetheart Chris. Déborah has now moved to the USA with Chris, where she works for fellow Alsatian and world champion baker, Pierre Zimmermann of La Fournette bakery, Chicago, who also features in this book.

Follow Deborah: Instagram, https://www.instagram.com/ deborah.ott.libs/

~Déborah Ott-Libs

11. Déborah's Braided Chocolate Raspberry Brioche

This recipe makes 52 brioches at 45 g each. Brioche freezes very well, so normally, the dough is divided. One half is processed after mixing and the other half is frozen for future use. This recipe takes 2 days to prepare. The dough is made on Day 1. The ganache's made and the dough is shaped and baked on Day 2. You'll also need an egg wash (1 egg and pinch of salt whisked together to break down the egg; let sit for 15 minutes before using).

Day 1: Preparing the Brioche Dough
Ingredients: Brioche Dough

1,000 g	Strong bread-making flour: AP or T–55
150 g	Sugar
20 g	Salt
45 g	Fresh yeast
500 g	Whole egg
90 g	Milk
500 g	Butter
70 g	Fresh mint (chopped into small pieces or blitz in a blender)

Making the Brioche Dough

The DDT is 24 °C.

1. In a planetary mixer with a dough hook, mix flour, sugar, salt, fresh yeast, egg and the milk for 5 minutes on 1st speed and for 7 minutes on 2nd speed.
2. Add the butter (room temperature, not from the refrigerator) over three stages.

3. Mix for 6 minutes again to clear the butter completely through the dough.

4. Add the chopped fresh mint and mix for 1 minute on 1st speed.

5. Place the dough overnight in the refrigerator at 3 °C.

Day 2: Preparing and Baking the Brioche Dough

Ingredients: Chocolate/Raspberry Ganache

120 g	Fresh double dairy cream (heavy cream)
38 g	Trimoline/glucose syrup (or honey)
45 g	Corn starch (sieve well in advance to remove lumps)
255 g	Dark chocolate 52% cocoa callets (drops or chopped/small pieces)
150 g	Raspberry purée (blend fresh raspberries down to a purée)

Making the Chocolate/Raspberry Ganache

1. Boil the heavy cream and trimoline in a saucepan.

2. Add the corn starch, followed by the dark chocolate and raspberry purée.

3. Chill in the freezer for 10 minutes before you're ready to use it, allowing it to harden.

Making the Brioche

1. Divide dough into 45 g pieces.

2. Pre-shape into long pieces and rest for 30 minutes at 2 °C in the refrigerator or for 10 minutes in the freezer until the dough becomes firm and easy to work.

3. Using a rolling pin, roll out the chilled dough into rectangles 15 cm in length and 4 cm in width (see Image 1).

4. Roll out the 23 g units of ganache into strings approximately 13 cm long and insert them into the centre of the rectangle (see Image 2). Keep the

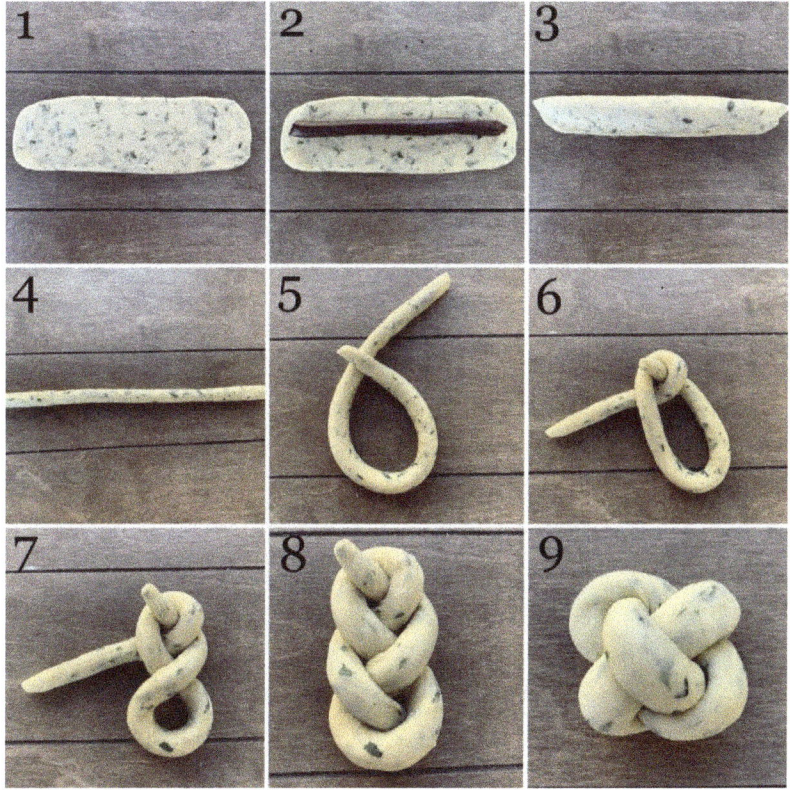

Recipes: Breads & Buns

ganache clear of the edges of the dough so it'll become enclosed when the dough is rolled in Step 5.

5. Roll each piece into a cylinder shape approximately 40 cm long and make a braid (one string plait; see Images 3-9).

6. Assemble on trays, allowing adequate spacing to avoid batching. Proof for 90 minutes at 25 °C and 70%–80% humidity.

7. Egg wash and bake at 170 °C in a fan oven for 12 minutes.

8. Allow to cool. Then, using a large scraper, mask ¾ of the brioche. Using a small sieve, dust the exposed ¼ of the brioche with icing sugar.

9. Garnish with a fresh raspberry and a leaf of fresh mint to finish.

Christian Vabret, Meilleur Ouvrier de France (France)

The son of a French artisan baker, Christian Vabret, grew up in the gentle warmth of the bakery beside his father who passed on to him the passion of his profession. An entrepreneur at heart, he

first moved to Aurillac at the age of 20. In 1986, he won the title of France's Best Workers in Bakery, Meilleur Ouvrier de France (MOF). In 1998, he opened a chain of shops named The Fournil Christian Vabret with nine stores in Santiago du Chile. Then, he realised his dream in 2011 by opening his first bakery in Paris, Au Pettit Versailles du Marais, a shop whose façade is classified as a historical monument in the heart of the Marais in Paris. A second bakery followed in 2015 in Paris, The Pain Acadamie. Then the Marie Antoinette Tea Shop in 2019. Those three businesses symbolize the soul of the baker Christian Vabret. Throughout his career, he's continued to honour artisan bakery worldwide. He created in 1992 the World Cup of Bakery, a major international competition with this in mind. After 27 years, the World Cup of Bakery has realised its intents: to promote the baker's trade, improve the quality of the products, and bring the world's bakers together to accentuate professional, friendly exchanges.

In 2002, Christian Vabret went to Ireland to present the World Cup of Bakery. It was during this trip that he met Jimmy Griffin, an atypical Irish baker. Since then, a great friendship was formed, where both have travelled the world, participating in global competitions and meeting to promote artisan bakery around the world. It's a beautiful story of friendship that unites bakers globally. Christian is also the founder of the Elite de la Boulangerie Internationale. Both inducted and presented Jimmy with his (EBI) medallion to recognise his service to the global bakery community over the past 2 decades.

Contact Christian at his school, L'École Christian Vabret – Boulangerie, Pâtisserie & Cuisine: Facebook, https://www.Facebook.com/profile.php?id=100010070081023

~Christian Vabret

12. Pain Surprise á La Provençale

The Provençal surprise bread is filled with a salad rich in raw ingredients. Because it transports easily, it's ideal for picnics—compact outdoor dining at its best. But don't discount it for sharing with friends in any friendly atmosphere with a glass of nice wine. Use your own favourite fillings to personalise your own Pain Surprise and impress your friends and colleagues.

Ingredients: Dough

1000 g	Flour T-65
600 g	Water
200 g	Fermented dough (overnight sponge or poolish)
18 g	Salt
10 g	Yeast
100 g	Olive oil

Making the Dough

The DDT is 25 °C when mixed for optimum fermentation.

1. Using a stand mixer with a dough hook, place all the ingredients in a mixing bowl and mix for 5 minutes on 1st speed.
2. Knead for a further 5 minutes on 2nd speed until the dough is smooth and soft.
3. Ferment for 1 hour at 25 °C.
4. Divide into 4 pieces of 480 g each and mould gently into balls.
5. Ferment for 30 minutes at 25 °C, covered in a machine bowl or container.
6. Shape into a ball, brush with olive oil, and sprinkle with basil.
7. Proof for 90 minutes at 25 °C and 70%–80% relative humidity.
8. Place in the oven and add steam to the oven. Bake at 250°C/260 °C for 15 minutes.
9. Drain the steam from the oven after 10 minutes to dry the crust.
10. The bread shouldn't be baked too much and should have a golden crust.

Salad Recipe Suggestion

After the bread is cooled, slice it near the top and scoop out the inside (similar to Bagnat bread). The fresh seasonal salad filling is made of mixed salad leaves, cucumber, beetroot, anchovies, asparagus, and shavings of Auvergne ham accompanied by a muslin sauce and a garlic-flavoured mayonnaise. Place the filling into the bread.

Pierre Zimmermann, World Champion 1996 (France & United States)

Pierre Zimmermann owns La Fournette, a wholesale and retail bakery in Chicago, Illinois. He's a native of Alsace, France, a master baker, and winner of the CDM de la Boulangerie (in 1996 as a team member). In 2008, as the French team coach, he guided France to world cup glory once more.

In 2015, he was appointed as the president of the Jury for the Louis Lesaffre Cup. Along with notable baker and former bakery USA team member Solveig Tofte, he co-founded the Intergalactic Bakers Federation (IGBF) in 2016. The IGBF is a new international organisation which aims to aid communities through education and volunteer work. Pierre was also inducted as a member of the Elite de la Boulangerie Internationale at CDM de la Boulangerie 2016 in Paris. Pierre and Jimmy met while at the CDM de la Boulangerie, where they had the chance to spend some time together when Jimmy was president of the jury at the 2016 CDM de la Boulangerie in Paris and Pierre was president of the Louis Lesaffre Cup.

Follow Pierre: Instagram, https://www.instagram.com/pierzim/?hl=en

~Pierre Zimmermann

13. Pierre's Alsace Beer Bread

Situated in France but close to the German border, Alsace is a region steeped in Franco Germanic history and culture. The local cuisine and baked products are an amazing mix of these rich cultures and histories. Pierre had the pleasure of visiting Strasbourg in Alsace on the occasion of Déborah Ott-Libs's wedding in June 2019. Accompanied by Xavier Honorin and Jimmy, Pierre ate local delicacies and drank Grimbergen (established 1128) Alsatian dark beer. He also ate Flammekueche, a local speciality made by pinning fermented dough into a rectangular or circular shape, similar to a pizza base, then covering it with crème fraîche, chopped onions, and lardons before baking it in a hot wood-fired oven for that special flavour that only a wood-fired oven bestows upon these types of baked goods. The highlight of his visit was to eat light desserts at the famous Naegel pastry shop and café, where Pierre served his apprenticeship as a young man. Local dark beer is used in the beer mixture for this bread, but stout or other dark beer will also substitute perfectly. This recipe takes 2 days to prepare. The pre-fermented dough is made on Day 1, and the beer bread dough is made and baked on Day 2.

Day 1: Pre-fermented Dough

Ingredients: Pre-fermented Dough

- 245 g   Strong flour
- 160 g   Water
- 5 g   Fresh yeast
- 5 g   Salt

Making the Pre-fermented Dough

1. Mix all the ingredients for 5 minutes on 1st speed and for 2 minutes on 2nd speed.
2. Let the dough rise in a container at room temperature, covered for 1 hour.
3. Punch down, cover again, and place in the refrigerator overnight at 3 °C–4 °C.

Day 2: Beer Bread

To make the beer bread, you'll need to prepare a beer mixture topping. It needs to be prepared for use before the final proofing stage but doesn't take long, so you can make it during the 15-minute resting period in Step 5 of Making the Beer Bread Dough.

Ingredients: Beer Mixture Topping

- 70 g   Rye flour
- 120 g   Alsatian dark beer (Guinness or dark beer)
- 3 g   Salt
- 5 g   Fresh yeast

Making the Beer Mixture Topping

1. Using a whisk, combine all the ingredients to make a smooth mixture: first, dissolve the yeast in the beer. Then, add the salt and flour.
2. The beer mixture should be spreadable but not too liquid.

Ingredients: Beer Bread Dough

330 g	Strong baker's flour (AP, T–55 or other strong flour)
170 g	Rye flour
320 g	Water
15 g	Fresh yeast
10 g	Salt
412 g	Pre-fermented dough (made on Day 1)
40 g	Potato flakes
130g	Water in which to soak the potato flakes

Making the Beer Bread Dough

1. Mix with a spatula the 40 g of potato flakes and the 130 g water.
2. When the flakes are fully rehydrated, add all the remaining ingredients together in dough mixer. Mix for 5 minutes on the 1st speed and for 4 minutes on the 2nd speed.
3. Allow the dough to ferment, covered, for 1 hour at room temperature.
4. Divide the dough into four equal parts of 350 g each, and pre-shape the dough into round balls.
5. Allow the dough to rest for a further 15 minutes at room temperature. (This is a good time to make the beer mixture.)
6. Shape the loaves into a triangle and place them on a wooden board lined with parchment paper.
7. Immediately after the final shaping, spread the beer mixture in a thin layer on the top of the bread using a brush or palette knife. Dust with rye flour.
8. Allow the dough to proof for 1 hour to 1 hour and 15 minutes at room temperature.
9. Bake at 250 °C for 15 minutes, vent closed, then for a further 25 minutes with the vent open.
10. Reduce the oven temperature to 225 °C at the end of the baking, if desired, to ensure a crispy crust develops. The beer bread must have a dark-brown colour.

Tobias Exner (Germany)

Tobias was born in 1975 in a country that no longer exists. He came from the former German Democratic Republic. His birthplace is the city of Leipzig. When he was 1 year old, his family moved from there to near Berlin; he's lived there ever since. His father is a baker, and so it turns out that he learned to bake from an early age. When he was 4, he was in the bakery every day to get some of the cake leftovers. Every day since then, he's had the aroma of hot bread in his nose. That's why he became a baker, as he loves this fragrance so much. In 1991, he started his apprenticeship in a small bakery near Hannover. Then, he moved to a bakery in Göttingen to gain more experience.

Since 1995, he's worked in both the family bakery (they have several shops) and the family business (they have a large distribution network). In 1998, he finished his apprenticeship as a master baker.

In 2001, Tobias returned to education and studied business administration in Frankfurt am Main. In 2019, he returned to the Baking Akademie in Weinheim to study once more and became one of only 93 bread sommeliers. The project work on his training included a challenge to eat a lot of bread for 90 days and prove that eating bread doesn't make you fat. It was a very interesting time, and it was great research. Besides baking bread, Tobias has a few hobbies, but he has three sons, which keeps him very busy.

Tobias met Jimmy in 2016 at the Bundesakademie der Bäcker in Weinheim. Of course, he was most impressed with Jimmy concerning his story about conger eels, an aerobatic pilot's dangerous life, and his impressive career as a baker and juror in baking competitions. He was also impressed with Jimmy's teaching methods as a lecturer in the bakery, and he learned to bake Jimmy's incredible conger eel bread with him. He also learned of other specialities unknown to him before meeting with Jimmy. Since then, Tobias and Jimmy follow each other on the usual social media sites, Facebook and Instagram. He's still looking for a suitable date to visit Jimmy in Galway, his hometown, and learn this special baker's secrets. Tobias is hopeful that perhaps someday Jimmy will just arrive in Germany in his plane, stand in front of his door and say, "Tobi! I am here!"

~Tobias Exner

14. Toby's Windmill Rye Bread

Tobias purchases his special rye mill flour from a 250-year-old windmill. The windmill is owned by a group of enthusiasts who dedicate their free time to keeping the mill in good working order. The rye flour for this special bread is produced at this windmill. You may, of course, use any rye flour, but T–1800 is recommended for this recipe. This recipe is for 3 loaves of 903 g each. This recipe takes two days to make. The sourdough preferment is prepared on Day 1, and the swell is made and the bread is baked on Day 2.

Day 1: Prefermenting the Rye Sourdough

Ingredients: Rye Sourdough

- 225 g Rye flour
- 300 g Water 34 °C
- 225 g Rye sourdough culture (See Judy Koh's starter: Recipe #29)

Making the Rye Sourdough

1. Mix the rye sourdough in warm water to activate it.
2. Add the rye flour and mix well with a hand whisk.
3. Place the sourdough in a sealed glass jar for 12–16 hours to mature.
4. Keep in a warm place 26 °C–28 °C during this time to develop the lactic bacteria.

Day 2: Making the Rye Bread

To make the bread, you'll need to make swell about 1–2 hours before making the bread dough.

Ingredients: Swell

- 33 g   Medium rye meal
- 98 g   Rye flour
- 34 g   Crystal salt
- 210 g Water

Making the Swell

1. Mix all the ingredients and bring to a boil in a saucepan until the mixture has a pudding-like consistency.

2. Cover the mixture immediately with cling film and let it cool.//
3. Allow to rest for 1–2 hours before use.

Ingredients: Rye Dough

760 g	Rye flour
160 g	Whole rye flour
800 g	Rye sourdough
4 g	Yeast
610 g	Water 24 °C
375 g	Swell

Making the Rye Dough

1. Using a stand mixer with a dough hook, mix the ingredients together. Cover and let rest for 45 minutes. The dough should somewhat increase in size.
2. Flour the work surface and carefully place the dough on the worktop.
3. If necessary, use plastic dough scraper to get the dough out of the mixing bowl.
4. Shape carefully, close/seam down, and place in a well-floured proofing basket. Cover the dough so it doesn't skin, and allow it to rise in a warm place for 2 hours.
5. For 2 hours, preheat a deck oven to 250 °C.
6. Carefully tip the dough out of the proofing basket. Place it directly onto the oven sole.
7. Pour a shot glass full of water onto the oven's bottom to generate steam and close the door immediately.
8. Reduce the oven heat to 230 °C.
9. After 10 minutes, reduce heat to 210 ° C and bake for 40 more minutes.
10. Open the oven about 5 minutes before the end so that the steam can escape and turn the temperature back up to 250 °C to obtain a crispy crust. That's it!

Max Kugel (Germany)

Max Kugel is a master baker and confectioner from Bonn, Germany. Through his veins flows not only blood but also a little bit of flour dust because he grew up in a family bakery that belonged to his parents. His hometown is Lahnstein, a small town on the edge of the Rhineland and the Palatinate. Here, Max spent the first 17 years of his life. He started working in his parents' family bakery at only 7 years of age. His job? To turn the dishwasher on and off every Saturday. Max continued learning his profession by working on the oven and the confectionery and by weighing out the dough. With every free minute, he helped where he could. At the age of 15, Max completed his training as a baker with his father. To lead the family business into the next generation, his father sent him on an apprenticeship journey to gain experience and become a better, more rounded professional. He started with additional training as a confectioner in Saarbrücken. Afterwards, he made a goal to become one of the best bread bakers in his country, and he gave everything he had to achieve this. He eventually decided against taking over his parents' bakery and instead opened a bakery that only bakes bread.

To gain all the necessary knowledge he would need to achieve his objective, Max travelled out into the world to learn from many bakeries that make magnificent and special bread. He lived and worked in many cities during this time, travelled to many countries, and met many amazing bakers and people who made him the baker he is today. Max got to know Jimmy in 2015 when Max attended a master class on baking Jimmy gave in Weinheim. The description of Jimmy's sourdough bread in the course description had made Max curious. From the first moment Max met Jimmy, they became friends. He describes Jimmy as a very friendly guy. In fact, when Max asked Jimmy if it was possible to visit his bakery in Galway, Jimmy

Recipes: Breads & Buns

immediately answered, "Yes!" A couple years later, in 2017, Max finally opened his own bakery, and true to his intentions, he sells 10 varieties of bread. No rolls. No cakes. Just bread. It's a simple formula. In his opinion, you can only do one thing very well, and you should concentrate on that one thing. For Max, that's bread!

In 2018, Max finally visited Jimmy in Galway and spent a week with him. Max was immediately embraced as a part of his family. He lived with Jimmy and his family in their house, had dinner with them, went to work with Jimmy at his bakery, and visited an Irish pub or two! It was an indescribably beautiful time in a great country. At the end of Max's visit, Jimmy even flew him in his plane over the Aran Islands and showed him the West of Ireland from above. It was fantastic. Max even got to fly the plane under Jimmy's expert guidance as a pilot. Friendships like Jimmy's have shown Max that you don't have to see each other often, nor do you have to live in the same city or country. In the best case, you must have similarities and even have a heart and a passion for the same thing, just like bread is for both men.

Follow Max: Instagram, https://www.instagram.com/max_kugel/

~Max Kugel

15. Heinz Rye Sourdough

Max's Heinz Rye Sourdough is a classic from his bakery. His loaf is a typical German strong rye bread with a wheat content. It's formed and baked as a 2.5 kg loaf and sold in quarters at Bonn's bakery. Because of its heavyweight and the long baking time, it has a great aroma and a very long freshness. It bears the name of Max's father, Heinz, as a tribute to him for the knowledge he gave Max on the way to becoming a master bake. The ingredients in this recipe are provided in quantities for making 20 loaves (1.25 kg each) and for making 2 loaves. This recipe takes 2 days to prepare. The sourdough (first stage), the poolish, and the mash are made on Day 1. The sourdough (second stage) and the bread itself are made on Day 2.

Day 1: Preparing the Sourdough (First Stage), Poolish, and Mash

Ingredients: Sourdough (First Stage)

20 loaves		2 loaves
1,400 g	Fine whole meal rye flour	140 g
1,400 g	Water 40°C – 45°C to activate the starter	140 g
140 g	Rye starter*	14 g

*Max recommends using your own starter or using Judy Koh's starter (see Recipe #29).

Making the Sourdough (First Stage)

1. Mix ingredients together in a spiral mixer for 5 minutes on slow speed. Cover and set aside.
2. Allow to rest for 18-24 hours at 25 °C.

Ingredients: Poolish

20 loaves		2 loaves
500 g	Wheat flour T-550/Strong bakers/AP	50 g
500 g	Water	50 g
5 g	Fresh yeast	0.5 g

Making the Poolish

The DDT is 23 °C.

1. Mix ingredients by hand until the mixture is smooth.
2. Allow to rest 18–24 hours at 5 °C.

Ingredients: Mash

20 loaves		2 loaves
1,300 g	Dried, ground bread (old bread)	130 g
2,600 g	Water	260 g
270 g	Salt	27 g

Making the Mash

Stir all the ingredients together by hand and leave to swell overnight.

Day 2: Preparing the Rye Sourdough Bread

Ingredients: Sourdough (Second Stage)

20 loaves		2 loaves
2,800 g	Sourdough (first stage)	280 g
2,800 g	Fine whole meal rye flour	280 g
2,800 g	Water	280 g

Making the Sourdough (Second Stage)

The DDT is 28 °C.

1. Mix all the ingredients together for 10 minutes on slow speed.
2. Allow to rest 3 hours.

Ingredients: Final Rye Sourdough

20 loaves		2 loaves
8,400 g	Sourdough 2nd stage	840 g
4,100 g	Swelling stage	410 g
1,000 g	Poolish stage	100 g
5,000 g	Fine whole meal rye flour	500 g
2,400 g	Wheat flour T-550	240 g
4,800 g	Water	480 g

Making the Final Rye Sourdough

The DDT is 26 °C –28 °C.

1. Temperature settings on an electric deck oven are 270 °C upper and 250 °C bottom heat, falling to 230 °C and 210 °C degrees, respectively.

2. After all the preliminary stages have been prepared, have matured overnight, and have been allowed to swell, everything is now put together into the kneader.

3. A long phase of slow kneading on 1st speed is important so that the whole meal flour can swell nicely and fully absorb the water. Kneading time is 15 minutes on 1st speed and 3 minutes on 2nd speed.

4. After kneading, allow the dough to rest for 30 minutes.

5. Scale the loaves at 1,250 g, round them in rye flour, and then place them in floured baskets to mature.

6. After 3/4 proofing, place the baskets on the oven setters and allow them to for 10 minutes. This process will allow the bread to develop slight cracks in the surface, resulting in a dynamic crust.

7. Put the loaves in the oven. Add steam. Bake for 70 minutes.

8. After 50 minutes of the bake, open the damper on the oven to release the steam (or open the oven door to purge the steam) so the crust will bake dry.

9. Remove the loaves from the oven and cool on wire racks.

Bernd Kütscher (Germany)

Bernd is a master baker and business economist with more than 35 years of professional experience in various functions in industry, as an entrepreneur, in voluntary work, and in the bakery trade organisation. In 2006, he was appointed Director of the Federal Academy of the German Bakery Trade in Weinheim. In October 2019, this Academy in Weinheim won the European Prize for Innovation in Vocational Education and Training, awarded by the European Commission. Bernd is also the coach of the German national bakery team and president of the jury at the UIBC World Championship of Young Bakers.

Appointed by the Federal Minister of Food and Agriculture, he's also part of the National Food Commission, which sets the rules for food processing in Germany. Since 2008, Bernd has also been managing director of the German Bread Institute in Berlin. This institute tests the quality of around 20,000 loaves of bread per year and keeps the German Bread Register with a recorded number of 3,200 different types of bread which are offered in Germany every day. The German bread culture is being included by the UNESCO Commission in the list of intangible cultural assets in Germany. Bernd is strongly committed nationally and internationally to the training of young people. Bernd and Jimmy met in 2007 at the National Academy in Weinheim and have been friends ever since. The last time that Bernd and Jimmy saw each other was in November 2019 in Shanghai, where they sat together on the jury for the Asian World Cup qualification for the bakery trade.

Contact Bernd: kuetscher@akademie-weinheim.de

~Bernd Kütscher

16. German Spelt Bread

This spelt bread is typical of Germany's southern area (Swabian), where spelt grows plentifully. This traditional recipe is enriched with some buttermilk, which makes the bread fresher and tastier. Bernd suggests that this bread is delicious with butter alone and doesn't require any other spread or topping. This recipe will make four loaves of 445 g each. This recipe takes 2 days to prepare. The pre-dough is made on Day 1, and the spelt dough is made on Day 2.

Day 1: Preparing the Pre-Dough

Ingredients: Pre-Dough

- 300 g   Spelt flour–white (not whole grain)
- 220 g   Cold water
- 5 g   Salt
- 2 g   Fresh yeast

Making the Pre-Dough

The DDT is 22 °C –24 °C.

1. On a stand mixer with a dough hook, mix the ingredients for the pre-dough slowly in the machine for 5 minutes on slow speed. Then place it in a larger bowl to ferment.
2. Cover the dough with a plastic sheet and let it rise for 15 hours at room temperature.

Day 2: Preparing the Spelt Bread

Ingredients: Spelt Dough

- 700 g   Spelt flour–white
- 320 g   Cold water
- 200 g   Buttermilk
- 10 g   Butter
- 18 g   Salt
- 10 g   Fresh yeast
- 527 g   Pre-dough (made on Day 1)

Making the Spelt Dough

1. After the pre-dough stage's fermentation is complete, mix the main dough, including the pre-dough, slowly for 8 minutes on 1st speed in a stand mixer with a dough hook. Depending on the flour's quality, knead briefly (1–2 minutes) at a faster speed until the dough is well kneaded.
2. Cover the dough again with a plastic sheet and let it rise for 2½ hours at room temperature, or 20 °C–22 °C.
3. During this bulk fermentation time, stretch and fold the dough 3 times, or every 30 minutes. The dough will be very soft, so you should handle it with wet hands only.
4. After the fermentation is complete, scale the dough, and then shape it into 2 or 4 pieces; depending on the bread size, you require 445 g for 4 pieces or 890 g for 2 large boules.
5. Mould the dough into a ball shape with your hands, which should be wet.
6. Fold the outer edges downwards continually until the balls are firm. Be careful to preserve the bubble structure inside the dough by gently moulding.
7. Place the dough balls on baking trays with silicone paper sheets.
8. Proof for 45–50 minutes 24 °C–26 °C covered with plastic.
9. Bake the bread, with steam, on the oven sole by sliding the silicone paper with the loaves on top onto the oven floor at 230 °C (446 °F).

10. The 445 g loaves require roughly 50 minutes' baking time. Larger loaf sizes require 10–15 minutes longer in the oven.

11. Open the oven door for a moment or pull the damper to release the steam 10 minutes before the bake is finished for a dry, crispy crust.

Daníel Kjartan Ármannsson (Iceland)

Daníel was born on the east coast of Iceland—Egilsstaðir, to be accurate. He found the love of baking by accident when he was 19 years old and got a job at the local bakery back home. He had no idea what this decision would lead him into. In 1999, he moved his apprenticeship training to the capital and the most popular and awarded bakery in Iceland, Mosfellsbakarí, where Mr. Haflíði Ragnarsson (Callebaut ambassador) was his mentor. That's when the ball really started moving for Daníel. Soon after, in 2001, he won the AEHT competition in pastry at Linz. He's competed in several competitions for Iceland over the years. In 2013, he won the baker of the year award in Iceland.

Daníel reflects on how, in 2017, in Stockholm, Sweden, he met with one of his favourite bakers, Jimmy Griffin of Ireland and Jury president. The Iceland team had preparations for their sourdoughs the evening before the competition, and as Daníel had hand-mixed his sourdoughs, Jimmy came to ask about his products. Jimmy's first impression was amazing because when Daníel was competing, he was using squid ink in one sourdough bread which was also infused with apples and tonka beans as a base flavour. Another sourdough variety Daníel made was with wild rice, honey, ginger root, soya sauce, and lemon zest. Instead of putting his ideas down, like 99% of the other judges, Jimmy, as the head of the jury, got Daníel believing in himself and that to "think outside the box" had great purpose and creativity.

Daníel remembers Jimmy coming over to say goodbye when the teams' preparations were complete with the words, "I am looking forward to tasting and seeing your products tomorrow". Daníel felt reassured knowing that a small country with no heritage in Nordic Bakery Cup, Iceland could make some waves at the event. Some months later, Daníel arranged for Jimmy to travel to Iceland and help train the Icelandic baking team, and they spent several very enjoyable and fulfilling days together. Daníel remarked that since the competition, it's been a real blessing to have Jimmy as a friend and advisor who's always available on "the hotline" to help him with his numerous activities, such as his job as Deputy Chief Expert at the Euro Skills competitions in baking. Jimmy and Daníel share the same passion for baking. Even though Daníel isn't working as a full-time baker anymore, his door in Iceland will always be open for Jimmy to visit.

Follow Daníel: Instagram, https://www.instagram.com/dannikjartan/

~Daníel Kjartan Ármannsson

17. Daníel's Fiery Icelandic Sourdough

I enjoyed tasting Daníel's delicious fiery Icelandic bread as chairman of the jury at the Nordic Bakery Cup 2017 in Stockholm. The flavours were an excellent combination of sourdough base flavour, spicy curry, Cayenne pepper, and added barley, which gave it a meaty bite and made it so interesting eat. I baked the recipe and had it with vegetarian pea and potato curry soup. It was wonderful.

This recipe takes 2 days to make. The boiled barley is made on Day 1, and the Fiery Icelandic Sourdough is made on Day 2.

Day 1: Preparing the Boiled Barley

Ingredients: Boiled Barley

130 g   Water
 80 g   Barley

Making the Boiled Barley

1. Boil the barley and water for roughly 20 minutes.
2. Cover and cool at room temperature and use the day after preparation in the dough.

Day 2: Preparing the Fiery Icelandic Sourdough

Ingredients: Daniel's Icelandic Dough

850 g	Water
675 g	Strong flour
320 g	Whole wheat flour
200 g	Boiled barley (above)
90 g	Linseed
9 g	Curry powder
2 g	Cayenne pepper (powder)
37 g	Salt
320 g	Sourdough 50/50 liquid sour (50% bakers flour/50% water)

Making and Proofing the Fiery Icelandic Sourdough

The DDT is 27 °C–28 °C

1. Using a stand mixer with a dough hook, combine all the ingredients together on slow speed for 7 minutes, then on 2nd speed for 4 minutes or until the dough is fully developed.
2. For the 1st bulk fermentation, place the dough in a covered, sealed bowl, and allow it to rest for 30 minutes.
3. For the 2nd bulk fermentation, stretch and fold the dough. Allow it to rest another 30 minutes.
4. For the 3rd bulk fermentation, stretch and fold the dough. Allow it to rest another 30 minutes.
5. For the 4th bulk fermentation, stretch and fold the dough once again. Allow it rest for about 3 hours at room temperature.
6. Scale the dough at 750 g and mould each piece into a ball shape.
7. Bench rest for 20 minutes.
8. Shape the dough into a cylinder shape and place each one in a banneton basket. (Use rice flour to prevent the bread from sticking to the banneton.)
9. Allow the dough to rest for 4–5 hours at room temperature.

10. Place the bread on the sole of an oven or baking stone, both heated to 280 °C.
11. Add steam to the oven and lower the temperature to 240 °C. Bake for 25 minutes.
12. Release the steam to dry out the crust and bake for 20–25 minutes more.
13. Remove the bread from the oven and cool on a wire tray.

Alternate Baking Option: Cold Fermentation

Cold fermentation gives the greatest flavour to this bread. To cold ferment the Fiery Icelandic Sourdough.

1. After Step 8, place the bread in a refrigerator (4 °C –6 °C), covered with heavy plastic to prevent skinning.
2. Cold ferment for 24–36 hours.
3. Allow the bread to return to room temperature before putting it in the oven.
4. Bake the bread following Steps 10-13.

Robert Humphries, World Champion 2006 IBA Cup (Ireland)

Robert is a graduate of the National Bakery School, Dublin. He worked in the industry for 10 years before joining the DIT Bakery School in 1985 as a lecturer in the bakery and pastry arts management programmes. Robert has won many National and International awards, including silver in the European Championships in Denmark in 2004 and, notably, gold in the International Baking Championships at IBA, Munich in 2006. He's a past president of the Institute of Irish Bakers (1990–1991). Robert first met Jimmy at the annual general meeting of the Institute of Irish Bakers in 1986, which was held at the Dublin Zoo. Since then, Robert and Jimmy have worked together as Baking Team Ireland team members, as lecturers at Technological University Dublin. They have also worked

together in Paris and Hungary at baking events and with students from the university. A true blue, Robert shares his deep knowledge of baking with everyone and has been an enormously influential figure for the university students, assisting them in competition training.

Follow Robert: Facebook, https://www.facebook.com/robert.humphries.33

~Robert Humphries

18. Robert's Potato and Dill Shamrock Bread

Created during the competition years, when Ireland was competing in the European and World Championships in the early 2000s, this bread not only signified Ireland with its catchy shamrock shape, but when cut, it had the colours of the Irish flag in the crumb. The addition of a small quantity of black pepper sets off the flavour of this wonderful bread. A sponge and dough making system is used to make this bread.

Day 1: Preparing the Starter

Ingredients: Overnight Cold Sponge Starter

- 250 g   Strong bread flour
- 170 g   Water
-   2 g   Fresh yeast

Making the Overnight Cold Sponge Starter

1. Disperse the yeast in the water and make it into a dough with the flour.

2. In a spiral mixer, mix for 2 minutes on slow and 2 minutes fast.

3. Refrigerate overnight at 3 °C.

Day 2: Preparing the Potato and Dill Shamrock Bread

Ingredients: Potato and Dill Dough

- 750 g Strong bread flour
- 475 g Water
- 420 g Sponge starter
- 20 g   Salt
- 3 g   Cracked black pepper
- 22 g   Fresh yeast
- 325 g Mashed potato
- 25 g   Olive oil
- 15 g   Fresh, chopped dill
-        Maize gritz

Making the Potato and Dill Dough

The DDT is 24 °C.

1. On a spiral mixer, mix together strong bread flour, water, sponge starter, salt, cracked black pepper, and fresh yeast for 2 minutes on slow and 6 minutes fast on a spiral mixer to a fully developed dough.

2. Add the mashed potato, olive, and the dill and mix for 3 minutes on slow to clear.

3. Allow for bulk fermentation with a stretch and fold after 35 minutes.

4. Scale 5 pieces at 400 g each and hand up gently into a ball shape.

5. Intermediate proof 15 minutes.

6. Press out on maize grits to about 20 cm and place on linen cloths to proof.

7. Final proof for 60 minutes at 28 °C with 70% relative humidity.

8. Set and cut into the shape of a shamrock and rest for 5 minutes.

9. Bake at 240 °C, dropping oven temperature to 210 °C with 10 seconds steam for 30 to 35 minutes.

Alternate Finish

For an alternate finish (see picture for this recipe), use Pierre Zimmermann's beer bread paste (Recipe #13). Paint the paste on the dough and dust it with rye flour before baking.

JP McMahon, Michelin Star Chef (Ireland)

JP McMahon is a chef, restaurateur, and author. He's culinary director of the Eat Galway Restaurant  Group, which includes Michelin-starred Aniar Restaurant, award-winning Spanish restaurant Cava Bodega, and Tartare Café &Wine Bar (Bib Gourmand). He also runs the Aniar Boutique Cookery School. JP is committed to the educational and ethical aspects of food, to buying and supporting the best of local and free-range produce, and engaging directly with farmers and producers. JP is the founder and plays host to one of the biggest and most talked-about international food events in Europe, Food on the Edge. The highly successful inaugural event took place in Galway in October 2015, followed by equally acclaimed 2016, 2017, 2018, and 2019 events. The event features the best international chefs from across the globe. Director, founding, and current chair of the Galway Food Festival, JP is an Irish food ambassador. He's also an ambassador for Spanish food in Ireland, promoting Rías Baixas' wines (Galicia) and Jerez. JP is currently a commissioner for Euro-Toques Ireland. He's also author and writer of *Tapas, A Taste of Spain in Ireland* and *The Irish Cookbook* (Phaidon 2020). He's a food writer and has a weekly column in the *Irish Times* on Saturdays. JP is a regular contributor to Radio One and Newstalk radio and has a monthly slot on RTE TV; he was twice the winning mentor for the RTE "Series Taste of Success".

JP and Jimmy met back in 1999 when JP worked in Fat Freddie's Pizzeria—Griffin's Bakery supplied Fat Freddie's with bread and flour. JP thinks Jimmy may also have developed the dough recipe for the Pizzas, and he has fond memories of his younger self carrying large bags of flour, one on each shoulder, from Jimmy's bakery, down Quay Street, Galway.

Follow and contact JP: Instagram, @mistereatgalway / @foodontheedge

~JP McMahon

19. Aniar's Irish Soda Bread with Stout and Treacle

Soda bread is one of those iconic loaves of bread which continues to be baked in many Irish households daily and weekly. It's also baked by the thousands of expatriates who bake it because it evokes childhood memories; the connection to home and Ireland lives on in the loaf's smell and texture. Every home baker, chef and baker has their own unique recipe and blend of ingredients. This JP recipe has added linseeds, pumpkin seeds, pinhead oatmeal, stout and treacle, giving a deep and rich colour and flavour to the bread.

Ingredients: Soda Bread

200 g	White flour soft wheat flour
800 g	Brown whole meal flour
12 g	Bicarbonate of soda (3 teaspoons)
150 g	Linseed
150 g	Pumpkin seeds
200 g	Treacle
850 g	Buttermilk
200 g	Stout
2	Eggs
20 g	Sea salt
50 g	Pinhead oatmeal (for the topping)

Making the Soda Bread

1. Mix all the dry ingredients together.

2. Add the eggs and buttermilk.

3. Add the stout until you achieve a good consistency.

4. Pour into two oiled loaf tins and bake at 130 °C for 90 minutes until hollow to touch and it sounds like a drum when tapped on the bottom.

Jimmy Griffin, World Silver Medallist Chocolatine 2019 (Ireland)

While I appreciate that many people may not have access to a 2 m oven, this bread can still be made and baked into smaller loaves of any weight. Because there's a story of survival and hope that gave birth to this loaf recipe, I share this story with you here and then provide the recipe and the process with you.

Conger Eel Attack (9th of June 2013)

One of the things I enjoyed pre-recession was occasional scuba diving. I hadn't dived in some time due to financial cutbacks, and I welcomed the opportunity for a free dive to test new diving equipment at an open day scuba event in Connemara. I looked forward to leaving my personal and professional troubles behind for a time and donned a brand-new shiny dive suit and set off for an enjoyable afternoon with several other divers. I drove to Connemara, accompanied by my mother-in-law, Dobrochna, and my youngest daughter, Sophie. They went off to the beach. I went diving. The skipper, and friend, Colin Hannon assigned me a diving buddy, Derek Bolton. Several other divers were on the boat as well. We set off to a well-known dive site named Inish Barna in the Killary Fjord. I'd dived several hundred times, without incident, but today was going to be different. Little did I realise that today was a day that would change my life forever.

The dive proceeded as normal, with everyone entering the water off the boat and commencing their descents into the Fjord's depths. As we descended, it began to get darker and darker; my dive buddy Derek and I were immersed in a thick algal bloom, which required the use of our dive torches. We turned around at 100bar of air pressure to return towards the dive boat drop-off point. The combination of the bloom and depth made for very poor visibility (less than a metre) at a depth of approximately 20 m. It was like diving in pea soup, the torches straining to illuminate the water ahead.

Thirty minutes or so into the dive, I was suddenly, without any warning, hit by a powerful force to the face. My head was jerked violently backwards, like getting hit by a punch. I peered to the left in the inky black-green depths, and to my horror, saw a blue-grey menacing shape that filled my view in the dive mask. I could see its blue-grey skin and large, black eyes. I knew in an instant that I was in the clutches of a giant creature. It started thrashing about, throwing me around like a ragdoll. It was a giant conger eel that had attached itself to my face and was tearing away at my cheek.

Vis Island, Croatia (2015). Courtesy of J. Kranjc, Svet Ronjenja.

I instantly reacted to protect myself. Judo training instincts kicked in, and, raising my hands, I wrestled with the creature from the deep, which was now firmly attached to my face and twisting violently. I remember screaming, not with fear, but with rage, thinking, how dare you bite me, you bastard!!! As I wrestled with it, I realised exactly how big it was—I couldn't wrap my hands completely around the circumference of its neck. The battle between us, both man and fish, appeared to progress in slow motion. I was being shaken about feverishly. The attack seemed to take forever although the entire event actually lasted only a couple of seconds. When the struggle was over, the eel and my cheek went one way while my regulator (air supply hose) mask and I went the other. As it swam away with a large chunk of me in its jaws, I estimated that the creature was roughly 2 metres (6 ½ feet) long.

The pain was excruciating, and the surprise attack and subsequent struggle with the eel had used up all the air in my lungs. My mask also had half-filled with cold seawater. My body was forcibly compelling me to breathe, and I knew that if I responded to my body's instinct, I would drown right there and then. I was deep, it was dark, and my dive buddy Derek did not see the initial attack, as visibility was so poor.

It had happened so fast, and I was alone in this. I realised I was dead unless I dealt logically with the issues facing me. Forcing my straining body not to breathe, despite it demanding I do so urgently, I searched for my regulator, as I was trained to do, and, finding it on the first attempt, I inserted the mouthpiece into my mouth. I took my first breath of air since the onslaught of the eel and used the first breath to satisfy my survival instinct, then used the first exhalation to reattach and clear my dive mask. I purged my regulator and took my first life-saving breath of air. It tasted so good—you have no idea! I knew that if I remained calm, I could survive this and return to my family, loved ones, and friends.

At this stage, I exhaled and partly realised how badly injured I was, as the bubbles left my mouth in an entirely different place than usual. The sound and direction of the bubbles I had exhaled was nothing like I had ever heard or felt before. The pain was increasing, and I felt like my head would literally split in two. Then, as I looked to the left, there was a black, inky cloud. I quickly realised it was my blood even though the red colour was filtered out and indecipherable at this depth. I knew I had to surface and get help, and soon. But there was another problem: I still needed to get to the surface without panicking. Looking at my dive computer, I confirmed that no decompression stop was required. At that point, I had a decision to make—a rapid ascent could still trigger a slow, painful death from the bends (decompression sickness from ascending too quickly), but a slow ascent would delay medical assistance. Again, my instincts were compelling me to get the hell out of there and race to the surface, but, thankfully, my head was thinking clearly, and discipline overcame my instincts. On reflection, I'm thankful for my calm dive buddy, Derek, and the combined training I possessed as a pilot, a divemaster, and a judo black belt, all of which kicked in and allowed me to cope with this emergency calmly and logically.

By now, Derek had come to my side, and I was trying to bring his attention to my bleeding face, but he couldn't see the blood in the dark, algal bloom at that depth. He thought my regulator was in free-flow because with each breath I took, half of the air was leaking out of the hole in my face. We held onto each other, and Derek offered me his spare regulator, as he feared mine had a malfunction. I refused, figuring he hadn't yet realised what had happened. It was clear, though, that he knew there was something wrong.

We began making a controlled ascent together to a depth of 10 metres. As we ascended, the visibility improved, and Derek finally saw the blood gushing from my face. His eyes widened, now fully understanding my plight. Now that he could clearly see both the blood and the horrific injury to my face, he hand singled to ask if I was okay. I replied with hand signals to tell him that I was *not* okay and that we should end the dive and surface. We were within safety limits and soon surfaced together after a controlled ascent.

During the ascent, my life literally flashed before me. All of my business and personal worries disappeared; they weren't important anymore. I worried about whether I'd ever see my wife and my children again. How would I be able to feed them later that evening? How would I drive home? It's amazing what goes in and out of your mind in times of crisis. All I wanted at that moment was a big hug from my little one, who was blissfully playing away, making sandcastles on the beach with her grandmother a half mile away, blissfully unaware of my plight. The dive boat was picking up the other divers some 100 m away, and Derek signalled that we urgently needed assistance.

As we surfaced, the spurting bright-red blood indicated an arterial bleed; I needed to get compression pads in place and quick. I was assisted by Derek, Jennifer Colin, and literally all hands on deck to take off my dive gear; I crawled onto the dive boat, in massive pain but alive. Jennifer Kealy, an instructor diver, was at hand, along with boat skipper and others who helped me place a dressing over the gaping wound. She lay me down on the boat and cradled me, holding the pad in place. I was still unaware of the extent of the damage inflicted, but the swooning, pale faces, and looks of great distress from the other divers confirmed my worst fears: this was not good. As the blood soaked through the first dressing, I demanded another, and I watched a diver on the boat turn milky white soon after a third dressing was required. I was bleeding badly.

I remember hearing Colin calling in the mayday distress call to the dive centre and instructing everyone to put on their lifejackets for the emergency boat trip back to shore. As I lay on the floor of the dive boat, I began to feel the cold. The blood loss was taking its toll; I was slowly going into shock, but because the adrenaline was still pumping, I was unaware of the shock and was just thankful for my survival at this point.

The boat reached the safety of the dive centre after a rapid return to shore; I remember walking unaided from the boat about 200 m to the dive centre. It felt so good to feel the earth beneath my feet. I was brought to the back of the dive shop where I sat on a chair, surrounded by worried looks, people on phones, speaking in haste, giving directions to the emergency services. The brand new dive suit I'd been given to trial had to be cut off me using scissors. It was after that when I started shivering uncontrollably. Breffni Grey swaddled me in blankets and warm clothes, and he, Jennifer, Derek, Markus, and some others huddled around me in a group hug, providing me with their much-needed collective body heat as the shock of the event and the blood loss took their toll. Eventually, the emergency services arrived: I could hear the clatter of the metal stretcher being removed from the ambulance as the drone of its siren shut down. The ambulance had travelled from Clifden, but due to a perfect storm of events, including the remote location, the first very fine weather of the season bringing out lots of traffic, narrow roads, and double-parked cars, there was a substantial delay in the ambulance reaching the dive centre.

My mind was also shutting down; my world was in slow motion, and the chatter about me seemed to have slowed down to a halt. I was almost stopped in time, waiting, anticipating my rescue. I remained calm throughout, slowing down my heart rate and breathing—a technique I had learned years before. I was fit, healthy, and athletic. I knew I could survive this.

I remember thinking that although my injuries necessitated I be airlifted immediately, the time between the attack and the arrival of the ambulance was several hours. I snapped from this state of thought when the first paramedic arrived. He was wearing a yellow fluorescent jacket and bellowing at me with questions. I then heard him shout, "Can I have a look at your injury"? I lifted up the layers of blood-soaked compression dressings to show him. He just turned his head sideways as if I did not exist and shouted to his colleague (who was getting the stretcher), "Paddy Joe [not his real name]. Holy Jesus, come here quick and see the huge fucking hole in yer man's face". He was clearly shocked. I didn't know at this stage whether to laugh or to cry, but I have to say, I did see the funny side of it and it gave me a lift.

I began texting a colleague who worked in University Hospital Galway, the regional hospital in Galway: Dr. David O'Keefe, a Galway Flying Club friend. He responded immediately to my text for help. The paramedics were going to bring me to Castlebar General Hospital. Dr. O'Keefe confirmed my wishes and strongly agreed that I shouldn't be taken there but rather to University College Hospital Galway (UCHG). I was offered a Panadol painkilling tablet to swallow, as the paramedics didn't have any morphine. I was in agony. I couldn't swallow anything in my state. The paramedics were still insisting that I go to Castlebar, but I refused to board the ambulance unless I was guaranteed arrival in Galway. My resolve won out at the end. I needed more than ever to be close to home and in the care of those I knew.

Within a few minutes, Dr. O'Keefe responded that a team of plastic surgeons had been contacted, and I'd receive the expert care I badly needed in Galway. I sought pain relief, as the pain, combined with the shock, was causing me to drift in and out of consciousness at this point. I was told that another ambulance with a doctor trained to administer morphine had to be called. Dr. O'Keefe arranged for an emergency ambulance to depart from Galway and meet my ambulance with a doctor carrying morphine for much-needed pain relief.

As the ambulance set off for UCHG, I lay on the metal stretcher. I heard and felt every bump as the vehicle negotiated the narrow twisting roads towards Galway. I found myself drifting in and out of consciousness as the 1 ½ hour journey to Galway got underway. Then, between Oughterard and Moycullen, the ambulance came to a halt. A doctor climbed aboard and administered the long-awaited morphine. I was now high as a kite and free of pain and smiling blissfully from ear to ear. Bloodied, high, and giggling, Batman's nemesis The Joker sprang to mind.

At UCHG, a team of medics greeted my arrival with professionalism and urgency. They had researched in advance to consider whether a conger eel bite was likely to carry any known infections. Thankfully, they didn't have any known toxins in their saliva. It was one less worry. Consultants whizzed in and out of my cubicle in the emergency department asking questions and providing reassurance. One lady from Dr. Padraig Regan's plastics team took some of the iconic photos that would go viral over the Internet in the coming days. The photo she took with my own phone was the first glimpse of the damage caused by the eel attack.

Where my cheek once was, there was a gaping, bloody hole, with part of my lip missing. My gums and teeth were visible. The razor-sharp teeth marks were also visible on the skin, which remained attached above and below the gaping wound. Dr. Regan's team and the staff of National University of Ireland, Galaway were wonderful and made me so comfortable. They cleaned the wound, hooked me up to an IV, and began administering antibiotics. I couldn't have received better care anywhere in the world. Dr. Regan explained that the commissure, the angle of the joint of the upper and lower lips, was gone, and there was now just a gaping void. He assured me that he would repair the damage and that I shouldn't worry. I was now in good hands and again began drifting in and out of consciousness and ecstasy as the morphine kicked in once more to dull my pain. I then remember being on the stretcher passing through doorways, watching white walls whizz by. Everything was now in slow motion, a haze. I was a mess. I arrived at the operating theatre and had friendly banter with my anaesthetist. He challenged me to count backwards from 10 to 1. I watched as he injected the creamy, milky, cold anaesthetic into the tube attached to my arm. I remember watching as it entered my hand. As I struggled counting down as I went under, I hoped that Dr. Padraig Regan and his team could help save what remained of the left-hand side of my face.

As I drifted off into oblivion, a friend of Jennifer Kealy, Ronan Fahy, drove Sophie and her grandmother back home to Galway in my car. My wife, Bogna, had gone to Poland that fateful weekend to visit her sister, Aga. The Scuba Dive West crew had managed to contact her and kept her up to date with my progress. As I awoke from the anaesthetic many hours later, a warm, familiar hand was holding mine with care and love, with a tender smile and teary eyes. Bogna had managed to make the last flight out of Poland that night, rented a car, and drove like a bat out of hell through the night to be by my bedside. It was a great feeling.

Later that morning, Dr. Regan, accompanied by his surgical team, explained that because the eel had taken most of my cheek and a part of my lower left lip, there was nerve damage. He further explained that he had to cut my neck and stretch the skin up to close the gaping hole in my face. He also removed a part of my upper lip, gave it a blood supply and grafted it onto my lower lip to form a new commissure. I resembled a damaged battleship from WWII that had been welded back together, but I had survived an ordeal that could have killed me so easily. The doctors also told me that my overall fitness at the time, which ensured that my heart rate remained very low at rest, also helped save my life after losing so much blood.

Five days after the accident, I would travel with my son Dillon and the DIT bakery students to the UK. I was invited to act as a guest bakery judge at the Alliance for Bakery Students and Trainees (ABST). This annual bakery students' competition showcases the work of baking students from Ireland and the UK. The conference was held in the East Midlands. Over 1,500 entries were received, and I was asked to judge eight separate classes during this competition. The highlight of the weekend was the fancy-dress party, with a pirate theme. Many people came up to me during the evening, speaking in drunken pirate accents, telling me that my scar makeup was fantastic. If only they knew what had happened, they would never have believed it.

I was grateful for a second chance of life and for the repairs performed by the surgeons. I couldn't eat properly for a few weeks and would require a mouth guard to be worn at night to prevent biting the now very tight skin inside my mouth. I was grateful to have survived and embraced my family, but I suffered the most horrific nightmares for many months. I would wake up screaming several times per night with a form of post-traumatic stress disorder, revisiting the moment I had been attacked, over and over again. In the dreams, it was as though I was a spectator in the cinema watching a movie, a few seats back from the screen. I could see myself in the water. I could see the eel approaching from underneath to the left on my blindside. I would scream at myself in the dream, "It's behind you!" Each time I was too late to divert the attack and woke shaking, screaming, and dripping with sweat. I was determined to overcome this life-changing event and was offered sleeping tablets by my doctor to help. Still, I decided to do without any medication, and, following the second session of corrective surgery some months later, the nightmares went away.

Following the accident, the incident made both local and world news. I was trending on social media in Australia, Asia, Europe, and South America. I was splashed all over newspapers, and some tabloids printed graphic photos of the wounds I had endured. In some cases, the headlines were just as graphic. One read, "Devil eel ate my face". There were several radio interviews and a feature on the attack in *Diver Magazine* in September, 2013. I never had time to dwell on it until I began to write this book. It proved to be a very emotional experience for me, as I relived each moment, felt every bite. I remember the sounds made as the eel feasted on my face. I remember my silent screams in the depths of the Atlantic at the horror that was unfolding. I recalled the struggle at 40 m deep, re-lived the excruciating pain and the worry of survival.

I was an emotional wreck when I finished writing this chapter and couldn't edit it for some weeks. At the time of the accident, I was left with minimal feeling on my face's left-hand side and was given a 30% chance of recovering full feeling there. The feelings never came back. Instead they were replaced with permanent pain and numbness, similar to a dental injection. The only difference is that my pain and numbness lasts 24/7, 365 days a year. Still, it's a small price to pay, considering I was lucky to come away from that day alive.

I returned to normal life and eventually to diving, thanks to encouragement from my wife, Bogna, and my family. I also received tremendous support from my brother, Mark; his wife Patricia; Bogna's sister, Aga; Aga's husband, Luke; and Bogna's mother, Dobrochna. I haven't forgotten the support from my many friends including Ciaran Scully, Jarlath Conneeley, his wife Ann, and Jimmy and Sinead Norman; my customers and work colleagues from Griffin's Bakery and DIT; and my scuba diving friends and colleagues: divers Jennifer Kealy, Colin Hannon, Kevin Derrig, and Breffni Grey who looked after me on that fateful day. Later during my recovery, I owe Janez Kranjc and his wife Ivana Orlovich much thanks for encouraging me to get back in the water once more.

I also have to thank Jeremy Wade of *River Monsters* fame. My bizarre story was featured in "Season 8: Sea Monsters, Mysteries of the Ocean" programme. The mutual support from all these people kept the fire lit to fuel my passion for life and rekindled my passion for diving. As I write today, I have just finished a 31 m dive in Montenegro. It wouldn't have been possible to recover to this extent without these wonderful people. I humbly and sincerely thank you all for your care and compassion. Here is the hyperlink to the episode of *River Monsters* (Season 8, Episode 6, 2016) on which my accident is featured: https://www.youtube.com/watch?v=286lYr-Lxug&list=PLOcWEiL3wAqrlGDRU67fgezwxIVIziebT&index=1

Today, I live with permanent pain and a physical scar from the event. The pain is a reminder of how lucky I am to be alive. The scar is a daily reminder that I am a survivor. I accept my fate and carry the physical scar, the constant pain, and the emotional scars of that day, which drive me to live my life and share it with my loved ones and friends. I walked out of the hospital 3 days later sore and weak but happy to be alive. The accident has taught me that life is for living and not to dwell on past accidents or misfortunes but to embrace and love life daily. I have since left the attack in the past where it belongs.

The Birth of the 8 Kg Conger Bread

In 2011, in Guangzhou, China, when I was a jury member at the Coupe Louis Lesaffre, I met a Chinese baker who told that one man's crisis is another man's opportunity. Remembering his wise words, I decided to take his advice and turn my personal crisis into an opportunity. The conger eel attack was indeed life changing, but I decided to celebrate my new chance at life and did so in true baker's fashion by forming an 8 kg piece of sourdough into bread the size of the creature that had attacked me: 2 m long! The sourdough bread, aptly named the conger loaf, became an overnight success and was sold in Griffin's Bakery and to many restaurants and cafés in the Galway area. I must say that I enjoyed daily watching the conger bread being sliced and sold in the bakery. The story spread far and wide and has enriched my life significantly.

In 2015, I was approached by model and Mares brand ambassador, Ivana Orlovic, to join her, her equally talented husband Janez Kranjc, world-class underwater photographers, and diving superstars to dive with conger eels in Viz Island in Croatia.

In the past couple of years, I've been invited to 18 many countries to demonstrate how I produce the bread. In Paris, conger bread was most notably featured at Le Fête du Pain, where the conger bread was made at the International Bread Festival in a large marquee outside Notre Dame Cathedral in March 2017, a little more than 2 years before the fire that destroyed it. The bread attracted hundreds of the many tourists at Notre Dame Cathedral, eager to have a selfie or a photo taken with the giant loaf. Obviously, the sheer size of the loaf is something to see, but, I think, the most amazing part is the story behind it.

~Jimmy Griffin

Team Ireland of DIT with Christian Vabret MOF in 2017 in front of Notre Dame, Paris. L-R: Shannon Dickson (missing from photo), Deirdre Gaffney, Vaarsha Baugrret, myself, Christian Vabret MOF, Jeremey Pastor, and Robert Humphries.

20. Jimmy's Conger Loaf

This spongy, open-textured bread was one of our all-time favourites with customers when Griffin's Bakery was in operation. The combination of preferment, sourdough, and yeast leads to a delightfully crispy crust and an open spongy bread with lots of holes in the texture. It was sold by weight and beautiful for open sandwiches.

This recipe requires a large oven with a setter or long wooden board to place the dough into the oven, a large couche cloth for resting the dough, and some liquid sourdough. You can use Judy Koh's starter (Recipe #29). The dough is made using a delayed salt technique. (You'll add the salt at the end.) I use a preferment for flavour, and a liquid sourdough of 1-part flour, 1-part water, a 1-part liquid starter for extensibility. I've included the original recipe for 1 full conger for commercial bakers and a scaled-down recipe which can be baked and enjoyed in the home.

This recipe takes 2 days to make. The preferment is made on Day 1. The dough is made on Day 2. The DDT is 24 °C–26 °C.

Ingredients: Preferment

Full loaf		Scaled loaf
480 g	Strong flour T–65/bakers flour/AP flour	120 g
320 g	Water	80 g
8 g	Fresh yeast	2 g

Making the Preferment

Using a stand mixer or spiral mixing machine, mix ingredients together on 1st speed for 2–3 minutes. Place in a sealed container and ferment overnight for 12–16 hours at 18 °C–20 °C.

Ingredients: Dough

Full loaf		Scaled loaf
808 g	Preferment	202 g
400 g	Liquid levain	100 g
4,000 g	Strong flour T-65/Bakers flour/AP flour	1,000 g
2,600 g	Water	650 g
62 g	Salt	12.5 g

Ingredients: Bassinage (Washing)

Full loaf		Scaled loaf
100 g	Water	25 g
50 g	Yeast	12.5 g

Making the Dough

1. Mix for 5 minutes at slow speed.
2. Stop the machine and cover. Autolyse for 30 minutes.
3. Mix the together the water and yeast for the bassinage using a hand whisk. Add the mixture to the dough.
4. Mix for a 5 minutes at slow speed.
5. Add the salt and mix for 2 minutes on 2nd speed to develop the dough.
6. Ferment a total of 90 minutes. Stretch and fold after 60 minutes.
7. After fermenting the dough, tip the dough out onto a well-floured table.
8. Flatten into a rectangle and roll up gently like a baguette, but loosely rolled.
9. The dough should now be a long cylinder of dough 130 cm long
10. Transfer and wrap well in a large couche cloth.
11. Intermediate proof in the cloth at 26 °C–27 °C for 20 minutes.

12. Reshape once more by flattening it out into a large rectangular shape and rolling it up tightly into a Swiss roll shape, just like a large baguette.
13. Place in a well-dusted couche cloth, wrap well, and proof for 60 minutes in the cloth.
14. Prepare the setter and roll the conger loaf onto the setter.
15. Gently elongate the dough to two meters and turn in the ends to make them neat.
16. Dust with wheat flour.
17. Using a sharp knife, slice into a crosshatch pattern with diagonal cuts.
18. Bake at 240 °C with steam, dropping the temperature to 210 °C for 55–60 minutes.
19. Drain the steam from the oven after 45 minutes to bake the bread with a dry crust.
20. When fully baked, remove from the oven and cool on wire racks.
21. The bread can be sold by weight if making a large loaf, or alternatively, you can bake in smaller units of 500 g or 1,000 g and proof in bannetons.

The 7th Generation

In most cases, 2020 is a year to remember for the wrong reason: the curse of COVID-19. I made a new starter, named it Covid Culture 2020, and baked the hell of it during the lockdown. In my case, the lockdown gave me something I never really had in the past: time to write, bake, and spend with my family.

In my baking studio at my home, we baked our way through the strict first lockdown. I had the opportunity to teach my son Dillon, a recently graduated honours degree dietitian from Robert Gordon University, Aberdeen, Scotland, how bread is made. It began when he had to return from Australia as countries closed their borders in March 2020. Dillon loved the sourdough bread I was making at home and took a keen interest, watching me tend to the many dough-making stages, stretching and folding right through to scarification and baking. He's taken to the task like a duck

to water, his genetic heritage coming to the fore. Dillon is now a skilled and avid home baker and makes bread weekly. He understands the process, the patience, and the work involved, and he's seen me in a different light as he never knew the complexity involved in manipulating just four ingredients that make great bread. He's now the 7th generation of baker in our family. Lockdown has permitted me to give him the gift of knowledge and procedure, a life skill to provide great bread to him and the family's next generation.

While not yet as interested in breads as Dillon is, Sophie, who turned 14 in 2020, loves to bake sweet cakes, brownies, and cupcakes. Recently, she started helping me bake traditional pan bread for her, as she doesn't like sourdough.

Baking is in my blood, and it seems the apple never falls far from the tree. Learning a skill such as making bread is something my family has done for seven generations.

I'm always happy to teach and pass on my knowledge not only to my children but to my students and colleagues as well. By nurturing others' interest in baking, my work will live on in my family for yet another generation, and hopefully, generations to come.

Derek O'Brien (Ireland)

Derek is a master baker and educator and is passionate about everything associated with baking art and craft. He became an indentured baking apprentice at age 18. Upon completing his apprenticeship, Derek gained a degree in baking technology at the South Bank University, London. He worked in management positions in both the UK and Ireland before joining DIT as a lecturer. He was appointed the head of the department and was responsible for promoting the craft of baking both within DIT and nationally.

Derek also introduced upskilling programmes for SMEs, including inviting baking experts to give seminars in Ireland and organising study visits to centres of excellence abroad. He's also encouraged interest in traditional baking by introducing popular professional baking programmes for the public at DIT. Together with Jimmy Griffin, he established the Irish affiliate of the Swiss Richemont Club, Richemont Ireland. This enabled Irish bakery personnel to visit centres of excellence and study quality baking in Europe. Derek was also instrumental in setting up the Irish National Baking Teams with Jimmy in the early 2000s. This involved training Irish bakers to the highest level of skill to enable them to compete in the World and European baking competitions.

On retirement from DIT, Derek joined Akademie Deutsches Bäckerhandwerk, Weinheim, Germany, as head of the diploma programme in German baking. He also established the Baking Academy of Ireland in Palmerstown Village, Dublin, where he and his team of baking experts taught both beginners and experienced students the art of baking. Derek was presented with a lifetime achievement award in 2011 by the Irish Food Writers Guild for his continuing dedication to ensuring that handcrafted bread-making skills are kept alive in Ireland. In 2013, he was bestowed with an honorary award by the German Bakers Confederation to recognise the many years of close cooperation, dedication and unique contribution to the continuance of excellence in the education and training of craft skills in Germany. He closed the academy in 2019 and is now enjoying a well-deserved retirement with his wife Carol and family.

Follow Derek: Facebook, https://www.facebook.com/derek.obrien.336

~Derek O' Brien

21. Derek's Barm Brack

The barm brack is traditionally made to celebrate Halloween, but Derek's brack is lightly fruited, so it's one of those things that calls for weekly indulgence. Wonderful, when lightly toasted and smothered with salted butter, Derek's brack has a colourful array of red glacé cherries and candied fruits of green, orange, and yellow. It can be enjoyed at breakfast time or evening tea. Wash the fruit the day before and place it in a closed container overnight.

Stage 1: Flour and Salt

375 g   Strong bread flour
  4 g   Salt

Blend together and use in Stage 2.

Stage 2: Starting the Dough

200 g   Water (32 °C)
 50 g   Whole egg
 10 g   Yeast (dried)
  8 g   Milk powder
400 g   Sultanas
100 g   A mix of cherries and mixed peel (other fruits may also be used)

Mixing the Dough

The DDT is 26 °C.

1. Mix the water, dried yeast, and the milk powder. Add the egg.
2. Add this mixture to the flour and salt mixture from Stage 1.
3. Mix on a stand mixer with the dough hook on 1st speed for 8–10 minutes.
4. The total bulk fermentation time is 45–55 minutes.
5. While the dough is fermenting, place the dried fruit on a tray and place the tray in a proofer or warm place to warm up the fruit so it won't slow down the dough's fermentation when added later in the process.

Stage 3: Butter and Sugar Preparation

  40 g Butter
  60 g Caster sugar (or any white, granular sugar)

While the dough ferments, cream together the butter and the sugar until it's light. Set aside.

Stage 4: Final Dough Processing Stage

1. After 20 minutes of bulk fermentation, add the butter and sugar mix to the dough. Mix it through the dough until fully incorporated.
2. Allow the dough to rest for 20 minutes.
3. Add the fruit and mix it through the dough gently. Be careful not to tear the dough or fruit.
4. Allow the dough to rest for 5 minutes.
5. Scale the dough at 2 pieces of 630 g each. Hand up into a ball shape.
6. Intermediate proof 10 minutes keeping covered with a tea towel or plastic sheet.
7. Final shape into a ball. Place individual dough pieces in prepared 6-inch (15 cm) round baking hoops and egg wash.
8. Proof for 55–60 minutes.
9. Bake at 190 °C–200 °C for 35–40 minutes.

10. When the bracks are finished baking and out of the oven, wash with bun glaze.

11. Remove the hoops and stand on a wire rack to cool.

Bun Glaze (Sugar Wash)

20 g   Water
30 g   Sugar
 5 g   Honey

Boil in a microwave oven for 30 seconds in a cup or container.

Dario Bertarini (Italy)

Dario owns and has run a 2nd-generation family bakery since 1988. Over the years, the company has evolved from a small country store managed by his family. Presently, he has more than 10 employees. He's been a member of Richemont Club Italia since 1997 when he participated in the European Bakery Championship in Nantes, where he and Jimmy met. He's been teaching in the ENIAP bakery school in Como for the past 25 years, and he brought Jimmy over to give a class of Irish bakery products in the school during 2015. Dario was president of the Bakers Association of the Province of Como for 5 years. He also taught Jimmy to make Panettone, and Jimmy has visited him in Italy several times over the years. Dario and his family have visited Jimmy in Ireland as well.

Dario and his friend Mauro met Jimmy in Como when Jimmy was flying a Seaplane at the school there. Dario is a wonderful man and friend who makes time for everyone, and Jimmy and he often meet at global bakery exhibitions. He's always friendly, supportive, and there for his colleagues when they need anything Italian clarified. Dario is one amazing and well-loved person.

Follow Dario: Facebook, https://www.Facebook.com/dario.bertarini

~ Dario Bertarini

22. Darío's Pan Tramvai

This recipe is an ancient method used in Como for the production of this particular raisin bread. The name is derived from the fact that it was consumed at breakfast on the tram (i.e., train) that brought the workers to Milan. Dario's pan tramvai is best consumed alone or with hot tea as *Rompidigiuno* (a snack), but it's equally delicious when served with tasty cheeses. It keeps for 2–3 days but is at its best the day after baking.

Ingredients

1,000 g	Italian bread flour W > 250 p/L 0.55(strong bread flour)
800 g	Water
30 g	Olive oil
10 g	Fresh yeast
10 g	Malt extract, powder, or honey if malt is not available
20 g	Salt
1,000 g	Raisins per each kg of dough

Making the Pan Tramvai

1. Dissolve the yeast in a small part of the water.
2. Add the malt to the yeast and the water.
3. Pour the flour and all the ingredients, except the raisins, into a container.
4. Mix a little by hand on a table. It's not necessary to knead the dough with a machine.
5. Final dough temperature is 24 °C–25 °C. Cold proof at 18 °C–20 °C for 12 hours.
6. Soak the raisins in cold water for 2 hours, then drain.

7. Pour the dough on the table.
8. Take 2/3 of the dough and knead it with an equal weight of soaked raisins.
9. Stretch the remaining 1/3 of the dough to form a cover over the dough with the raisins to prevent the raisins from burning during baking.
10. Proof on a floured table for 90 minutes.

11. Turn onto a frame or baking pan and bake at 230 °C for 45–60 minutes.
12. Cool on a wire tray.

Piergiorgio Giorilli (Italy)

Since 1987, Giorgio has been a master baker in the sector's professional schools, a teacher, and a specialist consultant. He holds the rank of Knight and Commendatore of the Italian Republic. His  bakery team ranked second in the world at the CDM de la Boulangerie 1994. He's been the team coach participating in many international competitions, winning podium placement six times. Since 1998, he's been teaching at CAST Foods in Brescia. He's the founder and honorary president of Richemont Club Italia and member of the Ambassadeurs du Pain, of the Confraternity of the Chaine des Rôtisseurs, with the title of Chevalier du Baillage d'Italie, of the Ticino Confraternity of Knights of Good Bread and Élite de la Boulangerie Internationale Club (EIB). He's a co-author and author of many publications on baking. Piergiorgio and Jimmy met as candidates and as jury members in Coupe d'Europe de la Boulangerie in 1995 and as Richemont Clubs International's presidents. Piergiorgio also invited Jimmy to give his first international demonstration, which was in Rimini in 1997. He's most widely recognised as a world authority on Panettone.

Follow Maestro Giorilli: Instagram, https://www.instagram.com/giorilli/

~ Piergiorgio Giorilli

23. Mafalda Sicilian Bread

In the peasant culture of pre-industrial Sicily, the real man ate *bread travagghiatu*, obtained, that is, with the sweat of his forehead. The homemade bakery was typically female job throughout Sicily:

on Saturday afternoons, when the farmer returned from the countryside, he found hot homemade bread and some pie or pizza with parsley and oil. Unlike other Italian regions, such as Sardinia, Sicily lacked the "bread room," and the oven was generally located in the kitchen. In western Sicilian farms, the oven also served as a pantry.

One of the most famous Sicilian traditional breads was, and still is, homemade with durum wheat semolina and characterised by a dense and minute flour. Its preparation requires specific machining, characterised by low-water hydration when compared to standard bread preparations. This type of bread has high preservability, determined by the low water content that makes it less sticky for the moulds. Sicilian homemade bread is also known as *scaniatu* because it's worked vigorously using traditional tools and methods. However, today, there is a production that is increasingly geared towards the use of modern techniques and equipment.

Among the most popular and widespread breads in Sicily, mafalda certainly stands out throughout the region. Mafalda is a golden-crusted bread with a delicate and characteristic sesame seed flavour, shaped in different forms, including "eyes Santa Lucia" and "Crown". The bread is made of semolina flour, malt, sesame seeds, brewer's yeast, and salt. The dough is worked vigorously and then allowed to rest before it's formed into the long cylinders that fold themselves on spirals four times, with the initial part placed on top of the bread. It's then dampened on top with water by spraying the surface, then sprinkling with sesame seeds and left to rest for at least 2 hours (at room temperature) to proof, then it's baked. Although this recipe uses brewer's yeast and malt in the recipe, both can be purchased at all home brewing stores. Bakers fresh yeast may be substituted, and honey can replace the malt if not available locally. This recipe will make 17 rolls scaled at 120 g each. This recipe takes 2 days to make. The preferment is made on Day 1. The dough is made on Day 2. Leaven temperature is 17 °C –20 °C.

Ingredients: Levain Preferment Starter

- 375 g Italian flour Type W 300 (or strong baking flour for bread)
- 170 g Water
- 3 g Brewer's (or bakers)yeast

Making the Levain Preferment Starter

1. Using a stand mixer, mix for 4 minutes on 1st speed. Transfer to a bowl.
2. Cover and ferment overnight for 16–20 hours, keeping the levain between 17 °C–20 °C.

Ingredients: Dough

- 480 g Preferment levain
- 1,000 g Strong bread flour
- 590 g Water
- 30 g Brewer's yeast (or fresh bakers' yeast)
- 29 g Salt
- 7 g Barley malt powder or liquid (or honey)

Making the Dough

1. Using a stand mixer with a dough hook, mix for 8 minutes on 1st speed, then for 4 minutes on 2nd speed.
2. Knead all the ingredients except the salt, which will be added to the dough after half the mixing time is complete. The final dough temperature should be 25° C.
3. Let the dough rest in bulk for about 20–25 minutes. Scale at 120 g.
4. Form the dough into a cylinder shape initially, and then elongate them until they reach approximately 60 cm. Fold in pleats of approximately 8 cm. The final pleat is stretched over the gathered pleats and pressed down with the thumbs to seal them together.
5. Dampen the top with water and sprinkle on or dip in sesame seeds and place on trays.
6. Let it stand for approximately 60 minutes in the proofer at 27 °C–28 °C.
7. Bake with steam at 220 °C for approximately 20 minutes. Open the damper for the final 5 minutes of baking to dry the product and get a nice crispy crust.

Watch how Giorilli shapes the dough: https://www.youtube.com/watch?v=yO6LJMHFcfk

Japan Home Baking School (Japan)

The Japan Home Baking School (JHBS) was founded in 1975, with its headquarters located in Osaka. The school educates, encourages, and promotes home baking throughout Japan. Many of its students now bake bread and cakes at home for family and friends. It has a varied curriculum and offers speciality courses to its students to teach them new bread, cake, and pastry skills. This process enables student development in different baking areas, and many students teach at their homes using the school's methods and equipment. At present, there are more than 15,500 people annually learning as members of the school. Focusing on increasing students' skills and creativity, JHBS holds annual summer seminars of roughly 30 days' duration each year in five major cities throughout Japan. These seminars are conducted by elite-level instructors from overseas, whom it invites annually. Additionally, it's also been inviting foreign instructors for occasional short-term masterclasses. JHBS has had encounters with many wonderful international instructors over the years, one of which was Jimmy Griffin. He has again been invited to visit the school during its summer programme in 2021/2022, COVID permitting.

Contact the JHBS: Instagram, https://www.instagram.com/japan_home_baking_school/?hl=en

~ Japan Home Baking School

24. Japan Home Baking School's Melon Pan

Melon Pan is a favourite pastry in Asia. It's unique, with fermented, enriched dough on the inside and a crispy cookie dough layer outside. The cookie dough can be infused with many colours and flavours, giving it a distinct look and taste. JHBS's melon pan is traditional, and the cookie dough is infused with melon essence. Still, you can use a variety of your own favourite colours and flavours to produce these light and crispy Japanese favourites. Be bold; experiment with your own favourite combinations. This cookie is

Recipes: Breads & Buns

delicious when eaten soon after cooling; the crispy outer cookie shell combines nicely with the soft internal dough.

Ingredients: Fermented Dough

- 300 g Strong bakers' flour (T–55)
- 6 g Fresh yeast
- 15 g Castor sugar
- 3 g Salt
- 15 g Milk powder
- 30 g Salted butter
- 45 g Whole egg
- 165 g Water

Filling

180 g Raisins

Making the Fermented Dough

1. Mix the ingredients for 20 minutes on slow speed using a stand mixer.
2. Ferment for 40 minutes.
3. Scale the dough at 45 g each for 12 pieces.
4. Intermediate proof 15 minutes.
5. Roll out the dough out into 8 cm disc shapes.
6. Place the raisin filling in the centre of each piece and remould into round balls, taking care to completely enclose the raisins in the centre of the dough. Set aside.

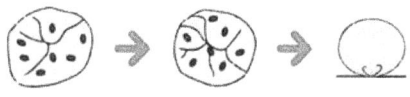

Ingredients: Cookie Dough

- 70 g Salted butter
- 65 g Sugar
- 30 g Whole egg
- 3 g Drops of melon essence
- 150 g Pastry flour (soft flour or biscuit flour)
- 1 g Baking powder

Making the Cookie Dough

1. Beat the butter and sugar together until it's light and fluffy.
2. Add the egg and melon essence over three additions.
3. Sift the flour and baking powder 3 times, and fold into the batter.
4. Mix well until the cookie dough develops a sticky consistency.
5. Scale the dough for 25 g for 12 pieces. Roll the pieces out flat. Then chill in the refrigerator for 30 minutes at 3 °C.
6. Roll out the cookie dough again into 9 cm disk shapes with a thin rolling pin.
7. Place the yeasted bread rolls with raisin filling on the round cookie disc and wrap with the cookie dough to enclose.
8. Dust well with castor sugar and score with a steel scraper.
9. Place on trays, allowing room for expansion and proof.
10. Proof for 20–25 minutes –26 °C.
11. Bake at 150 °C–160 °C for 13–15 minutes.
12. Remove from the baking tray and cool on wire racks.

Antonio Arias Ordóñez (México)

Antonio Arias Ordóñez is currently president of the UIBC, holding that position since 2014. He's the third generation of bakers on his mother's side and the second generation on the father's side. His father founded "Panificadora La Panera" in Mexico City more than 55 years ago. Antonia has run the bakery for the past 43 years. He's been an active member in the Mexican Association of bakers, CANAINPA, where he held the presidency during 2006–2008. He's a strong promoter of Mexican bread around the world. He's an active member of CIPAN and actively participates in the international nutrition congresses promoting bread from a nutritional and health perspective. He's participated as a jury member in various competitions such as the Louis Lesaffre Cup, the SIGEP Cup, and the TIBS Cup, among many others. He was awarded the EBI medal in Paris, 2016.

Antonio met Jimmy in 2007 as a representative of the bakers and confectioners of Ireland. From that time, a great friendship formed and continues to this day, coinciding in different international events worldwide, always seeking to improve and enhance bakers' profession.

Follow Antonio: Facebook, https://www.facebook.com/lapanera.panificadora

~ Antonio Arias Ordóñez

25. Antonio's Pan de Muerto

Pan de Muerto (bread of the dead) is a Mexican sweet bread, typical of the Day of the Dead. It's a traditional bread and one of the most representative of Mexico. Its origin is related to the gastronomy of the Catholic dates of All Saints and the Dead Faithful, November 1st and 2nd, respectively. In Mexico, it's said, "The passage to the beyond is lived with joy".

The bread consists of a small sphere in the centre of the upper part representing a skull and four or eight arms called quills representing bones. The bread of the dead season usually starts mid-August and continues until mid-November. This recipe takes 2 days to make to accommodate proofing.

Ingredients: Dough

5,000 g	Strong baker's flour/AP/flour/T–55
2,300 g	Butter
2,000 g	Whole egg
50g	Salt
1,500 g	White sugar
200 g	Fresh yeast
80 g	Orange zest
75 g	Whole milk powder
680 g	Water

Ingredients: Butter Sugar Mixture for Decoration Post-Baking

800 g	Butter (melted)
1,000 g	White granulated sugar

Making the Dough

1. In a mixer with a dough hook, mix together all the dry ingredients except the sugar.

2. Add the egg and the water and mix on 1st speed.

3. When all the ingredients have been integrated, mix on 2nd speed for approximately 10 minutes until the dough is silky and has developed a windowpane.

4. Add the sugar little by little and continue mixing until the sugar has been completely incorporated. Check for the windowpane to confirm dough development.

5. Take the dough out of the mixing bowl and allow to rest at room temperature, covered, for 20 minutes of intermediate proofing.

6. Cover dough with a damp cloth. Refrigerate overnight.

7. The next day, set aside a piece of dough (about 150-200 g) to form the decorative quills and small ball for the top of the bread. Divide the dough into 9 pieces of approximately 15 grams each. This will give you 1 small ball and 8 quills.

8. Scale the remaining dough into 800 g portions.

9. Roll the dough, place it on trays, and put a little lard on the top of the rolled dough.

10. After resting for approximately 10 minutes, spread the dough pieces with your hands to give them strength.

11. Make the quills by moulding the dough pieces between your fingers. Make balls without separating the dough.
12. Place the quills on top of the bread, but don't put the small ball on top yet.

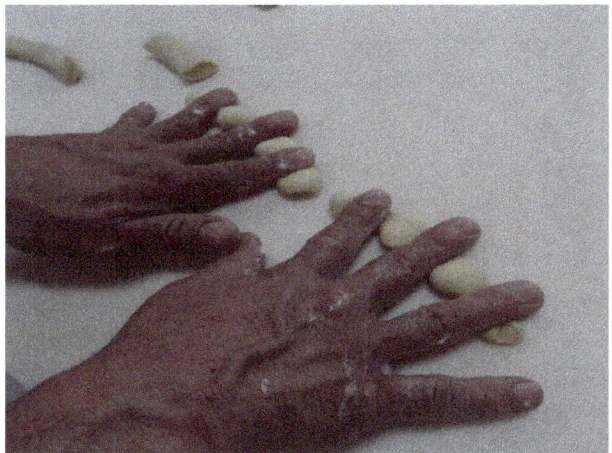 

Step 11. Shaping the quills   Step 12. Placing the quills

13. Ferment the bread until they're double in volume. Ferment the small balls at the same time but apart from the bread for the same amount of time you ferment the loaves.
14. When the bread is fermented, gently moisten the ball with a little egg and place it on top of in the quills in the centre of the bread.

Step 14. Placing the small centre ball

15. Bake for 45–60 minutes at 150 °C, considering that not all ovens behave the same.
16. When the bread comes out of the oven, paint it with melted butter and dust with the white sugar to finish. You can split them in half and add some filling (cream, jam, etc.).
17. Place on wire racks to cool, eat, and enjoy.

Recipes: Breads & Buns

Peter Bienefelt, World Champion 2018 (Netherlands)

Peter Bienefelt is the owner of Atelier du Pain. Peter is a 5th generation Master baker. His business is training and developing bakers to bake with more knowledge and pleasure. Besides his training and consultancy, he has own Bakery and Training Centre. His impressive resume includes a gold medal in the European Championships, The Pellons d'Or in Amsterdam, Netherlands in 2012. In 2013, he won Master Baker of the Netherlands; in 2018, he became one of the elites to win the coveted title of World Master Baker 'Nutritional Bread' in Paris, France; and in 2019, he was the coach of the Dutch Boulangerie team, Coupe d'Europe in Nantes, France.

Peter met Jimmy for the first time with the Irish bakery team in Nantes, France in the hotel's bar while attending the Coupe d' Europe 2006. The rest is history. They have remained friends since then.

Contact Peter: Riederhof, 322993 XJ / Barendrecht, Netherlands / 0031 657 384 922 / email, Info@atelierdupain.nl / www.atelierdupain.nl

~ Peter Bienefelt

26. Peter's World Master's Wow Bread, 2018

This bread was developed for the World Masters competition in 2018. The intention was to make bread that would "WOW" in all areas. It has a great and crispy crust and stunning colours on the inside, and with every bite, you'll get a different taste experiences. Because it's made with purified seawater and algae, this bread is also a "wow" on the nutritional declaration. Being low in salt and high in nutritional values, this bread has definitely helped Peter to become number one in the world!

Ingredients: Base Dough

800 g	Wheat flour T-65
282 g	Wheat liquid levain (flour 125 g; water 125 g; sourdough 32 g)
565 g	Purified seawater
8 g	Fresh yeast

Making the Base Dough

The DDT is 25 °C.

1. Place the ingredients together in a stand mixer with a dough hook and mix for 8 minutes on low speed and an additional 2 minutes on high speed.

2. Divide the dough into 2 pieces for further mixing: 1 piece of 850 g for making the black dough and 1 piece of 800 g for making the green dough.

Ingredients: Black Dough

850 g	Mixed dough
48 g	Olive water (the liquid with the green olives in the jar)
5 g	Squid ink
96 g	Green olives

Making the Black Dough

1. Add the squid ink to the 850 g portion of dough and mix it through the dough.

2. Add the olive water and then gently blend the olives into the mix. Clear the dough. The dough will be black in colour.

3. Place the dough in a plastic container. Cover and refrigerate at 3 °C–5 °C for at least 12 hours.

4. After the overnight fermentation, scale the dough into 250 g pieces.

5. Gently shape into long strands like small baguettes.

6. Place the dough in a plastic container. Cover and allow the dough to bulk ferment for 60 minutes.

Ingredients: Green Dough

800 g	Dough piece
12 g	Green algae
96 g	Water
115 g	Currants

Making the Green Dough

1. Add the algae to the 800 g portion of dough and mix it through the dough. The dough will be green in colour.

2. Add the water. Mix to clear.

3. Add the currants to finish the dough.

4. Place the dough in a plastic container. Cover and refrigerate at 3 °C–5 °C for at least 12 hours.

5. After the overnight fermentation, scale the dough into 250 g pieces.

6. Gently shape into long strands like small baguettes.

7. Place the dough in a plastic container. Cover and allow the dough to bulk ferment for 60 minutes.

Making the Wow Bread

1. Take a piece of the black dough and piece of green dough. Place the green dough on top of black dough and mould the pieces like a baguette about 45 cm long. Decorate it with Panko breadcrumbs.

2. Rest the dough for 90 minutes in a couche cloth for final proofing at 24 °C –26 °C.

3. When proofed, bend the baguette-shaped dough into a horseshoe shape. Dust it with flour and cut with scissors.

4. Bake it with steam at 230 °C. After 20 minutes, remove the steam from the oven and reduce the oven temperature to 220 °C. Bake for an additional 15–20 minutes.

5. Remove from the oven and cool on wire racks to avoid the bottom sweating. Enjoy my world-class healthy bread.

Anna Gribanova (Russia)

Anna Gribanova is a chef-baker from Russia. She possesses enormous talent and has competed at the world's highest level, representing Russia at the CDM de la Boulangerie. She lives in Siberia, in the city of Krasnoyarsk. Extraordinarily talented, she's the four-time champion of Russia in baking. For 20 years, she's been working in the Khlebny Dvor bakery. She's been a participant in European and World Championships: Coupe Louis Lesaffre, 2015; IBA cup, 2015; CDM de la Boulangerie, 2016; Bakery Masters, 2018. She teaches master classes in Russia and also does consulting for other bakeries. She met Jimmy in 2016, in Paris, France, at the CDM de la Boulangerie, when Jimmy was the jury president. Jimmy was well impressed with her talent and innovation during the competition, where she was the viennoiserie candidate from the Russian team.

Follow Anna: Instagram, https://www.instagram.com/anna.baker.anna/

~ Anna Gribanova

27. Anna's Russian Taiga Bread

This recipe was created for those who want to surprise their guests with wonderful traditional Russian bread. It does take a lot of time to make because you need to prepare it many stages, but the result will please you, and your time won't be wasted. This recipe will make three 680 g pieces. For proofing, you'll need three wooden banneton baskets or three medium bowls lined with tea towels.

Recipes: Breads & Buns

Combined Ingredients: Russian Taiga Bread

- 300 g Spelt flour (Whole meal)
- 820 g Flour T-1370 (Medium rye flour)
- 800 g Water
- 60 g   Fermented rye malt
- 40 g   Rye starter (Use your own or see Judy Koh's starter: Recipe #29)
- 60 g   Honey
- 20 g   Salt
- 10 g   Dry pine shoots

Stage 1: Semi-Finished Products

Ingredients: Boiled Flour

- 120 g Flour T-1370 (Medium rye flour)
- 60 g   Fermented rye malt
- 360 g Water (very hot) 80 °C –100 °C
- 10 g   Dry pine shoots

Making the Boiled Flour

1. Prepare the boiled flour the night before baking. Mix the T-1370 flour, malt, and the pine shoots. Add the boiled water. Mix thoroughly.

2. Place the dough in a warm place at 65 °C for saccharification for 4 hours.

Ingredients: Rye Sourdough

- 40 g   Rye starter
- 400 g Flour T-1370
- 250 g Water

Making the Rye Sourdough

1. Mix ingredients together. Ferment overnight for 12 hours at 28 °C with 60% humidity.

2. Reserve 40 g of the matured sourdough for the next batch of bread making.

Blending the Boiled Flour and Rye Sourdough

1. In the morning, mix the boiled flour (550 g) with the rye sourdough (650 g) and set aside in a warm place for an additional 4 hours of fermentation.

2. The sourdough with boiled flour is ready to use when it has doubled in volume.

Stage 2: Dough

Ingredients: Dough

1,200 g	Sourdough with saccharified boiled flour
300 g	Spelt flour
300 g	Rye flour T-1370
190 g	Water
20 g	Salt
60 g	Honey

Making the Dough

The DDT is 28 °C.

1. Place all the ingredients together in a stand mixer with a dough hook.
2. Mix at 1st speed for 15 minutes.
3. Ferment for 40 minutes. Cover the dough with a lid or plastic cover.
4. While the dough ferments, prepare the bannetons or shaped moulds for the bread. Dust them very well using a fine sieve and rye flour.
5. Dust the table with rye flour. Divide your dough into 3 pieces of 680 g each.
6. Make 3 balls. Put them in the bannetons or shaped moulds.
7. Proof for 1 hour in a warm place at 32 °C.
8. Place parchment paper on a wooden board or oven peel. Carefully, turn the proofed dough over onto the wooden board.
9. Put your dough, on the parchment paper, in the oven preheated to 260 °C. It's best to bake the bread on an oven stone or on the oven's sole.
10. At the beginning of the baking, add a little steam.
11. Bake for 25 minutes at 210 °C and for an additional 20 minutes at 180 °C.
12. Remove from the oven. Cool on wire racks for 6 hours before cutting.

Haif Hakim (Senegal)

Haif Hakim is of French, Senegalese, and Lebanese extraction. He's been a master baker for 24 years. His training includes a diploma from the EBP (School of Bakery and Patisserie of Paris), 1992; pastry, chocolate, and glacier in France, 1993; preparation of the master's certificate in pastry-bakery and cooking, 1993–1995; and trainer at EBP, 1993–1996. From 1996–1999, Haif was pastry chef and baker at the Duc d'Orsay in France. In 2000, he opened his bakery, Aux Fins Palais, in Dakar, North Africa.

In 2004, Haif competed in the CDM de la Boulangerie, and in 2011, he was manager and coach of the Senegal team in pastry and bakery. In 2011, he was a winner of the African Cup of Bakery; in 2012, finalist at the Bakery World Cup in Paris; and, in 2014, he was a finalist at the Master of Viennese Art in Paris. In 2016, he was inducted as a member of the EBI. Haif met Jimmy when were both members of the CDM in 2016. In 2017, he was selected as a member of the Intergalactic Bakers Federation in Chicago.

Follow Haif: Facebook, https://www.Facebook.com/aux.palais

~ Haif Hakim

Haif's Pain de Mie au Moringa

The *Moringa oleifera* tree gets its name from the Tamil language, where *Murungai* means *twisted pod*. This small tree is native to India but also is cultivated in many other parts of the world. Moringa powder is considered a superfood and is generally harvested from the dried leaves of the plant. Dry moringa is green in colour and is a known source of antioxidants and vitamins, including zinc, iron, vitamin C, magnesium, vitamin A, and some B–vitamins.

Recipes: Breads & Buns

28. Haif's Pain De Moringa

Haif's Moringa bread is unique and colourful with an interesting green and white crumb. The bread's mottled interior is a precursor to its unique flavour and all the underlying health benefits that this bread bestows. Sitting on a table for dinner, Haif's bread is sure to be a conversation starter and a curiosity which both family and guests are sure to enjoy. This recipe makes 3 loaves of 750 g each.

Ingredients: Dough

1,250 g	Flour T-55
125 g	Sugar
25 g	Salt
62 g	Fresh yeast
125 g	Butter
750 g	Water

Ingredients: Moringa Paste

18 g	Moringa powder
25 g	Water

Making the Moringa Bread

1. Mix all the dough ingredients in a machine bowl for 3 minutes on the 1st speed and 5 minutes on the 2nd speed.

2. From the dough, scale 1 piece at 300 g.

3. Mix the Moringa paste into the 300 g dough piece using a small stand mixer and a dough hook. The green dough portion will weigh 342 g.

4. Divide the green dough into 3 pieces and place them in the refrigerator.

5. Scale the rest of the white dough into 6 balls of 250 g each.

6. Proof in the refrigerator at 3 °C for 20 minutes.

7. Remould the dough and reproof for 20 more minutes in the refrigerator.

8. Roll out the 9 pieces of dough (3 green and 6 white) and overlay 3 alternate layers of white (250 g), green (114 g), and white (250 g) dough into rectangles approximately 1 cm thick to form 3 layers of colour.

9. Divide the dough further into 3 equal pieces. Mould them into an oblong cylinder shape, and then place them into pan-shaped frames with a lid (pain de mie mould or Pullman pan shapes).
10. Proof at 25 °C for 40 minutes.
11. Bake for 40 minutes at 200 °C on the oven sole.
12. Cool for 20 minutes in the baking tin, remove.
13. Cool on a wire tray.
14. Slice as required.

Judy Koh (Singapore)

Judy Koh founded The Creative Culinaire School and Caffe Pralet 14 years ago. Her forte is in creating recipes for bread, cakes, and pastries with a strong Asian influence. She's also engaged in extensive research on food ingredients for several international food companies and has published several recipe books. Frequently, she's invited as a judge for national and international bakery and pastry competitions. Judy also is passionate about educating and sharing knowledge with those who have a keen interest in bakery and pastry.

Trained in Asia, America, and Europe, Judy also has worked in several bakeries, hotels, and other food industries. In 2008, she received the award for World Guinness Book of Records for Tallest Chocolate Sculpture. In 2008, she received the award for World Guinness Book of Records for Tallest Chocolate Sculpture. She also has led her team to break several Singapore Book of Records awards such as Biggest Birthday Cake (2008), Tallest Christmas Tree of Cupcakes (2009), Longest Swiss roll (2010), and Largest Logo of Cupcakes (2011). The most recent achievement was in October 2020 when Judy organized and led 33 companies in Singapore to set a record for the longest packaged bread, which were all distributed to families in need.

Judy first connected with Jimmy at the Taipei International Bakery Show, 2018. Jimmy and his dear friend Günther Koerffer were the international jury members, and he introduced Jimmy and Judy. She was truly impressed by not only his works of art on pastry and bread, which he posted on Facebook, but also by his reflections on life and people. They point to a keen, intelligent and outstanding chef. Of course, Judy follows his Facebook posts with great interest. His recent work, *The Art of Lamination*, is indeed an amazing legacy to the world of bakery.

Judy's recipe requires the use of liquid rye sourdough, and she details the preparation, refreshment, and maintenance of her sourdough. Once mature, the bread can be made, or a similar sourdough may be used if you use and maintain your own sourdough with little or no adjustment required.

Contact Judy: www.creativeculinaire.com
17 Eng Hoon St., #01-03/04 Eng Hoon Mansions, Singapore 169767
Tel: 6324 1663, Fax: 6324 9490, email: j.jireh@creativeculinaire.com

~ Judy Koh

29. Growing Your Sourdough Starter with Judy Koh

1. Give your sourdough an endearing name like *darling* or *my dear*. It helps you be personable about it—to think and care about it as it's a living thing.

2. Day 1: Mix 100 g of rye flour or whole meal flour with 150 g unchlorinated or filtered water in a clean, preferably sterilized container like in a glass jar. Cover slightly and set aside for about 24 hours in a cool place at about 20 °C (39 °F). Mark the dough start level on your container with an elastic band to monitor progress.

3. Day 2: If you don't see bubbles or any activity, don't get discouraged. Weigh 100 g of starter, discarding the rest. Feed with 100 g of unbleached flour and 100 g of water. Mix well, cover, and set aside for 24 hours in a warm place.

4. Day 3: By now, you might see some activity in the form of bubbles, and the starter may have expanded. Start feeding the starter twice a day, 12 hours apart. Measure 100 g of the starter, discarding the rest. Feed it with 100 g water and 100 g unbleached flour. Monitor the elastic band to check the expansion of the dough.

5. Day 4: Repeat Day 3 schedule, feeding twice a day.

6. Day 5: Feed the starter twice a day. Measure 100 g of starter, discarding the rest. Feed it with 100 g water and 100 g of flour. Fix the elastic band on your jar at the top of the dough when it has settled in the jar. By the end of the day, the starter will expand to double its volume. Bubbles will appear, and a sour, acidic smell can be detected although it shouldn't be unpleasant or overpowering. If there are none of these signs, continue to feed the starter twice a day for Day 6 and Day 7, or for as long as it takes to be bubbly, vigorous, and risen, all signs indicating the starter is ready to use.

7. When the starter is ready, feed it one final time. Measure 100 g of the sourdough, discarding the rest. Feed it with 100 g of water and 100 g of flour. Rest for 6–8 hours at about 20 °C (39 °F). The bubbles should be apparent and active.

8. To begin making sourdough bread, weigh out the amount needed for the recipe. Keep the rest in the refrigerator. Feed your sourdough once a day until it becomes established. Once established, the sourdough can be fed 3 times a week, or less, when it becomes very strong and vigorous

*Important note: Smile at your sourdough starters. They're your babies and the "mums" and "dads" of many delicious loaves of bread to come. They need to know they are loved, cared for, and appreciated. They will always come through for you when needed as reliable and dependable partners.

30. Judy's Turmeric Chilli Crab Bread

Judy's bread is the foundation of this marvellous seafood dish. Getting the bread right is half the battle and will enhance the flavour of the filling. The filling will remain inside the bread and won't leak out through the crust when made properly with decent sourdough bread. Judy uses a crab stencil on her bread. Stencils can be cut out of hard card paper, which often can be found in art stores. To apply a stencil, simply place the stencil over the loaf. Spray with a mist of water from a water spray container and then dust with flour. The flour will stick to the water sprayed layer and keep the stencilled shape intact on the bread. This recipe makes 10 loaves.

Ingredients: Crab Paste

340 g	Fresh chillies, deseeded
50 g	Dried chillies, deseeded
360 g	Shallots
130 g	Garlic
40 g	Shrimp paste
30 g	Blue ginger
240 g	Oil
90 g	Dried prawns
30 g	Fermented bean paste

Making the Crab Paste

Make ahead of time / while the dough is fermenting.

1. Blend the ingredients together in a food processor until very fine.
2. Cook the mixture over medium heat, stirring all the time until fragrant.
3. Set aside to cool before storing either chilled or frozen.

Ingredients: Chilli Crab Filling

1,200 g	Chilli crab paste (either store-bought or made from scratch)
1,250 g	Water
750 g	Tomato sauce
100 g	Corn starch dissolved in 100 g of water
10 no	Whole eggs (10 eggs approximately 550 g)
750 g	Crabmeat chunks

Making the Chilli Crab Filling

Make ahead of time or while the dough is fermenting.

1. Place the chilli paste, water, and tomato sauce in a sauce pan and bring to a simmer.
2. Add the corn starch mixture, stir, and cook until thickened.
3. Break the eggs in a bowl and whisk thoroughly.
4. Carefully stir the eggs into the chilli paste mixture.
5. Add in the crab meat chunks.

6. When the mixture is cool, divide into 10 equal portions.

7. Wrap the chilli crab filling: layer a piece of baking paper with a piece of aluminium foil followed by another baking paper layer on the top.

8. Secure carefully (a piece of string can be used to tie the ends) to prevent the filling from spilling during proofing and baking. Chill until ready to use.

Ingredients: Dough

3,000 g	T-55 flour
2,000 g	Japanese flour/strong bakers flour/AP flour
50 g	Dried yeast
90 g	Salt
100 g	Turmeric powder
2,500 g	Water
1,500 g	100% hydration sourdough starter (See Judy Koh's starter: Recipe #29)
300 g	Unsalted butter
200 g	Olive oil

Making the Dough

The DDT is 29 °C.

1. Place the water and sourdough starter in a spiral mixer.

2. Add in the flours and autolyse for 1 hour.

3. Add the yeast and mix for about 2 minutes. Add the salt and turmeric powder.

4. Add the butter and olive oil. Knead until it's well developed.

5. Bulk ferment for 1 ½ hours. Stretch and fold twice during fermentation (every 30 minutes).

6. Divide into 865 g pieces. Round each piece of dough and set aside.

7. One by one, flatten each piece and wrap the dough around each packet of chilli crab filling.

8. Lightly spray the dough with water and sift some flour over a crab stencil.

9. Proof at 28 °C for approximately 1 ½ hours.

10. Bake in a preheated oven at 230 °C with steam for about 30 minutes until golden brown.

11. To serve, make cuts on the bread to create 8 sections and spread the segments open to reveal the chilli crab filling packet embedded in the bread.

12. Fold the paper and foil attractively and serve hot.

William Woo (Singapore)

William Woo is from Singapore. He's an artisan baker and teacher. For about 6 years, William had a baking academy in Singapore called Bakerz@Work. Since ceasing operations, he now focuses on teaching in this geographic region with his new enterprise L'Ecole Artisanale. All of William's life,

he's been surrounded by bread. He loves to focus especially on natural bread, using natural ingredients, and on infused bread baking, with varieties of fresh ingredients available in the local Asian markets. Additionally, he loves to play with natural and long fermentation to see how much one can push the limit of the process of bread baking.

William finally met Jimmy at Europain 2020 in Paris, several years after connecting with Jimmy on various social media platforms. William says that Jimmy has been such an inspiration to his personal baking journey and that he's come to know Jimmy as an awesome chef who is willing to help everyone, share his baking experiences and knowledge, and give sound guidance and advice in his bread baking journey. William remembers well, just last April 2020 when he posted that he would be ceasing operations of Bakerz@Work baking school, though thousands of kilometres away, Jimmy was the first person who connected with him and extended his helping hand and motivation to move forward. William is sincerely thankful to Jimmy for that moment as it has helped him move forward and take steps to continue in his bread baking journey during these difficult COVID times for everyone.

William's been trying to get the maximum goodness and richness in this bread, a process which often reminds him: artisan baking is an eternal learning journey—it's a progression, it's bread without borders!

William is honoured to share his bread baking experience in this wonderful book and has shared one of his favourite recipes that includes local and easily available ingredients, is healthy, and has a soft, chewy texture that the Asian market likes. He hopes you'll enjoy it as much.

Follow William: Instagram, @lecole_Atrisanale

~ William Woo

31. Williams Pumpkin and Oat Sourdough

One of Williams' many innovative creations, this pumpkin oat sourdough is the complete package. Its stunning looks, the magnificent burst of the seam during the bake, and the underlying rich colours that lurk just below the tantalising crust make this bread one you simply can't wait to taste.

Using pumpkins, sourdough, and whole wheat flour as base ingredients, the combination excites the taste buds and draws your eyes to its texture and colour. The pumpkin not only imparts stunning colour and texture to the bread, it also adds vegetable fibre for health benefits and natural moisture that gives the bread great shelf life. This recipe takes 2 days to prepare. The sourdough starter and toasted wheat are made on Day 1. The dough is made on Day 2.

Day 1: Preparing the Ingredients

Ingredients: Sourdough Starter

150 g	Bread flour
150 g	Water
30 g	Liquid starter culture

Making the Sourdough Starter

1. In a clean bowl, mix all the ingredients until well combined.
2. Allow the starter to ferment for 1 hour at 25 °C–26 °C.
3. Refrigerate at 16 °C for 15 hours before use.
4. Alternatively, you can allow the starter to ferment at a room temperature (25 °C –26 °C) for about 6 hours before use.

Ingredients: Toasted Wheat

100 g	Whole-wheat flour

Making the Toasted Wheat

1. Preheat the oven to 200 °C for 20 minutes.
2. Spread the whole wheat flour evenly onto a baking tray with parchment paper and bake the flour for about 20 minutes at 180 °C.
3. Allow to cool before use.
4. This process is best done 1 day in advance.

Day 2: Making the Pumpkin and Oat Sourdough

Ingredients: Pumpkin Purée

3,000 g	Fresh pumpkin
100 g	Brown sugar
200 g	Rolled oats

Making the Pumpkin Purée

1. Wash the pumpkin with the skin intact. Then cut it in half. Discard the seeds and fibres.

2. Put 50 g of brown sugar and 100 g of rolled oats in each raw half pumpkin. Put the pumpkin pieces on a baking tray.

3. Bake at 200 °C for about 10 minutes. Remove the pumpkin from the oven and mix the rolled oats with the soft pumpkin to promote thorough cooking of the oats.

4. Continue to bake for 15 minutes or until the pumpkin is soft and cooked.

5. Set aside and allow to cool before scooping out the pumpkin filling. Cool completely before use.

Ingredients: Final Dough

900 g	Bread flour
100 g	Toasted whole wheat
300 g	Liquid sourdough starter
22 g	Salt
1 g	Instant yeast (optional)
1,000 g	Pumpkin purée mixture
550 g	Water
50 g	Toasted pumpkin seeds

Making the Final Dough

1. In a mixing bowl on low speed, mix all the ingredients, except salt and pumpkin seeds, with 400 g of water (additional water depending on the purée) for about 4 minutes.

2. Gradually, add in the necessary amount of water until the dough is moist and has good dough tension. This will take about 4–6 minutes on low speed.

3. Increase to medium speed and continue to mix until the dough has achieved a good gluten development. Normally this takes 3–4 minutes, but it's better to constantly check the dough by feeling the gluten development.

4. Once the dough's gluten is well developed, gradually add in salt at low speed for about 2 minutes. Increase to medium speed for 30 seconds or until salt is fully absorbed.

5. On low speed, sparingly drizzle the toasted pumpkin seeds into the dough and ensure that they are well distributed.

6. Transfer the mixed dough to a lightly oiled plastic container. Do a simple fold to even out the dough in the container. Cover the dough. Bulk ferment for about 45 minutes.

7. Perform a good stretch and fold to give the dough more tension and to regulate the dough temperature. Rest again for 30 minutes.

8. Pour the dough to a lightly dusted worktable. Cut the dough into 420 g (7 pieces). Lightly shape it into a simple cylinder, then rest for another 20 minutes.

9. After the bench rest, final shape the dough into a sharp batard shape. Proof on a linen proofing cloth for about 60 minutes at 24 °C–26C°.

10. Preheat oven to 240 °C for about 30 minutes.

11. Once the dough is fully proofed, turn the dough onto a wooden peel, score once in a straight line, and bake with steam for about 20 minutes.

12. Drain the steam after 14 minutes to dry out the crust. Cool on a wire rack and serve.

Ricky Ellis (South Africa)

Ricky Ellis is a chef/ baker who resides in Johannesburg, South Africa. Ricky has been baking for 25 years. He's currently heading up the bakery department of a five–star hotel group and overseeing three other five-star hotels, plus a large 15,000-person-capacity convention centre. Ricky is accustomed to baking for celebrities, states of nations, delegates, and ministers. He was invited to represent South Africa in the 4th International Festival du Pain in Tunisia, 2019. Ricky is heavily involved in assisting and tutoring students and bakers. He's also a member of many prestigious related trade organizations. He's a professional member of the South African Chef Association (SACA), the World Association of Chef Society (WACS), and the South Africa Bakers Association (SABA). Ricky is also the founding member of Sourdough SA; Sourdough & Craft Bakers, South Africa; Gluten-Free Sourdough & Gluten-Free Baking, South Africa. Ricky also does bakery consultation, up-skilling of bakers, and streamlining of bakeries in South Africa. He hosts bread and baking workshops in his free time and engages in food product development and test baking. Although Jimmy and Ricky have never met in person, they do follow each other on social media and admire each other's work. They also, of course, share their mutual passion for baking.

Follow Ricky: Facebook, https://www.facebook.com/ricky.ellis.359
Follow Sourdough & Craft Bakers South Africa: Facebook, https://www.facebook.com/groups/SourdoughSA

~ Ricky Ellis

32. Ricky's Potbrood

Potbrood is one of South Africa's traditional loaves of bread and dates back to the early settler's era of the 1820s. During that time, there were no electric ovens or mixers and no advanced bakery equipment. This bread was mixed traditionally by hand on a flat stone surface covered to ferment and baked in a cast-iron pot over an open fire of wood coals, which gives the bread an amazing flavour. During those times, the settlers ground their own wheat, which they grew on their land. It was a prime example of the field to oven baking, a concept that is now being embraced once more by many European farmers looking for ways to lower their carbon footprints. This recipe makes one large loaf of 900 g in a 10-inch cast-iron pot with a lid.

Ingredients: Potbrood Dough		Baker's %
500 g	Stoneground white bread flour	100%
10 g	Salt	2%
30 g	Oil	6%
350 g	Water	70%
10 g	Yeast	2%

Making the Potbrood Dough

1. Dissolve the yeast in the water.
2. Mix all the ingredients together to make a soft, developed dough.
3. Cover and ferment for about 2 hours until the dough doubles in size.
4. Shape the dough into a ball. Cover and proof until the dough doubles in size, approximately 1 hour.
5. While the dough is proofing, brush the cast iron pot with fat to prevent sticking.
6. Transfer the proofed dough to the fat-lined pot. Place the lid on the top.
7. Place the pot on warm coals. Cover the side of the pot and lid with coals.
8. Bake for approximately 1 ½ hours or until you've achieved the colour you desire.
9. When baked, release from the pot, and cool on a wire rack.

Arturo Blanco (Spain)

Arturo Blanco is the coach of Los Espigas (the spikes), the Spanish baking team, technical advisor, and one of the most prominent voices in the bakery world. He's also a technical advisor to the Confederation of Bakers of Spain (Ceop-pan), working for example, on the writing of the bread quality standards and the implementation of the latest module of specialization in the bakery for professionals training. Arturo also collaborates with leading

national and international companies in the sector. His career as a baker began when Arturo was young and he joined what has been a family tradition that goes back four generations. He's participated as a coach in numerous international bakery competitions where his role as technical advisor and jury member has been of special relevance.

At national and international conferences, he's shared his scientific work on sourdough cultivation for free. As the national team coach to Espigas, he's been involved for 5 years with this project, about which he's very passionate. He's proud of having helped make the team that, in addition to comprising great professionals, looks and feels like a family. That's a big reward for him. Arturo reminds us that we must not forget all the team's bread promotion actions, which all its members carry out with all the love and dedication that this wonderful job deserves.

Arturo met Jimmy at the UIBC conference in Sao Paulo in 2016. They immediately became friends. How could it be otherwise between two fanatics of bread and bakery? Since then, Jimmy and Arturo have had the opportunity to meet at various events, and they always enjoy each other's company. Arturo has also enjoyed visiting Galway, where he was welcomed by Jimmy with traditional Irish hospitality.

Follow Arturo: Instagram, https://www.instagram.com/arturoblanco.pan/

~ Arturo Blanco

33. Pan Murciano With Durum Wheat

The Pan Murciano is made with rich Durum wheat and was developed by the Murcian Bakers Association to promote durum wheat consumption in the area. It has a unique flavour all of its own. The bread is best complimented by ham, with tomato and olive oil spread onto the bread. The combination of bread and fillings make this elaboration an authentic Spanish delicatessen item. This recipe makes 20 loaves of 500 g each.

Ingredients: Sourdough Starter

1,000 g	Durum wheat flour
600 g	Water
1 g	Liquid sourdough (See Recipe # 29)

Making the Sourdough Starter

Mix ingredients together and ferment for 12 hours at 24 °C.

Ingredients: Dough

5,000 g	Durum wheat flour
3,500 g	Water
1,601 g	Sourdough
110 g	Salt
5 g	Fresh yeast

Making the Dough

The DDT is 22 °C–24 °C.

1. In a spiral mixer, mix all the ingredients together.

2. Knead for 8 minutes on 1st speed and for 1 minute on 2nd speed.

3. Let rest in bulk fermentation for 90 minutes at 26 °C.

4. Scale at 500 g each and preform into a cylinder. Rest for 15 minutes.

5. Form 500 g chuscos (batons) and leave the pieces to ferment for 2 hours at 26 °C in couche cloths or use floured tea towels.

6. When proofed, cut down the centre with a sharp blade.

7. Bake at 220 °C with steam for 50 minutes. Release steam for the final 15 minutes of the bake.

8. Cool on wire racks, split, fill, and enjoy!

Vicente Sancho Colomer (Spain)

Vicente is an artisan baker from the beautiful city of Valencia. He speaks French and Spanish as well as his mother tongue, Valencian. He was the first teacher at the Depanaderia School of Valencia from 1988 to 1995. He completed a specialist teaching course at The National Employment Institute, National Vocational Training Centre and is a founding partner of club Richemont España. He's an active member of Les Ambassadeurs du Pain, a global organization that promotes bakery excellence through global competition and international conferences. Vincente was the champion of Spain in 1993 and 1995 and won 4th place in Third European championship in 1995. His bakery, Colomer, was founded in 1948 by Fernando Colomer, a 4th generation baker. The company is currently owned by Vincente's mother Amparo Colomer, a 5th generation baker, and managed by Vincente, who is now the 6th generation baker in his family. It's a small business where tradition and craftsmanship are paramount to this amazing bakery family. Vincente first met Jimmy during the Coupe d'Europe de la Boulangerie in Nantes, 1995, when he was a Spanish national bakery team member. They have continued to be friends ever since. Both have visited each other's cities, and Vincente helped organise a master class in Valencia for Jimmy when he travelled there in 2017 to the famous and historic El Gremio School in the city centre.

Follow Vincente: Facebook, https://www.Facebook.com/vicente.sanchocolomer
Contact Vincente: lartdepa@hotmail.com

~ Vicente Sancho Colomer

34. Huerta Bread

Among the large number of varieties of rustic bread enjoyed in Valencia, the most typical is Valencian bread, known at least since the 17th century. It consists of a well-hydrated dough and is formed into four or more shapes including the orchard bar, a rustic bar-shaped bread with a longitudinal cut; the bun, a typical round bread with 3 cuts; the roll, a variant of the bun but with a small slit in the centre for improved baking; and the pataqueta. This recipe makes 6 loaves.

Ingredients: Dough

950 g	Bakers flour/strong flour/AP flour
50 g	Flour T–80
700 g	Water
20 g	Salt
100 g	Sourdough
10 g	Fresh yeast

Making the Dough

The DDT is 24 °C–26 °C.

1. Put all the ingredients together and mix for 1 minute on 1st speed or mix by hand to just hydrate the flour.
2. Bulk ferment for 90 minutes.
3. Perform a 10–minute 1st speed kneading. Continue mixing for 8 minutes on 2nd speed.
4. Place the mixed dough in a sealed container and allow for bulk fermentation for 1 hour.
5. Divide the dough into 300 g portions by hand or in a volumetric, low stress divider.
6. Give some pieces a small pre-shape and round others.
7. Pre-ferment for 20 minutes.
8. Form the loaves without overtightening. Form the pataquetas and the rolls.
9. Final proof for 1–1 ½ hours (depending on conditions).
10. Cut the orchard bar and rolls with a longitudinal cut, make a cut in the pataquetas, and give the buns 3 cuts.
11. Put the loaves in the oven at a strong starting temperature of 250 °C. Steam and bake on a falling oven to 220 °C.
12. Allow the loaves to cool and enjoy this delicacy.

Josep Pascual (Spain)

Josep is an international master of bakery and pastry and works as an international consultant and a jury member in world championship and other global tournaments. He also works as a technical trainer and coach to many international teams. Josep is the technical director of Pastry Revolution magazine and a collaborator in many other specialized magazines worldwide. He's had a very

exciting and varied career. He's worked as a teacher at the bakery school in Barcelona and at the German bakery school in Weinheim, and he was responsible for the coordination and pedagogical management at the bakery school in Santiago de Chile.

Josep's also worked as a teacher in several schools in Italy. Josep was a member of the Spanish national team in the European Championship in Nantes, France, 2013. He's had many important roles as a jury member, such as in the international championships of bakers in the Golden Bread Cup in Italy, 2013 and in the Word Championship, Europain, France, 2012. He's been a coordinator and trainer of international teams since 2010, winning 3rd prize in the SIGEP Bread Cup in Rimini, 2009, in Italy. He's a spirited competitor, winning 1st prize in the championships held in Lille, 2008, France when he was the Spanish national team captain. He also competed in the Louis Lesaffre Cup of national teams. He's been captain of the Spanish national team at the world championship in Villepente, France.

Historically, as a competitor, he's amassed great success and experience in the competitive world, winning 1st prize for the best exposition of traditional bakery and pastry products at the SIGEP Bread Cup, Rimini 2007, Italy. He was the Spanish representative at the European Festival of Bread in Oporto, Portugal, in 2007, and won 1st prize in the World Championship of Bakery held at SIGEP, Rimini, Italy in 2006. He also won 1st prize in the Spanish Championship of Bakery Schools. He regularly attends conferences and has delivered many technical demonstrations in several countries worldwide, such as Portugal, Italy, Holland, Belgium, Israel, Finland, México, Germany, Russia, Chile, Guatemala, Argentina, Sweden, India, Luxembourg, and Canada.

Recipes: Breads & Buns

Josep met Jimmy for the first time at the SIGEP trade fair held in Rimini, Italy, in the early 2000s. Spain and Ireland participated in the event, and of course, among the Irish contingent was Jimmy, who also speaks Spanish. They became friends, and ever since, they have been meeting at different events, fairs, and competitions throughout Europe, either as participants in some competitions or as judges in other competitions, such as the Bakery World Cup.

Contact Josep: jpascforner@yahoo.es

~ Josep Pascual

35. Josep's Organic Spelt Bread with Butterfly Stencil

Spelt bread is a very versatile product. It goes very well with meat and fish but adapts to all meals. It's also excellent alone or with jams or chocolate spread. Decorative stencils can be made by cutting them out on thin cardboard, and a nice selection of stencils are available from art supply stores and can be purchased online. (See Judy Koh's Turmeric Chilli Crab Bread, Recipe #30). Try for plastic ones, which can be washed and reused over and over again. This recipe takes 3 days to prepare (the sourdough must be prepared 2 days in advance) and yields 18 spelt rolls scaled at 100g each.

Ingredients: Sourdough

150 g   Organic spelt grains
300 g   Warm water

Making the Sourdough

1. Mix ingredients by hand.

2. Cover and leave to ferment at room temperature for 24 hours to become active.

3. The following day, crush everything together and leave to ferment at room temperature for another 24 hours.

Ingredients: Dough

- 650 g Organic spelt flour
- 100 g Organic whole spelt flour
- 100 g Sprouted whole spelt flour
- 500 ml Water
- 450 g Sourdough made from organic spelt grains
- 16 g   Salt
- 5 g   Fresh yeast

Making the Dough

1. Using a spiral or stand mixer with a dough hook, knead for 6 minutes on slow speed and 3 minutes on fast speed.

2. Remove the dough from the bowl and give it a few folds over to give it consistency and strength.

3. Rest the dough in a covered container for 120 minutes, stretching and folding at 30–minute intervals (4 times). Cover after each stretch and fold.

4. Scale the pieces at 100 g each and roll them slightly into loose balls.

5. Rest the balls sheltered from drafts for 20 minutes for intermediating proofing.

6. Roll round once more to build strength and allow to rest for 5 minutes.

7. Prepare a tray with a damp cloth and another with seeds, such as poppy or sesame.

8. Slightly squash the ball and run the edge of each dough ball using your finger and thumb through the wet tray first and then through the seeds, to coat them.

9. Ferment in a chamber at 26 °C with 80% humidity for approximately 1 hour.

10. Dust with flour using decorative stencil or leave plain.

11. Bake at 235 °C, falling to 210 °C. Apply steam at the beginning for a crusty bake. Release the steam after 12 minutes

12. Bake for 16 minutes until light and crispy

Beesham Soogrim (Sweden)

Beesham is a life-long vegetarian chef with a passion for sourdough baking and natural fermentation. He travels the world to share his love of baking and has run workshops in Holland, Belgium, Bulgaria, Denmark, France, Israel, Italy, Mauritius, Netherlands, Norway, Singapore, Spain, and Taiwan. His workshops become fully booked as soon as they are advertised on his Facebook page. Beesham and Jimmy met when Jimmy was the jury president for the World Cup of Baking, Le CDM de la Boulangerie, in Paris, in 2016. They also met in Stockholm, Sweden, when Jimmy was jury president at the Nordic Bakery Cup 2017.

In 2020, Beeshams' Instagram page was hacked and held for ransom. Unwavering, Beesham declined and was cut off from his circa 40,000 followers. In just a few months, he's built up his followers once more to over 24,000. He's a lovely person and dedicated to his passion for all things in baking.

Contact Beesham: beeshamthebaker@gmail.com, https://beeshamthebaker.com/

~Beesham Soogrim

36. Beesham's Seeded Nutrition Bread

Beesham's nutty Kamut bread is a beautifully crunchy bread loaded with mixed seeds—you can choose your own favourite ones to put into this delightful bread. Kamut is an ancient grain that has become popular in recent times due to its rich nutty flavour. Enjoy the nutty bread as breakfast bread or later in the day as a sandwich bread with cut meats and cheeses. This bread takes 2–3 days to prepare, depending on how long you soak the seeds. This recipe makes 2 loaves at 605 g each.

Day 1: Preparing the Nut Mix and Preferment

Ingredients: Nut Mix

- 150 g   Whole Khorasan* grain or whole wheat grain
- 100 g   Mixed seeds
- 100 g   Water

Preparing the Nut Mix

Soak the seeds overnight (or for at least 6 hours) in 100 g of water.

Day 2: Preparing the Preferment

Ingredients: Preferment

- 250 g   Strong wheat flour
- 100 g   Spelt flour
- 200 g   Liquid sourdough starter (see Recipe# 29)
- 400 g   Water 300 g to make the dough
- 11 g   Salt

Making the Preferment

1. Using a stand mixer with a dough hook, mix the two flours and water for 2 minutes at slow speed. Autolyse (rest) for 45 minutes.

2. Add the sourdough starter and mix for 5 minutes on low speed.

3. Add the soaked seeds and salt. Mix for another 10 minutes still on low speed.

4. Mix at high speed for 2 minutes.

5. Transfer the mixed dough into a container and do the first stretch and fold. Cover and repeat the stretch and fold twice, at room temperature, at 45-minute intervals.

6. Leave the entire dough overnight in the refrigerator for bulk fermentation at 3°C –4 °C.

Day 3: Making the Bread

1. The following day, divide the dough in half or leave whole if you prefer a big loaf.

2. Shape as you desire or put in a baking tin. Proof for 2–3 hours at room temperature (22 °C–28 °C).

3. Bake at 250 °C with steam for 15 minutes. Then, reduce the oven heat to 200 °C and bake for another 30–35 minutes. Drain the steam for the last 10 minutes.

4. Take the loaves from the oven and allow the baked bread to cool down on a wire tray before cutting. (Finally, and most importantly—enjoy!)

Ellen Yin (Taiwan)

Born into a family baking business, Ellen officially entered the baking profession in 1995. She enjoys connecting with baking professionals all around the world. She's passionate about the biology, chemistry, and physics behind the baking craft and

engineering thinking behind improving the process. Ellen is proud to have been the first female in multiple leadership positions in various organizations, making a difference in the industry globally. Ellen received her bachelor's in economics at the University of Washington and her master's in management at Boston University. Her baking industry career is most impressive. Ellen was the chairperson of the Taipei Bakery Association from 2007 to 2010 and has since been the honorary chair. She was the vice president of the UIBC from 2011–2019 and participated in jury selection for the CDM de la Boulangerie Europe, 2019. Ellen was a board member at UIPCG from 2007– 2012, and was the founding chairperson of the Taiwan Baking Competition Council in 2010. She is the CEO of Florida Bakery Ltd., 福利麵包公司, established in 1949, and president of Fabrica Tortilla Ltd., 多提亞食品, established in 1999.

Ellen first met Jimmy at the UIBC meeting in Verona in 2011. The two have met up annually at the meetings ever since. In 2019, Ellen was travelling in Ireland with her family and visited Jimmy at his bakery, where they enjoyed his delicious butter croissants and conger bread.

Follow Ellen: Instagram, https://www.instagram.com/ellenyin/

~ Ellen Yin

37. Ellen's Tapioca Tea Bread

Also known as Bubble/Boba Tea Bread, this bread was featured in several publications and magazines throughout Asia. It's a fun fusion of Asian creativity and innovation. Merging cookie dough (the top) with fermented dough in a drinking cup and giving it the appearance of an iced drink is really unique and clever. The moist custard filling, soft spongy dough, crunchy cookie dough, and tapioca pearls combined with the base of heavy cream provide a refreshing taste sensation. It's fun and easily made, and the assembly can be completed using long edible wafers as straws for decoration.

This recipe is a 2-day process. The preferment is made on Day 1. The cookie dough can be made the day before. It's best to make the custard and chill it in advance. The brioche dough is processed on Day 2. The black tapioca pearls are available online or from Asian food shops. (Baking note: Both the bottom and the top are made with the brioche dough, which is filled with custard and black tapioca pearls. The top portion of brioche is also wrapped in cookie dough.)

Additional Supplies

- 22 Plastic drinking cups (height 135 mm, top width 90 mm, bottom width 60 mm)
- 22 Cookie straws
- 22 Tulip muffin shapes   or   Large muffin tins

top width: 70 mm

height: 75 mm

bottom width: 60 mm

Day 1: Preferment & Prepping Ingredients

Ingredients: Preferment for the Brioche Dough

- 660 g Strong flour
- 20 g   Fresh yeast
- 386 g Water

Making the Preferment for the Brioche Dough

1. Bloom the yeast in water (18 °C). Mix the flour through to form a dough.
2. Allow the dough to ferment overnight at 19 °C – 20 °C.

Ingredients: Custard Filling

- 160 g Instant custard powder
- 12 g   Darjeeling tea powder
- 560 g Whole fat milk

Making the Custard Filling

1. Blend all the ingredients together using a hand whisk or stand mixer.
2. Chill in the refrigerator at 3 °C until required to fill the brioche doughs.

Recipes: Breads & Buns

Ingredients: Cookie Dough

100 g	Unsalted butter
100 g	Icing sugar
100 g	Whole eggs
5 g	Darjeeling tea powder
200 g	Pastry flour

Making the Cookie Dough

1. Using a stand mixer with a cake beater, cream the butter, icing sugar, and tea powder until it turns lighter in colour.

2. Add the eggs in 3 additions of 1/3 at a time, scraping down the bowl well and mixing to clear each of the 3 times you mix the batter.

3. Add the 200 g of pastry flour and mix to clear.

4. Wrap in cling film and chill at 3 °C for half an hour before using. The cookie dough can be made on Day 2; however, it's easier to handle when chilled.

Day 2: Baking and Assembly

Ingredients: Brioche Dough

1,066 g	Preferment
330 g	Strong flour
180 g	Sugar
5 g	Salt
10 g	Yeast
10 g	Darjeeling tea powder
194 g	Chilled water
100 g	Salted butter

Making the Brioche Dough

The DDT is 26 °C.

1. Bloom the yeast in water. Except for the butter, mix all the brioche dough ingredients together using a stand mixer with a dough hook on 1st speed for 5 minutes to form a dough.

2. Add the preferment and mix on the 1st speed for 5 minutes and on the 2nd speed for 8 minutes to fully develop a windowpane. *Do not add the butter until a windowpane is developed.*

3. Add the butter and mix to clear completely, approximately 2–3 minutes on 2nd speed.
4. Allow the brioche dough to bulk ferment in a covered bowl for 45–60 minutes.

Scaling the Doughs

1. Scale the brioche dough to 22 × 50 g pieces for the bases and 22 X 30 g pieces for the top.
2. Shape round all 44 of the brioche dough pieces. Rest for 10–15 minutes, covered with plastic.
3. Scale the cookie dough to 22 × 15 g pieces for the cookie dough coating for the top.

Filling the Dough

1. Using the 15 g cookie dough portions, roll out to a disk 2–2 ½ mm thick.
2. Place the cookie dough disk in the palm of your hand. Then place 1 portion of the 30 g brioche dough on top and in the centre of the cookie dough in your hand.
3. Stuff each 30 g brioche dough portion with 10 g of custard filling and 5 g of Boba pearls. To do this, pinch the brioche dough around the custard filling and tapioca pearls with your right hand until they are completely enclosed in the brioche dough (like filling dumplings) while spreading the cookie dough around the outside of the brioche dough with your left hand until the cookie dough covers 2/3 of the brioche dough.
4. Using the 50 g brioche portions, roll out to disk 2 mm thick.
5. Stuff each 50 g brioche dough portion with 20 g of custard filling and 10 g of Boba pearls. To do this, pinch the brioche dough around the custard filling and tapioca pearls like a little purse, ensuring the seam is sealed so the filling won't leak out. Reshape round and place into the large muffin tins or tulip muffin papers to form the bases.

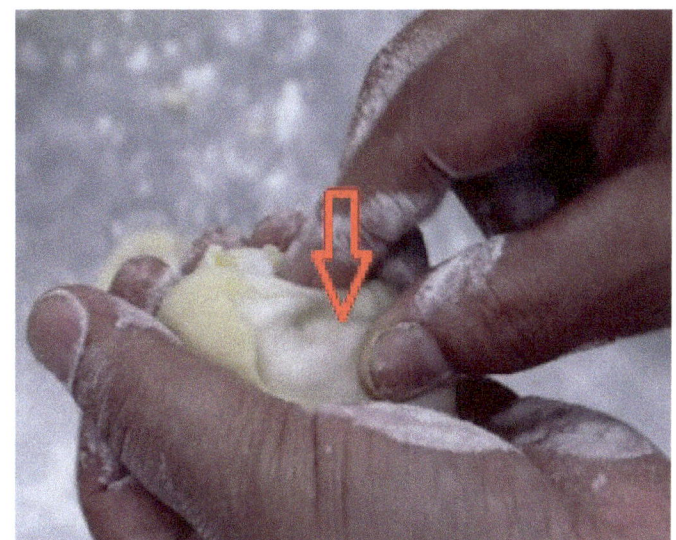

Proofing and Baking

1. Proof the 50 g brioche dough bases for 50–60 minutes at 27 °C –28 °C and 75%–80% humidity.

Recipes: Breads & Buns

2. Proof the 30 g brioche pieces with the cookie dough wraps on top of the oven *without moisture*, so the cookie coating will remain crunchy after baking. When fully proofed, the cookie dough coating will crack.

3. Bake the dough at 180 °C until golden brown. Bake the 50 g brioche dough bases for 15 minutes. Bake the cookie-dough-wrapped 30 g brioche dough pieces for 12 minutes.

4. Allow the bases to cool. Remove them from the tins/tulip muffin papers. Move the cookie dough tops to wire racks to cool.

Ingredients: Final Decoration and Filling

300 g Boba tapioca pearls
120 g Whipping cream

Assembling the Tapioca Tea Bread

1. Place the baked dough base at the bottom of a clear cup.

2. Pipe in a layer of whipped cream.

3. Add a layer of tapioca pearls.

4. Place the cookie crusted bread (Bolo bread) on top and insert rolled cookie straws.

Gülten Yağmur (Turkey)

Gülten is a food engineer. Her interest in bakery started 13 years ago when she started to work for Lesaffre at the Baking Centre in the Middle East and in Central Asian regions. Since then, she's worked on different bread types from all over the world. Gülten has studied various baking methods, gaining valuable practical experiences and knowledge, especially in the Middle East and Central Asian regions. She completed her doctoral study on Turkish sourdoughs in 2013.

Gülten has worked to fulfil her dream of sharing the science behind this ancient art with Turkish bakers and raising awareness about it to bring this ancient profession to the status it deserves. In 2015, Gülten became the first woman coach of the Turkish national bakery team. The Turkish team won Louis Lesaffre in 2015 and qualified to participate in the 2016 World Bakery Competition held in France. In 2016, Gülten met Jimmy at the CDM de la Boulangerie when he was jury president. Since then, they have been in contact with the same objectives: to share their passion for baking and spread it to all.

Contact Gülten: https://www.facebook.com/gulten.yagmur.3

~ Gülten Yağmur

38. Gülten's Simit

The Turkish simit is a bread made using Pekmez, a type of molasses. The sweet syrup can be made from a variety of fruits, although it's most commonly made from grapes. Thickening agents are used to achieve the rich consistency. Pekmez can be enjoyed plain as a syrup, but people also enjoy having it for breakfast mixed with tahini. Using Pekmez in this recipe is what gives it its interesting and tasty flavours. This recipe makes 9 rolls.

Ingredients: Simit Dough

- 1,000 g   Flour T–65/bakers flour/AP flour
- 550 g   Water
- 15 g   Salt
- 30 g   Compressed fresh yeast

For the outside decoration, you'll need toasted white sesame seeds and Pekmez for securing them.

Making the Simit Dough

The desired DDT is 22 °C–26 °C.

1. On a stand mixer, mix all the ingredients for 3 minutes on 1st speed.

2. Knead for 5 minutes on 2nd speed until the dough is smooth and soft.

3. Bulk ferment in a bowl for 45 minutes, covered.
4. Scale the dough for 9 pieces at 120 g each and gently mould each piece into a ball.
5. Roll out the dough pieces until they are each 50 cm in length. Place 2 sides parallel to each other and pinch the open ends.
6. Roll in opposite directions to make a twist.
7. Tie together the ends of both sides to form a circle.
8. Dip the shaped dough into the Pekmez. Ensure the dough is thoroughly coated.
9. Dip the dough into the toasted sesame seeds until the dough is fully coated.
10. Place them on trays.
11. Final proof for 45 minutes at 25 °C.
12. Place in the oven and bake at 240 °C for 15 minutes in a deck oven with steam.
13. Cool on wire racks after removing from the oven.

Gülten's Recipe Suggestion

This is a basic traditional simit recipe. This recipe can be enriched by adding cheese, sausages, or figs into the dough during the shaping stage to increase the food's flavour and value. To consume as a sandwich, you can cut the bread horizontally from the side and use different fillings such as olive paste, cheese, tomato, or carved meats.

Wayne Caddy (United Kingdom)

Given that Wayne started his baking career as a test baker for a large bakery producing thousands of hot cross buns, it's quite fitting that Wayne chose to share his version of the hot cross bun. Wayne initially met Jimmy in 2014 at the Master's in Paris. Wayne was representing the UK, and Jimmy was a jury member. The two have remained friends ever since. In 2018, Wayne invited

Jimmy to be a guest lecturer, the viennoiserie specialist, at the world-famous School of Artisan Food in the UK. Jimmy and Wayne regularly socialise and are in touch weekly over social media profiles to share teaching ideas and methods.

Follow Wayne on Instagram: https://www.instagram.com/wayne_caddy/

~ Wayne Caddy

39. Wayne's Spiced Apple Streusel Buns

This recipe is based on a British classic, the hot cross bun, which was historically produced at Easter for Good Friday, to represent Christ's crucifixion. Using a highly hydrated milk-based fermented sponge dough (similar to poolish), gives these buns their lighter and moister texture. Simultaneously, the butter and honey round off and carry all of the sweet, zesty and aromatic flavours from the apples, sultanas, and mixed spices. A slice of baked apple brushed with a super sticky bun glaze, a liberal sprinkling of the baked streusel, and a white chocolate cross finish on top all add extra visual depth and interest. These buns truly are a treat for the senses. This recipe takes 2 days to prepare and makes 30 rolls.

The preferment is made on Day 1, and the dough is made on Day 2. In addition to the listed ingredients, you'll also need white chocolate (for the crosses).

Day 1: Preferment

Ingredients: Milk Sponge Preferment

- 300 g Organic bread flour
- 300 g Milk (4 °C)
- 1 g Fresh compressed yeast

Making the Preferment

1. Combine all ingredients and mix by hand until no visible lumps of flour remain.
2. Store in a sealed tub for 12 hours at 22 °C.

Making the White Chocolate Crosses

1. Melt the white chocolate in a bain-marie. Deposit into a piping bag with a fine nozzle.
2. Evenly pipe the white chocolate into cross shapes on baking parchment-lined trays and allow to set until needed to garnish the buns.

Preparing the Dried Apples*

1. Keeping the skins on, remove the apple cores (retain for glaze) and slice into 8 rings. Place the apple rings in lemon juice to stop browning.
2. Slice the apple rings into smaller rings about 5 mm thick.
3. Place apple rings onto a lined baking tray and place the tray into a fan-assisted oven at 80 °C for 3–5 hours with the door slightly open. Dry until slightly leathery.
4. Store in cool conditions in an airtight container for up to a week. For best results, freeze apples for up to 3 months. Ensure they're thoroughly defrosted before use.

*The number of apples you need will vary. Typically, you can make 8 apple rings from a medium sized apple. You would need 4 apples to make enough rings for 30 buns. Adjust quantities as needed based on the number of apple rings each apple produces.

Ingredients: Sticky Bun Glaze

3	Apple cores
800 ml	Water
700 g	Caster sugar
1	Vanilla pods
1	Cinnamon sticks
2	Cardamom pods
1	Star anise
100 g	Honey

Preparing the Sticky Bun Glaze

1. Place all the ingredients into a pan and cook on a low to moderate heat for approximately 4 hours on a gentle rolling boil at 115 °C to 120 °C until a honey-like amber colour is achieved and the glaze coats the back of a spoon.

2. Sieve immediately and apply to warm buns or store in a cool environment in an airtight container. Warm before using.

Ingredients: Streusel/Crumble Preparation

100 g	Unsalted butter
100 g	Castor sugar
50 g	Ground hazelnut
100 g	Plain flour
2 g	Cardamom

Making the Streusel/Crumble

1. Mix the cold butter and flour together using the beater attachment on a mixer until a sandy texture is achieved or mix by hand.

2. Add the remaining ingredients. Stop mixing when a fine-to-medium particle size is reached.

3. Bake the streusel on a lined baking tray at 200 °C until golden brown.

4. Allow to cool and crumble into a medium-to-fine consistency.

5. When cool, place in an airtight container until ready to use.

Ingredients: Dough Stages 1-3

		Stage
700 g	Organic bread flour	
350 g	Water	1
30 g	Fresh yeast	1
601 g	Milk sponge	1
80 g	Liquid whole egg	1
15 g	Fine sea salt	1
150 g	Butter	2
150 g	Honey	2
300 g	Dried apples	3
300 g	Sultanas	3
20 g	Grated orange zest	3
20 g	Grated lemon zest	3
25 g	Mixed spice (Speculaas)	3

Making the Dough

The DDT is 24 °C.

1. With a spiral mixer, mix all the Stage 1 ingredients on 1st speed for 5 minutes or until the dough develops good strength.

2. Add the Stage 2 ingredients and mix on 2nd speed for 5 minutes until cleared and dough shows a smooth, silky gloss.

3. Add the Stage 3 ingredients and mix on 1st speed for 2 minutes until evenly distributed.

4. Bulk ferment at 22 °C for 60 to 90 minutes.

5. Use a 30-piece bun divider moulder to divide the dough or scale manually at 90 g of dough per piece. Pre-shape the dough round and rest for 10 minutes.

6. Final shape into round balls. Place the buns on a medium-sized, lined baking tray ensuring even spacing to avoid batching.

7. Place a 3 mm-thick piece of sliced apple on top of the rounded bun.

8. Final proof at 22 °C for 60–90 minutes.

9. Bake at 230 °C for 13 minutes or until golden brown. Right before removing the buns from the oven, heat the bun glaze.

10. While the buns are still hot, evenly brush the buns with the bun glaze, and liberally sprinkle with baked streusel.

11. When totally cooled, add the chocolate crosses and sprinkle with a touch of icing sugar.

Jacob Baggenstos (United States)

Jacob Baggenstos is a most talented baker from Seattle, USA, who has spent time at wholesale and retail bakeries throughout the USA. In 2016, he competed for Team USA at the CDM de la Boulangerie in the Artistic Design category and returned to compete for the USA in the World Bakery Masters 2018. He first met Jimmy when Jimmy was President of the jury for the CDM de la Boulangerie 2016 in Paris. Jimmy was well impressed with the clean-cut young bakers on team USA. Mannerly, interested, and passionate about their profession, Jacob enjoyed hanging out with Jimmy and the team talking shop and telling jokes.

Follow Jacob on Facebook: https://www.facebook.com/jpbaggenstos

~ Jacob Baggenstos

40. Jacob's Earl Grey Ciabatta

Ciabatta is a classic Italian flatbread. Ciabatta itself translates into slipper/or slipper bread, resembling the shape and length of slippers. Ciabatta bread has been enjoyed globally in recent years, gaining ground on the French baguette as one of the most internationally recognizable bread in the marketplace today.

Jacob's ciabatta has been pimped with the addition of Earl Grey tea levain, black tea powder, and honey. This innovative bread is wonderfully light, flavoursome and has a beautiful open texture with a thin crispy crust.

Ingredients: Preferment

132 g	Water
10 g	Tea leaves
132 g	T-85 Yecroa Flour
20 g	Sourdough starter (See Judy Koh's starter: Recipe #29)

Making the Preferment

1. Boil the water and soak the tea leaves for 5–10 minutes.
2. Allow to cool to 38 °C.
3. Mix the flour and the culture into the tea leaf/water mixture.
4. Knead until smooth on a stand mixer with a dough hook.
5. Ferment at 21 °C (70 °F) for 8 hours.

Ingredients: Dough

300 g	T-55 bread flour
200 g	T-85 flour
5 g	Instant yeast
15 g	Salt
5 g	Black tea powder
75 g	Honey
294 g	Tea levain preferment from above
381 g	Water

Making the Dough

1. Using a stand mixing machine with a dough hook, knead in all the ingredients on 1st speed for 5 minutes, and then on 2nd speed for 3 minutes.

Recipes: Breads & Buns

2. Transfer to an oiled bowl and cover with plastic to prevent skinning.

3. Ferment for 1 hour at room temperature. Stretch and fold the dough.

4. Ferment for another hour at room temperature. Stretch and fold the dough.

5. Ferment for 1 more hour.

6. Cut into 2 pieces of 635 g each. Shape as for ciabatta.

7. Proof the dough until almost doubled in size.

8. Place on a setter or silicone parchment and slide on to the oven sole.

9. Bake at 240 °C (460 °F) with steam for 12 minutes.

10. Remove the steam from the oven and continue to bake for a further 13 minutes or until a reddish-brown colour.

11. Remove from the oven and cool on wire racks.

Jeffrey de Leon (United States)

Jeffrey de Leon is a pastry chef and baker based in Los Angeles, California. After building a strong foundation for himself while baking with Chef Thomas Keller, he's travelled the world seeking to perfect his craft. This journey has led Jeffrey on a path he never thought possible. His efforts paid off in 2016 when he was fortunate enough to be selected by the Bread Bakers Guild of America to be a part of the team representing the USA at the CDM de la Boulangerie, competing under the Viennoiserie category. He was extremely honoured to be invited back for the Master's de la Boulangerie competition in 2018. While his career's providence has led to many mentions and accolades, it's all been the consequence of doing something he truly loves. Jeffrey just had the luck to put himself in the right places at the right times.

Jeffery likes to create pastries that are equally tasty and beneficial without being unnecessarily sweet or over-indulgent. He believes that one of the greatest privileges bakers have in the craft is the knowledge people are taking in and ingesting our art. It's a deeply personal experience, and Jeff doesn't take it lightly. He wants to be sure if someone is to eat something he makes, the experiences will be enjoyable.

Jeff's spent a lot of time baking within the confines of restaurants and for savoury chefs. He believes he's benefitted from this because it's exposed him to many different flavour profiles and combinations that he might not necessarily have known while working solely in a bakery or pastry shop. It's also forced him to adapt different pastries to various ingredients while keeping the foundation of the pastry at heart.

Jeff takes advantage of his good fortune to live in Southern California were every season's harvests are bountiful. Farmers' markets always provided him with various fruits and vegetables with which to play. These opportunities let Jeff have some versatility in his pastries so he can best accommodate the hard work each of the farmers has to offer.

Jeff met Jimmy in 2016 at the CDM de la Boulangerie, where Jimmy was the president of the jury. While that started off as a much more formal relationship, the two quickly became friends. They were reunited in France, where Jimmy was a guest speaker and technical presenter at the Masters' de la Boulangerie 2018. Over the past few years, he's collaborated with Jimmy, trading late-night formulas and talking shop from halfway across the globe. Jeffrey says that he's humbled to be able to call Jimmy a friend and a colleague. Jimmy's hard work and dedication are a testament to his baking spirit. Jimmy shines bright in a world of stars and is proven to be a champion among all bakers.

Follow Jeffrey: Instagram, https://www.instagram.com/xxjeffydxx/

~ Jeffrey de Leon

41. Jeffrey's Turmeric Bee Pollen Brioche Feuilletee

The recipe for the Turmeric Bee Pollen Brioche Feuilletee was inspired by an espresso drink that a barista once served Jeff during brunch service at a restaurant for which he was baking at the time. Jeff was looking to create something naturally beneficial for his guests to drink as they enjoyed their breakfast pastries but also wanted to create a pastry that was equally beneficial.

The ingredients for this special pastry were thoughtfully chosen. The curcuminoids found in turmeric have beneficial medicinal properties with anti-inflammatory and antioxidant effects, which help fight disease. Black pepper aids the body in the absorption of the curcuminoids. Organic bee pollen contains more than 200 biologically active substances, including antioxidants, vitamins and minerals, proteins, carbs, lipids, fatty acids, and enzymes. While these ingredients may seem like a random set, their individual attributes help each other to radiate. This recipe takes 3 days to make. The osmotolerant starter and brioche dough are made on Day 1. The brioche dough is prepared on Day 2. The dough is laminated and baked on Day 3.

Day 1: Preferment and Dough

Ingredients: Jeffrey's Osmotolerant Starter   Bakers%

59.82 g	Bread flour	100%
35.89 g	Water 26 °C	60%
9.57 g	Sugar	16.7%
11.96 g	Sourdough starter	20%

Making Jeffrey's Osmotolerant Starter

1. Add the warm water to the starter to stimulate fermentation.

2. Add the sugar and the flour. Mix well.

3. Place in a sealed glass jar with a lid in a warm place (28 °C–30 °C) for 12–16 hours.

Ingredients: Brioche   Bakers%

Amount	Ingredient	Bakers%
435.03 g	Bread flour	80%
108.76 g	Whole wheat flour	20%
24.47 g	Water	4.5%
42.96 g	Milk, whole	7.9%
271.89 g	Whole egg	50%
65.25 g	White sugar	12%
10.88 g	Trimoline	2%
11.96 g	Yeast, Lesaffre gold	2.2%
13.59 g	Sea salt, fine	2.5%
3.26 g	Malt, non-diastatic	0.6%
117.24 g	Osmotolerant starter	21.6%
244.7 g	Butter unsalted	45%
284 g	Lamination butter	21%

Making the Brioche

The DDT is 25 °C–26 °C.

1. Mix all the dry ingredients by hand in a bowl and add them to a stand mixer with a dough hook or a spiral mixer.
2. Dissolve the yeast in the water.
3. Excluding the butters, add all the wet ingredients to the dry ingredients.
4. Intensive mix the dough until the dough develops a windowpane. You're looking for an opaque window with constant gluten development.
5. The suggested mixing times are 2 minutes on 1st speed and 4–5 minutes on 2nd speed.
6. Add the room temperature unsalted butter in 2 additions, mixing the dough to clear with both butter additions.
7. Remove the dough from the mixer and press it out into a prepared pan or tray.
8. Cover with plastic and cool in a refrigerator at 3 °C. Rest overnight.

Day 2: Lamination

Laminating the Dough

1. Prepare the laminated butter block. Set aside.

2. Laminate the dough using 2 double (book) folds.
3. Rest for a minimum of 2 hours, covered, in a refrigerator at 3 °C.

Ingredients: Turmeric Pastry Cream

366 g	Milk
1	Vanilla bean, scraped
60 g	Egg yolks
75 g	Sugar, granulated
37.50 g	Pastry cream powder
64 g	Butter, tempered
26 g	Turmeric, ground
1.50 g	Black pepper, ground

Making the Turmeric Pastry Cream

1. In a saucepan, bring the milk, vanilla bean, and ½ the sugar just to a boil.
2. In a bowl, combine ½ sugar, pastry cream powder, turmeric, and black pepper. Then, add the egg yolks.
3. Temper the milk into the egg yolk mixture. Return to the saucepan.
4. Over medium heat, whisk the cream mixture until it thickens (approximately to 82 °C).
5. Add the cooked cream to a mixer bowl. Mix on high speed with a whisk attachment.
6. Once the mixture has stopped steaming, add the butter. Mix to combine.
7. Remove cream from the bowl. Spread onto a plastic-lined tray. Cover with plastic and place in cooler to set at 3 °C.

Ingredients: Flat Icing

500 g	Confectioners' sugar
120 g	Heavy cream
10 g	Vanilla paste

Making the Flat Icing

Combine all ingredients in a mixing bowl until the icing is smooth and without lumps. (Adjust the thickness of your icing by increasing or decreasing the amount of heavy cream you use.)

Ingredients: German Streusel

250 g	Granulated sugar
250 g	Butter
500 g	All-purpose flour

Making the German Streusel

1. Cut chilled butter into approximately 1/4" cubes.
2. Combine all ingredients in a mixing bowl until a crumbly mass forms. Be sure to keep ingredients cool. Do not over-mix.
3. Spread streusel crumbs evenly across a parchment-lined sheet pan. Place in refrigerator to set.
4. Store on a covered sheet pan or in a container until ready to use.

Assembling the Buns

1. On a worktable or sheeter, widen the dough to 45 cm. Turn and sheet to 4 mm.
2. Trim dough to 40 cm wide.
3. Apply 225 g pastry cream evenly across the brioche.
4. Sprinkle cinnamon sugar (60/40) mix evenly across the pastry cream. You can add as much or as little here as you would like.
5. Roll the brioche firmly lengthwise and mark it in 45 mm segments.
6. Cut length of brioche into 2 or 3 segments and place on a pan and put into the freezer until firm enough to portion.
7. After portioning, use immediately or store in freezer.

Proofing and Baking

1. Place 75 mm ring moulds evenly across a sheet pan. Spray liberally with non-stick spray.
2. Set portioned brioche into mould. Proof at 26 °C and 80% humidity.
3. The dough is fully proofed and ready to bake when it fills the mould and doesn't spring back when touched.
4. Garnish with German streusel.

5. Bake at 177 °C in a convection oven for 18–20 minutes with high fan. To test for doneness, a probe thermometer inserted into the centre of the pastry should read about 88 °C.

6. After baking and while still warm, remove from moulds and top with flat icing and garnish with bee pollen. Allow to cool at room temperature.

Notes on Turmeric Pastry Cream Process

The turmeric will cause the pastry cream to thicken more than usual. This is normal and will help aid in the overall makeup of the pastry. Hot process pastry cream powder, such as Elsay from Patis-France, is what was used in this formula. If it's not available, corn starch is a suitable replacement. Be aware of the freshness of the turmeric. It loses essential oils and pungency over time if it's not stored correctly. If available, use fresh turmeric, as it will have a stronger, more well-rounded flavour. Grate it on a fine microplane or in a spice grinder for best results.

Alan Negrete (United States)

Alan has always been around the restaurant and bakery worlds. His dad had a restaurant when he was growing up as a Latino teenager. At the time, Alan often fought with his dad about having to work in the family restaurant. (Ugh!) The arguments never went well. As time moved on, Alan found himself working in fast-food joints not intending to do anything else except make a buck. He always found work. Many of the owners would ask him how much he wanted to be paid. He told them he' work 1 day for free and then they could pay him what they thought he was worth. The strategy always paid off.

Soon after leaving high school, Alan was working in a warehouse in a go-nowhere job. It didn't take long before he was back working in the food industry, where he excelled. He found that restaurant/bakery owners trusted him, and he would often be assigned the task of opening and closing the locations. Even though they knew he would go out and party, they could count on him to be at work on time. It wasn't unusual for Alan to sleep in his car in the restaurant/bakery parking lot after a long night partying. He may have been a little hung over, but he was on time and kept the crew going. Alan refers to these youthful times as his Culinary Mercenary Days.

When Alan was working for a couple of French chefs, they convinced him to fill out a scholarship application for the French Culinary Institute in New York. The scholarship included the programme in New York and a 90-day internship programme at the end of the education programme. To Alan's surprise, he won the scholarship, and, 18 months later, found himself working at Poilâne Bakery in Paris, France. Alan was one of 30 interns. This was a challenging time for Alan, who worked as many shifts as possible and barely made ends meet—somehow, he made $500 last for 3 months. Wow! Eventually his hard work paid off and he was noticed by the owner who offered him the job. Alan stayed in Paris for an additional 2 years. He has worked as a baker for his entire professional career, working his way up to become a leader in all bakeries he's worked in including Bread Only (Los Angeles, CA; 1993–1996), La Brea Bakery (Los Angeles, CA; 1996–1998), and Andre Boudin Bakery (San Francisco, CA; 1999–2013).

Alan's earned certificates from the San Francisco Baking Institute, the American Institute of Baking, and the French Culinary Institute. He earned his CMB from the French Boulangerie Council. He is a member of the Culinary Professional Education Board at the Orange County School of the Arts, is a key member of a company that has been in business since 1833 (seems like it should be named if it's tossed out there), and was a member of Le Cordon Bleu Professional Education Board, having an influence on the bakery education at the Hollywood and Pasadena CA campuses. He opened Disney's California Adventure—Boudin Bakery, and is the featured chef for Disney's food and wine culinary events. He was the winner of the Disneyland Culinary and Pastry Competition for 9 years in a row and also won the Maple Leaf Pastry Competition in Canada. Alan has been included in the stock footage of the FoodNetwork and has been the featured chef in multiple television segments: "Great Chef Series BBC", "At the Chef's Table BBC", and "Into the Fire". Alan appreciates the opportunities he's had to mentor key bakery staff and develop leaders in all bakeries he's worked. He truly enjoys working with bakery layouts to maximize performance and ensure quality standards. Alan is affiliated with The American Bread Bakers Guild, International Food Technologist, and Culinology.org.

Alan first met Jimmy Griffin in 2007 at the Bread Bakers Guild of America's event "Camp Bread" at the San Francisco Baking Institute. Alan snuck into Jimmy's class, "Authentic Irish Baking" and introduced himself. Alan was amazed at Jimmy's presentation of bread samples. After striking up a conversation, the two became friends and have kept in touch over the years since. Occasionally, they are lucky enough to have their paths cross. Alan will never forget the night he was listening to the radio and work at heard the story about the scuba diver who was attached by a conger eel. It was Jimmy Griffin! Alan had always thought Jimmy had a strong sense of character—as a true baker must have to live the baker's life. He's grateful that social media has made it easier to keep in contact with his friend.

Contact Alan: www.thecalbakehouse.com

~ Alan Negrete

42. California Sourdough Bread

For this recipe, Alan likes to use local Californian red grapes, unbleached high gluten flour (≈14% protein; King Arthur, Sir Lancelot brand), and purified filtered water to make the sour starter. Ingredient weights are provided for commercial baking as well as scaled down home and small quantity baking. This recipe takes 14 days to make. The sourdough starter is made on Days 1–11. The mother starter dough is made on Day 12. The final sourdough is made on Day 13, and the California sourdough bread is made on Day 13. This recipe yields 20 loaves at 505 g. A small mix yields 2 loaves at 505 g. You can scale at whatever weight suits your production/customers' requirements.

Stage 1: Sourdough Starter

Ingredients: Sourdough Starter

20 loaves		2 loaves
1,000 g	High gluten flour, unbleached	100 g
500 g	Purified filtered water, room temperature	50 g
250 g	Red grapes, organic if available	25 g

Making the Sourdough Starter

1. Pour the water into a 4 litre (8 quart) container at room temperature.

2. Add the high gluten flour. Stir by hand until it creates a liquid slurry. This should be in a very liquid state. Set aside.

3. Place the red grapes on a rectangular length of food-grade cheese cloth.

4. Roll up the cloth with the grapes and tie off the ends with string or a knot.

5. Pound the rolled cloth with a rolling pin to break up the grapes and allow the juice to escape through the cheesecloth.

6. Place the cheese cloth package of smashed grapes into the flour/water slurry in the container. Be sure to totally submerge the cheese cloth.

7. Cover the container and store in a location with an ambient temperature around 21 °C–26 °C (70 °F–80 °F) for 11 days. Fermentation will begin very quickly.

Stage 2: Mother Dough

Ingredients: Mother Dough

20 loaves		2 loaves
1,000 g	Hi gluten flour, unbleached	100 g
450 g	Purified filtered water, room temperature	45 g
800 g	Sourdough starter	80 g

Making the Mother Starter Dough

1. Pour the water into a mixing bowl. Add the sourdough starter and then the flour.

2. Mix on slow speed to incorporate all ingredients—no more than 8–11 minutes.

3. Place in a container with a lid and cover. Allow to rest in the refrigerator for 24 hours. (You can make bread with this "mother dough" after 9–15 hours of it fermenting, but it can cause you to lose strength in the dough. Ideally, it should ferment for the full 24-hours.)

Ingredients: Californian Sourdough

20 loaves		2 loaves
5,000 g	Hi gluten flour, unbleached	500 g
3,000 g	Purified filtered water, room temperature	300 g
2,000 g	Mother starter dough	200 g
112.5 g	Salt	11.25 g
pinch	Ascorbic acid	pinch

Recipes: Breads & Buns

Making the California Sourdough

The DDT is 21 °C–24 °C (70 °F–75 °F).

1. Load the ingredients into the mixing bowl in this order: water, mother dough, salt, and flour.
2. Mix on slow speed for 2 minutes to incorporate ingredients. Then mix on medium speed for 8–11 minutes until the dough has developed to a medium development level (i.e., a windowpane is developed).
3. Let the dough rest in a container with a lid for 15–20 minutes.
4. Scale the dough into desired sizes and shape them the portions into round balls. Ensure there is some tension in the dough by moulding it tight.
5. Leave dough portions on a table and cover with plastic wrap or towel.

6. Let dough rest for at least 20 minutes.
7. Final shape the dough into round or long loaves as desired.
8. Place the loaves onto a pan that has been prepared with oil or pan spray.
9. Cover the dough and let it rest for 1–2 hours at room temperature and then for 24 hours or so in a refrigerator at 3 °C.
10. Score the loaves with a sharp knife to achieve an appropriate scoring pattern.
11. Place the tray of bread in the oven. , spraying around the oven to create a steam pocket. And close the oven door.
12. For 600 g pieces, bake at 204 °C–210 °C (400 °F–410 °F) for about 20–30 minutes. Bake with steam for the first half of the bake. If you don't have a steam feature on your oven, use a spray bottle to spray down the loaves with water before putting them into the oven.
13. After baking, cool on wire racks. The sourdough flavour will continue to develop as the bread cools.

Mike Zakowski, World Silver Medallist (United States)

Mike Zakowski is a graduate of the Culinary Arts programme at Kendall College in Chicago, Illinois. When he owned Kraftsmen Baking in Houston, Texas, he was named Best Baker in Houston and won the Best Bread award for his *pain biologique* during the bakery's first year of operation. Mike was the operations manager at Artisan Bakers in Sonoma, California, for 5 years and currently owns his own bakery, The Bejkr. He markets his creations at local farmers markets in Sonoma County, CA.

Mike is a Bread Bakers Guild Team USA member and competed at the 2010 Louis Lesaffre Cup and the 2012 CDM de la Boulangerie in the Baguette and Specialty Bread category, where he and his teammates brought home the world silver medal. He was then selected to compete in the Master's de la Boulangerie 2014, representing the USA as one of six competitors worldwide.

Mike and Jimmy met at the CDM de la Boulangerie in 2012 when his team competed, and Jimmy was a jury member. Then they met again in 2014 when Mike competed for the Master's du Boulangerie, and Jimmy was the jury president. It was during this second encounter the two got to know each other better. They shared time together chatting at the competition when Mike wasn't competing and also at the gala dinner event for the competitors and jury members. Mike fondly remembers his competition days in Paris and remarked that "his time competing was very memorable, and the time spent getting to know Jimmy better was great fun".

Follow and contact Mike: The Bejkr, www.thebejkr.com and Instagram @thebejkr1

~ Mike Zakowski

43. Mike's Einkorn Bread

Mike has been selling his amazing baking at the farmers' markets for years. His Einkorn bread is a thing of legend and one of the first pieces of bread to sell out from his stall. Mike uses flour milled from ancient grains as they are known to have been used to produce this bread. Ancient grains have not been genetically modified or bred solely to provide a big harvest yield. They are grains that have been cultivated and harvested for tens of thousands of years and baked into delicious nutty flavoured breads.

Mike's recipe will make 2 delicious Einkorn loaves weighing 800 g each. This recipe takes 2 days to make. The soaker, sesame seeds, and the sourdough are prepared on Day 1. The dough is made, proofed, and baked on Day 2. You'll require 2 large 2-pound rectangular loaf/Pullman tins or similar, lightly greased to prevent sticking.

Day 1: Ingredients Preparation

Ingredients: Einkorn Porridge Soaker

- 323 g   Water for the soaker
-   4 g   Salt
- 64 g   Cracked einkorn
- 64 g   Sesame seeds

Making the Einkorn Porridge Soaker

1. Toast, separately, the cracked einkorn and sesame seeds.

2. When making the porridge, cook the toasted, cracked einkorn with the water and salt until most of the liquid is absorbed in the grain.

3. Switch off the heat and add in the toasted sesame seeds.

4. Mix the porridge to disperse the sesame seeds throughout.

5. Make the porridge at the same time as you make the liquid levain sourdough.

6. Allow to cool. Then cover and leave overnight.

Ingredients: Levain*

100 g   Einkorn flour
 75 g   Water (18 °C –20 °C)
  1 g   Liquid sourdough starter

*Zacwas is the Polish word for Levain.

Making the Levain

1. Mix the water with the starter using a hand whisk to agitate it. Thoroughly blend together.

2. Add the flour. Mix to clear and set aside in a warm place covered, ideally in a glass jar overnight for 12–14 hours.

Day 2: Making and Baking the Einkorn Bread

Ingredients: Einkorn Bread

549 g   Einkorn flour
414 g   Water
 16 g   Salt
171 g   Liquid sourdough starter
455 g   Porridge soaker

Making the Einkorn Bread

The DDT is 21 °C.

1. Mix ingredients on a stand mixer with a dough hook on 1st speed for 10–12 minutes.

2. Bulk ferment for 1 hour.

3. Stretch and fold the dough once. Continue fermentation for 1 more hour.

4. Prepare the loaf shapes. Scale the 2 loaves at 800 g each.

5. First, shape into a boule. Rest for 20 minutes. Keep the dough covered to prevent skinning.

6. Degas the dough and form into a cylinder. Place into the tins with the seam facing down.

7. Proof at 22 °C–24 °C for 90–120 minutes. Dust with flour or stencil (optional). (Loaf shown here dusted using diamond stencil.)

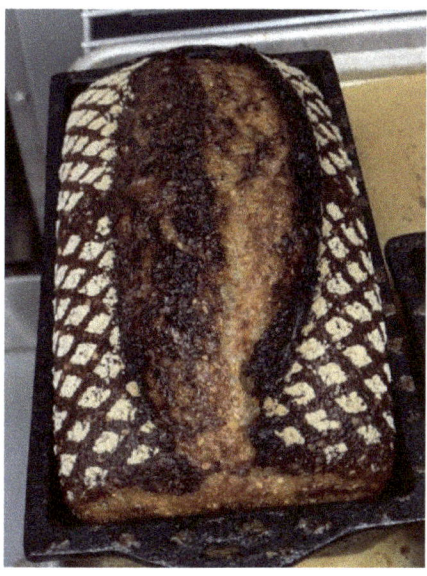

8. Score in the centre with a sharp blade and bake with steam (damper closed) for 55 minutes at 260 °C.

9. Release the steam from the oven and bake for a another 10 minutes with the oven damper/door open until the bread is a nice dark brown colour and has a dry crust.

10. Empty the loaves from the baking tins and stand on wire racks to cool completely.

Hector Facal (Uruguay)

Hector started to learn how to bake when he was 21 years old and began to work at his father-in-law's (Pablo Samuele) bakery. In 1985, he bought his first bakery with his wife, Rosa, where they stayed until 1992. In those past years, Hector began to dabble in CIPM (Centro De Industriales Panaderos De Montevideo). In 1990, he joined the said centre's board of directors, which later became the current CIPU (Centro De Industriales Panaderos Del Uruguay). In 1992, Hector and his wife partnered with a former long-time employee of their bakery, Francisco Antelo, and bought another bakery they named Verdun. In 2016, Hector and Rosa became the sole owners. This year marks the 28th year Hector has baking with his family at Verdun.

During these years, Hector participated in meetings, competitions, and national and international congresses representing the CIPU as a member of the school commission of the CIPU. In 2000, the commission founded the current bakery school in Uruguay based in the CIPU, called ITP (Technological Institute of Bread). Hector also participated in the first world bakery congress in New York City, being secretary of the CIPU (2006), and as a jury member at the National Bakery Championships. In 2008, Hector attended the congress of CIPAN and UIB, in São Paulo, Brazil. Hector served as president of the CIPU in 2010 and during 2011 at the alternate meeting of UIB and CIPAN at the Madrid congress of UIBC. In 2012, he attended the CIPAN meeting in Verona, Italy as well as the International Bread Convention in Mexico. In 2013, Hector attended the alternate

meeting of CIPAN in Uruguay. In 2014, Hector was a member of the Master De La Boulangerie jury in Paris, France. Then, in 2015, he attended the congress of CIPAN in Porto Alegre, Brazil.

In 2011, Hector had the opportunity and pleasure to briefly meet Jimmy in a hotel cafeteria in Verona in 2011. Then, in March 2014, both of them joined the jury and colleagues from other countries around the world for the Masters Boulangerie 2014, held as part of Europain in Paris (organised by Mr. Christian Vabret). During that time, Hector and Jimmy shared hours of work and learning but also moments of recreation and celebrations. Since that meeting, they have communicated through social media networks and emails, exchanging knowledge and other instances of their lives. These reunions make Hector reflect on how important it is to participate in meetings, fairs, congresses, and similar experiences. Their friendship is linked to their passion and their noble profession of which they are proud to make their daily bread.

Contact Hector: Bakery and confectionery "Verdun"; Montevideo, Uruguay
Mobile: +598 94 416 654, email: hectoranibalfacal@gmail.com
Instagram: https://www.instagram.com/facalhector/

~ Hector Facal

44. Hector's Corn Bread with Blueberries with Rum

The five-string plait's been a favourite at Hector's bakery ever since the bakery opened its doors in 1985. This bread stands out as a signature loaf of his geographic area and the plentiful ingredients and raw materials available locally. Corn is the staple diet of many South American countries and using cooked cornmeal in this bread adds a lovely natural yellow tinge of colour to each slice. The sun-ripened blueberries that have marinated in rum add the final touches of colour and flavour to the beautiful bread.

The Blueberry and rum plait's an ideal product to consume in winter or all year round. This bread is delicious and can be enjoyed for breakfast, a quick snack, or at teatime. Enjoy a slice to eat on its own, or spread it with red fruit jam or another of your favourite spreads.

The bread can be made into a loaf shape or other smaller plaits, such as a 3-string (175 g each strand) or a 4-string plait (131 g each strand). This recipe will make 10 5-string plaits of 525 g each (105 g each strand). This bread takes 2 days to make. The poolish is made and the maize and blueberries are prepped on Day 1. The bread is made on Day 2.

Day 1: Preparing Ingredients

Ingredients: Poolish

- 250 g   Baker flour/strong flour/AP flour
- 250 g   Water
- 2 g   Fresh yeast

Making the Poolish

1. Mix ingredients together with a whisk to form a dough.
2. Allow to rest at room temperature between 15–18 hours for fermentation.

Ingredients: Cornmeal Porridge

- 500 g   Water
- 250 g   Cornmeal
- 2.5 g   Salt

Recipes: Breads & Buns

Making the Cornmeal Porridge

Cornmeal in gastronomy carries 3 times its weight in water and is creamy. In Italy, it's called polenta, and it's typically served with a sauce made from minced meat and tomato. In this case, we cook the cornmeal and salt (99:1 ratio) with twice its weight in water.

1. Boil the water with the salt.
2. Add the cornmeal to the boiling water, stirring with a wooden spoon until it thickens and comes to a boil again. Remove from heat immediately.
3. Transfer to a plastic or stainless steel container and store in the refrigerator overnight at 3 °C. (You can prepare the cornmeal porridge the day you bake the bread; however, because the cornmeal tends to hold heat, you'll need to ensure you allow ample time for it to cool completely before using: a minimum of 4–5 hours. Using warm cornmeal porridge in the dough will affect the dough temperature.)

Ingredients: Rum Soaked Blueberries

- 600g   Blueberries (fresh)
- 150 g   Rum

Making the Rum Soaked Blueberries

Soak the blueberries in rum to marinate overnight at room temperature.

Ingredients: Dough

- 502 g   Poolish
- 2,000 g   Bakers strong flour
- 600 g   Cold cooked cornmeal
- 40 g   Salt
- 400 g   Sugar
- 50 g   Honey
- 40 g   Gluten
- 600 g   Water
- 140 g   Yeast
- 150 g   Butter (delayed addition)

Making the Dough

The DDT is 24 °C–26 °C.

1. Except for the butter and the blueberries, place all the ingredients and the poolish in the mixer.
2. Knead on 1st speed 5 minutes, until the dough comes together, then, continue mixing for 3–5 minutes until you obtain a soft, elastic dough and have developed a proper windowpane.
3. Add the butter in 2 additions and mix to completely clear.
4. Add the marinated blueberries to the dough. Gently mix until fully integrated.
5. Place the dough in a plastic container greased with vegetable oil or butter.
6. Allow to stand for between 90–120 minutes depending on the ambient temperature.
7. Empty the dough onto a table. Scale the dough at 105 g each. (You can scale at other weights to make 3 strand plaits.)
8. Roll into balls and rest for 15 minutes of intermediate proofing.
9. Roll out to a long strand of 30 cm and make 5 string plaits using sequence: 2 over 3, 5 over 2, and 1 over 3. Repeat this sequence until the dough is entirely plaited. Tuck the ends in neatly.
10. Place on smooth, flat trays and paint with egg wash.
11. Sprinkle with granulated white sugar. Then proof until it's doubled in size.
12. Bake with steam at 185 °C–190 °C for 25–28 minutes.
13. Glaze with syrup or sugar glaze upon removal from the oven.
14. Cool on wire racks.

Kao Sieu Luc (Vietnam)

Kao Sieu Luc is the general director and founder of Asia Bakery & Confectionery (ABC) Company Limited (Vietnam) and Emeritus Chairman of the International Federation of Chinese Bakery & Confectionery Association (IFCBCA). Kao began his career in bakery products at the age of 28. Today, with more than 3 decades' experience in the bakery and confectionery industry, the ABC company is now a significant business entrepreneur in Vietnam and is the primary supplier for all international fast-food chains and convenience stores in Vietnam, such as MCD, Burger King, Lotteria, KFC, Jollibee, 7-Eleven, Ministop, and Family Mart. Kao is a passionate baker and has made his hobbies of work and engineering his life. In 2012, he received the Labour Medal III for outstanding citizens from the Socialist Republic of Vietnam president.

In 2016, he was a member of Club Elite de la Boulangerie Internationale. In 2016, he also won a Lifetime Achievement Award in Baking Arts. Jimmy and Kao met as fellow jury members for the World Bakery Masters in Paris, 2010. In 2018, Kao invited Jimmy and Günther Koerffer to Vietnam before the Taipei International Bake Show (TIBS), and he hosted them in Ho Chi Minh. He brought them both around his extensive and impressive factories and his many shops throughout the city. A kind and generous man, Kao took time out of his very busy schedule to spend time with Jimmy and Gunther, bringing them around Ho Chi Minh City to see all the fantastic sights and museums.

Follow the ABC Bakeries: Facebook, https://www.facebook.com/abcdamsen

~ Kao Sieu Luc

45. Kao's Vietnamese Baguette (Banh Mi)

The Vietnamese French baguette, also known as Banh Mi, was derived from a French recipe introduced in Vietnam during the colonial period in Vietnam. The original recipe was modified and since then has become a typical and favourite food in the country. It's usually airy, with a thin, crispy crust and typically is served as a sandwich with special Vietnamese pork rolls, ham, cucumber, and pickles. This recipe makes 6 baguettes when scaled at 300 g per piece.

Ingredients: Poolish

- 200 g   Bread flour
- 245 g   Water
- 0.3 g   Dried yeast

Making the Poolish

1. Mix all the ingredients together by hand.
2. Ferment for 12–16 hours at room temperature.

Ingredients: Dough

600 g	Bread flour (strong flour or AP flour)
200 g	Cake flour (soft, pastry or biscuit flour)
0.79 g	Dried yeast
1.97 g	Salt
0.79 g	Maltose (glucose or honey)
427 g	Water
445 g	Poolish stage

Making the Dough

The DDT is 24 °C–26 °C.

1. Combine all the ingredients, including the poolish, together. Using a stand mixer with a dough hook, mix the dough on slow speed for 12 minutes and on 2nd speed for 1 minute.
2. Allow the dough to rest for 45 minutes.
3. Scale the dough at 300 g each piece and round each into a ball.

4. Allow the dough to rest for another 20 minutes.
5. Final shape into a baguette shape cylinder 55 cm–60 cm. Place on trays and proof for 50 minutes at 26 °C–28 °C.
6. When proofed, make several incisions with 3, 5, or 7 cuts (depending on the baguette's length) before baking.

7. Place the baguette in the oven and apply steam by spraying with a mist of water using a spray gun.

8. Bakr for 20 minutes at 200 °C bottom heat and 240 °C top heat.

9. Reduce the oven temperature to 210 °C–220 °C after steaming.

10. Open the oven door or damper to release the steam after 14 minutes and bake dry for the final 6 minutes.

11. Remove from oven and cool on a wire rack.

 Cakes

Jack Hazan (Israel)

Jack Hazan, chef, master baker and the president of the Israeli Bakers & Pastry Association, began his professional baking career more than 30 years ago as a pastry chef at the five-star Dan Hotel Tel Aviv, Israel. He graduated with an MA in agriculture science at the Israeli Hebrew University. In 2005, Jack became the Israeli baking champion at the national baking championships. Ever since, he's a leading R&D influence figure, well respected for his tremendous knowledge in baking, pastry innovation, and consulting both in Israel and internationally. Jack is the master baker at Sharon Puratos, the Israeli division of Puratos International.

Jack is president of the Union International De La Boulangerie, Israel and a member of the Elite de la Boulangerie International. He met Jimmy as a fellow jury member at CDM de la Boulangerie in Paris in 2012. They have remained great friends ever since and regularly meet up during Europain, as they did in January 2020.

Follow Jack: Facebook, https://www.Facebook.com/jack.hazan.3

~ Jack Hazan

46. Jack's Israeli Fancy Cheesecake (for Jewish Religious Festival)

Jacks refreshing cheesecake is easy to make, bake, and assemble. You can use all of your own favourite fruits on the top to garnish. Jack uses locally sourced figs and frozen raspberries for his signature dish, giving a fresh and tangy edge to his delicious cheesecake. The recipe here will make 2 rectangular cheesecakes in baking dishes measuring 23 cm L × 10 cm W × 5 cm H.

Ingredients: Pastry Base

300 g	Flour T -405 (soft pastry flour)
200 g	Melted butter
100 g	Icing sugar
50 g	Whole egg
Pinch	Lemon zest

Making Pastry Base

1. Place all the ingredients except for the flour in a stand mixer with the beater attachment and mix for 3 minutes on 1st/slow speed.

2. Using a dough hook, add the flour slowly and knead for 3–5 minutes on 2nd/medium speed until the pastry is smooth.

3. Roll out the pastry into a rectangle. Line the 2 baking dishes, and place them in the oven. Bake for 12 minutes at 180 °C.

4. Remove from oven promptly when baked.

Ingredients: Cream Cheese Topping

600 g	Fresh cream cheese
30 g	Custard powder
100 g	Sugar
550 g	Milk
200 g	Whole eggs
125 g	Melted butter

Making the Cream Cheese Topping

1. Place all the ingredients in a stand mixer with a whisk attachment.
2. Mix for 3 minutes on 1st speed until the entire mixture is smooth.

Finishing the Cheesecake

1. Add 800 g of cream cheese topping to the top of each of the baked pastry bases.
2. Bake for 5 minutes at 200 °C.
3. Reduce the oven temperature to 160 °C, and bake for another 25 minutes.
4. Allow the cheesecake to cool completely.
5. Finish with fig slices (3), raspberries (3), and mint springs (2). Cut a fresh fig into 1/3 and place them on the top of the cake, facing upwards. Add the raspberries, fresh if available, and then the fresh mint sprigs.

Second Topping Suggestion

The addition of yoghurt cream adds a beautiful flavour and texture to this dish. Mix together 80 g of fresh yoghurt and 20 g of sugar with a hand whisk. Add it to the top of the baked cake immediately after removing it from the oven. Then, place it back in the oven for an extra 5 minutes, baking at 160 °C until the yoghurt cream is stable. Bon Appétit!

Günther Koerffer (Sweden)

Royal confectioner Günther is a master confectioner and president of the CEBP; his father did not like the bakery trade, so he decided that Günther should be a confectioner. He also picked the place where Günther would serve his apprenticeship. After 3 years, Günther obtained his degree as a confectioner. He subsequently served 1 year as a baker. He has a passion for both bread and pastry. Though born in Germany, Günther moved to Sweden as a young man, where he now owns his own bakery/pastry and coffee shop. He's settled into life in Sweden, where he's made his home in Ulricehamn. Günther also made Victoria, the Crown Princess of Sweden's wedding cake, and he regularly supplies the royal palace with his confections. Günther and Jimmy met in 2011 as jury members in Guangzhou, China, for the Louis Lesaffre Cup world quarterfinals. Since that time, they have worked together as jury members and made many demonstrations together in Germany, Taiwan, Spain, and Brazil. If you have the time and the patience, you can bake a cake fit for a royal Princess. Günther's cake is spectacular in flavour and appearance and worth the time for a very special occasion.

Follow Gunther: Instagram, https://www.instagram.com/guntherkoerffer/

~ Günther Koerffer

47. Günther's Royal Princess Cake

I'm fortunate to have had the pleasure of working alongside my dear friend and colleague Günther. He assisted me as I set up my demonstration in Brazil, and when I was finished, I got to help him with his preparations. I also watched and assisted him in making this cake in Germany at IBA. While it's complex and involves many stages, it's truly a masterpiece. The many layers, infusions, colours, and textures are so rewarding. The work involved is worth it all. Günther's Castle Cake recipe makes 2 cakes (size 22 cm) of 10 servings each.

Ingredients: Crisp Nougatine Layer

- 50 g   Almond nougat
- 99 g   Feuilletine*
- 6 g   Cocoa butter
- 35 g   Milk chocolate

*You can buy Cocoa Barry brand feuilletine crunch mix or make if from scratch: https://www.youtube.com/watch?v=Q899UgdSuEE

Making the Crisp Nougatine Layer

1. Melt the chocolate, butter, and nougat. Mix with the feuilletine and flatten the mixture between 2 plastic sheets. Roll extra thin (2 mm–3 mm). Cut into a 20 mm circle. (The disc will shrink to16 cm–18 cm during baking.)

2. Bake 180 °C until golden brown, about 7–10 minutes.

3. Cool after baking and then freeze to −18 °C.

Ingredients: Champagne Mousse

- 500 g   Mascarpone (at room temperature)
- 200 g   Champagne (at room temperature)
- 45 g   Marc de champagne
- 16 g   Gelatine 4–5 leaves
- 159 g   Egg yolk
- 230 g   Sugar
- 65 g   Water
- 800 g   Whipped cream 36%–40% fat

Making the Champagne Mousse

1. Soak the gelatine leaves in ½ litre of cold water.

2. Whip the cream very lightly.

3. Boil the water and sugar together to 118 °C.

4. Whisk egg yolks until they're like mayonnaise. Slowly add the boiled sugar-water mixture.

5. Add the gelatine mix to the warmed egg yolks.

6. Add a little of the egg yolk mixture (1/3) to the mascarpone (room temperature) to soften it. Then, add the rest of the egg yolk mixture and mix slowly using a whisk until it's blended.

7. Add the champagne (room temperature) and the marc de champagne. Whisk to clear.

8. Finally, add the whipped cream and whisk by hand to clear with a spatula to finish the champagne mousse.

Ingredients: Almond Daycaise (4 Layers 22 cm Each)

225 g	Egg white
75 g	Granulated sugar
20 g	Icing sugar
205 g	Ground almonds
1	Lemon zest (approximately 10 g)

Making the Almond Daycaise (Sponge)

1. Whisk the egg whites with the icing sugar for 5 minutes at a low speed until it rises.

2. Add the granulated sugar and whisk to make a stiff meringue at medium speed.

3. When the meringue has reached a peak, by hand, add the almond powder and grated lemon zest.

4. Bake in a 22 cm tin in a deck oven at 170 °C for 15–18 minutes with the damper open.

5. Freeze after baking to −18 °C.

Ingredients: Wild Strawberry Curd (2 Layers)

200 g	Strawberry purée
69 g	Egg yolk
75 g	Whole egg
90 g	Granulated sugar
75 g	Butter
5 g	Gelatine

Making the Wild Strawberry Curd

1. Soak the gelatine (3 leaves) in ½ litre of cold water.

2. Place the strawberries in a casserole and warm up to 45 °C.

Recipes: Cakes

3. Mix the egg yolk, granulated sugar, and the egg by hand using a hand whisk until combined.
4. Place this mixture with the heated strawberries in a double-jacketed saucepan. Heat to 85 °C until it thickens.
5. Squeeze the gelatine of excess water and add the gelatine to the warm mixture.
6. Add the butter (room temperature) to the warmed mixture. Using a hand whisk, mix slowly to blend all the ingredients into a homogenous mixture.
7. Place the mixture into a stainless-steel bowl. Cover and place in the refrigerator at 3 °C.

Ingredients: Strawberry Fruits Compote

200 g	Strawberry purée*
69 g	Egg yolk
75 g	Whole egg
90 g	Granulated sugar
75 g	Butter
5 g	Gelatine

*Any forest fruits will work for this compote layer.

Making the Forest Fruits Compote

1. Soak the gelatine (3 leaves) in ½ litre water to soak.
2. Place all ingredients into a casserole and bring to a boil (100 °C) on medium heat.
3. Squeeze the gelatine of excess water and add the gelatine it to the boiled mixture using a hand whisk.
4. Pour the mixture into 2 plastic moulds of 16 mm–18 mm.

Ingredients: Fragilete (2 Layers)

100 g	Egg white
150 g	Granulated sugar
100 g	Almond paste 50/50
50 g	Milk

Making the Fragilete

1. Soak the almond paste with the milk and mix to soften.

Recipes: Cakes

2. Whisk the egg whites and sugar to a peak.

3. Add the softened almond paste and the milk to the meringue. Mix using a spatula and pipe to 16–18 cm circles on silicone paper.

4. Bake at 155 °C to dry for 18–25 minutes with the damper open until they are hard and slightly brown.

Royal Wedding Cake Assembly

1. Begin with one 22 cm sponge in a 22 cm ring.

2. Pipe the strawberry curd onto the sponge, allowing a gap of 1 cm at the edge of the sponge.

3. Cover with the champagne mousse.

4. Place the next layer of sponge on top of the mousse. Then, place the crisp nougatine disc (16 cm–18 cm) on the sponge.

5. Add the second layer of champagne mousse.

6. Add the third layer of sponge and place the frozen layer of strawberry compote on top of it.

7. Cover with champagne mousse. Use the piping bag to fill the sides with the mousse. Shake the ring to settle the layers and cover the top completely with more mousse.

8. Add the fragilite on top of this and then completely cover with the champagne mousse using a piping bag.

9. Freeze overnight to −20 °C.

10. The mousse will shrink in the freezer, so the following day, use the rest of the mousse to fill the shape and, using a palette knife smooth it off to fill the ring perfectly and freeze again.

Finishing the Royal Wedding Cake

1. Take the cake from the freezer. Using a blow torch, gently heat the ring to release the cake.

2. Lift the ring and immediately spray the sides and top of the cake with melted tempered white chocolate (50/50 white chocolate/cocoa butter) at 45 °C. If you wait too long to spray the cake, you'll lose the furry surface needed to finish the cake.

3. Decorate with a crown and/or add fresh fruit as you like. Enjoy!

Tarts

Benny Swinnen (Belgium)

As a young man, Benny was involved in the family business with his parents. His father and mother encouraged him not to become a baker, but he persisted with it and became both a master baker and a master confectioner. Benny has a passion for chocolate making, bread, and viennoiserie. He explains that, in the 1840s, half of Europe was Austrian. Alternatively, we could imagine that Austria was half of Europe. Thus, it represented an immense empire. The first successes in commercial pastry occurred in a very wealthy environment, among people who had the means of buying those things. Therefore, the evolution of pastry baking culture began with the rich in Vienna and Paris. The baking culture spread throughout Europe and gave rise to the culture and bakery shops across Europe and the world today.

Benny and Jimmy met as candidates in Coupe D' Europe de la Boulangerie in Nantes, France, in 1995. In the past 25 years, they've shared an enduring friendship, worked as jury members together all over the world, and have been to visit each other's homes and friends. Laughter breaks out all the time when these two get together. Benny is a warm, and friendly enigmatic character loved worldwide. Benny appreciates that Jimmy has told him it's an honour and a pleasure to have him in his life and in this book. Competitive baking brought them together and, to this day, ensures that their friendship endures.

Follow Benny: Facebook, https://www.Facebook.com/benny.swinnen

~ Benny Swinnen

48. Belgian Sweet Rhubarb Tart

This tart is a Belgian speciality from the Flemish Brabant region. It's one of Benny's favourites, so it's no surprise that he brought it with him to The Japan Home Baking School in Osaka, Japan, when he gave his summer school classes there in 2016. When his bakery shop was open, it was one of Benny's customers' favourite treats. Rhubarb is freshly available in the summertime, but tinned rhubarb can also be used to make the tart. Don't be afraid to get adventurous with this recipe and use apple, berries, pears, or any other soft fruit when in season.

Ingredients: Yeasted Dough

5 tarts		1 tart
600 g	Butter	120 g
60 g	Sugar	12 g
60 g	Fresh yeast (or 30 g/6 g dry yeast)	12 g
1,000 g	Bread flour (strong flour)	200 g
5 g	Salt	1 g
250 g	Water	50 g

Making the Yeasted Dough

1. In a mixer with a beating attachment, mix the butter, sugar, and yeast until it forms a paste.

2. Add the flour and the salt. Mix well together.

3. Add water. Mix to clear (until the water is fully absorbed).

4. Divide dough into smaller balls according to tin size

    - 15 cm = 120 g
    - 19 cm = 190 g
    - 22 cm = 240 g
    - 26 cm = 330 g

5. After rolling the dough into the required dimensions, place it directly into the tin and allow it to rise for 15 minutes before adding the rhubarb filling.

Ingredients: Rhubarb Filling

5 tarts		1 tart
2,000 g	Fresh rhubarb (chopped in cubes)	400 g
400 g	Flour (soft wheat flour)	80 g
400 g	White sugar	80 g
pinch	Cinnamon	pinch

Marking the Rhubarb Filling

1. Peel and slice the rhubarb stems. Cut the rhubarb into small cubes.
2. Add the cinnamon and flour to the rhubarb and mix.
3. Place the rhubarb directly into the pastry bases. Be sure the rhubarb mixture covers the entire pastry.
4. Bake in the oven at 190 °C for 30 minutes.

Ingredients: Meringue

5 tarts		1 tart
500 g	Egg whites	100 g
600 g	White sugar	120 g

Making the Meringue

While the tarts are baking, make the meringue using a stand mixer and the whisk attachment. Whip the egg whites with the white sugar into a meringue.

Finishing the Sweet Rhubarb Tart

1. Remove the tart from the oven and cover it with the meringue, piping small swirls to cover the tart.
2. Bake once more for 12 minutes.
3. Take the tart out of the tray as soon as possible and let it cool down.

4. Serve the tart warm, with whipped fresh cream or a selection of ice creams and forest berries, and a nice, chilled Rosé wine.

Erica Roessing Almeida (Portugal)

Born in Manaus, in the heart of the Amazon rainforest in Brazil, Erica began and progressed her sales career. During this time, Erica met her future husband Kleber and the father of her two daughters Beatriz and Esther. Having discovered Beatriz had gluten intolerance, in 2012, Erica decided to learn how to bake slow-fermented bread at home. This hobby turned into a passion as she began sharing her loaves with neighbours. In 2015, Erica and her family relocated to Portugal, where Erica continued to bake for her new friends and neighbours. She soon realised this passion could be turned into a career and began researching opportunities to study and develop her bread baking skills, discovering The School of Artisan Food, nestled away in the Nottinghamshire countryside in the UK.

During her time at the school, alongside learning how to bake numerous bread and pastries, Erica gained valuable work experience working in established bakeries. Her desire to one day own her own bakery grew. Following her time in the UK, Erica returned to Porto, Portugal, and has been instrumental in opening a new bakery in the city centre and developing a range of products. The bakery has seen a very successful launch. One day, Erica plans on having her own bakery, sharing her love for artisan bread, pastries, and sweet treats and teaching others how to create their own products through a series of workshops and courses. Erica and Jimmy first met in 2019 at The School of Artisan Food in the UK, where Jimmy taught the Advanced Diploma students how to make brioche and laminated pastries. They have remained friends and remain in contact with social media ever since.

Follow Erica: Facebook, https://www.Facebook.com/erica.rmatos and Instagram, https://www.instagram.com/ericasbread/ and

~ Erica Roessing Almeida

49. Erica's Ultimate Portuguese Custard Tart

Portugal's classic and traditional pastry, this iconic tart has been enjoyed by the Portuguese people for generations. Recently, the millions of sunseekers who holiday in Portugal every year seek it out as a local delicacy to be enjoyed over a coffee in the many cafes and bakeries in the major tourist resorts. It has become a mainstream global product in the past number of years, such is its popularity. This recipe will give you 12–15 tarts in 8 cm (W) × 2 cm (H) aluminium custard tart moulds.

Custard Filling Ingredients

- 20 g   Corn starch/cornflour
- 250 g   Whole milk
- 100 g   Heavy/double cream
- 150 g   Caster sugar/white sugar
- 75 g   Water
- 100 g   Egg yolks (4)
- 3   Pared strips of fresh lemon peel
- 1   Cinnamon stick

Making the Custard Filling

1. In a saucepan, add the milk, cream, starch, lemon peel, and the cinnamon stick.
2. Place on medium heat, stirring with a hand whisk until it thickens and starts to boil.
3. In a second pan, add water and sugar and prepare a sugar syrup to the thread stage (103 °C/217 °F) without stirring.
4. Slowly add the sugar syrup to the prepared cream mixture. Allow to cool.

5. Add the egg yolks and mix well before passing through a sieve to discard the lemon peel, cinnamon stick, and other lumps. Set side.

Ingredients: Puff Pastry

250 g	Flour plain/all-purpose/T–55 flour
150 g	Coldwater
3 g	Salt
200 g	Butter unsalted

Making the Puff Pastry (3-3-3 / 3-3–169 layers in total)

1. Place the flour, water, and salt in a bowl. Mix until there is no dry flour.

2. Place the dough on a clean surface and work it until it's elastic or mix on a stand mixer for 2 minutes on slow speed and a another 3 minutes on 2nd speed.

3. Shape into a ball, cut a cross on top of it, and let it rest for 30 minutes in a refrigerator.

4. Make a 10 × 10 cm butter block with the cold butter. Do this by putting the butter between sheets of baking paper and and rolling out with a rolling pin.

5. Place the dough on a cold surface dusted with little flour. Roll the dough out into a rectangle using a rolling pin until it's double the size of the butter (20 × 20 cm).

6. Place the 10 × 10 cm butter in the middle of the dough and close it so that butter is totally wrapped inside the dough. There will be 3 layers at this stage: dough-butter-dough.

7. Sheet out the dough in a rectangular shape, reducing in thickness to 7 mm.

8. After rolling out the first rectangle, fold it in 3 like a letter, a half-turn, or a 3-fold. Then turn it 90° and roll it out again. Fold it again and place it in the fridge for 30 minutes. Repeat this process 2 more times. After the final sheeting process, the dough needs to rest in the fridge for at least 2 hours before making the tarts. (For a detailed explanation of the lamination process, see *The Art of Lamination* or this YouTube tutorial: https://www.youtube.com/watch?v=rKvDjMQDySY)

Assembling the Tart

1. Roll out the dough in a rectangular shape to 5 mm thick. Make a thin roll of the pastry by rolling it up like a Swiss roll. It will have the form of a long cylinder of pastry.

2. Divide and cut the cylinder into 1.5 cm slices, about 38 g–46 g per tart for each tart tin.

3. Using wet thumbs with water, press the slice, cut side up, into the bottom of each tin and work it around, leaving edges a little bit thicker than in the centre (about 8 cm diameter and 2 cm in height).

4. Preheat the oven at 250 °C (482 °F) or maximum temperature. (Heat top and bottom with a fan if this function is available on your oven.)

5. Pour the filling into tins but not all the way to the top—leave a gap of about 3 mm.

6. Place the tins on a tray and place it on the oven sole so that the pastry will puff up and the filling gets ever so slightly burnt on the outside but remains light and creamy on the inside.

7. When the edge of the pastry gets golden brown and the filling is slightly scorched on the top, remove them from the oven.

8. After the tarts cool down a little, use the tip of a knife to release the tarts from the tins.

9. Sprinkle cinnamon powder on top and enjoy with your favourite beverage!

Olivier Hofmann, European Gold Medallist (Switzerland)

Olivier is the owner of Hofmann's Bakery-Pastry-Confectionery, of Reconvilier, Switzerland. His family business was established in 1882. Olivier is a 4th-generation master baker. His impressive record of awards includes 1997 Swiss Master Baker, 1999 European Champion, and Pellons d'Or in Nantes, France, 2011. He also was the coach of the Swiss World Champion team, Mondial du Pain, in St-Etienne, France. Olivier is also a specialist and world authority of baking with ancient grains and has given classes worldwide, spreading his tremendous knowledge. Jimmy and Olivier met in Nantes, France, at Coupe d' Europe, 1999 when Switzerland won the gold medal.

They have remained friends ever since and have met up at the Swiss Bakery Cup several times over the past 20 years. Olivier has also generously hosted the Irish baking team members at his home and bakery for training during competition years. He's a kind and generous man, very knowledgeable, and respected globally as an expert in his chosen profession.

Contact Olivier: https://boulangerie-hofmann.ch/

~ Olivier Hofmann

50. Olivier's Pumpkin Tart – Gold Medal Winner

For this recipe, you'll need orange marmalade to spread on the base of the tart and approximately 225 g of short pastry for each pumpkin pie. You can use John Slattery's recipe for shortcrust pastry (see Recipe #51), which will be sufficient to line the 7 tartlet shells achieved from this recipe. The tartlets are 22 cm in diameter.

Ingredients: Sponge Base

50 g   Eggs
35 g   Sugar
35 g   White soft pastry flour.

Making the Sponge Base

1. Mix the egg and sugar. Warm to 45 °C, remove from heat, and then beat until it's cold.

2. Slowly add 70 g of the white soft pastry flour. Blend gently.

3. Place the sponge in 16 cm circle tins or moulds and bake at 190 °C for 20 minutes.

4. Remove from oven and cool completely.

5. Once the sponge is cold, cut it into 7 thin slices for the pumpkin tarts.

Stage 1: Egg Mixture

Ingredients: Egg Mixture

- 100 g Whole egg
- 25 g Egg yolks
- 150 g Sugar
- 50 g Dextrose
- 50 g Orange paste or orange marmalade
- 15 g Mixed ginger
- 5 g Vanilla
- 2.5 g Salt

Making the Egg Mixture

1. Combine ingredients in a medium saucepan.
2. Warm to 45 °C and beat together with a hand whisk.

Stage 2: Filling

Ingredients: Filling

- 75 g Flour T -40 (soft pastry flour)
- 75 g Wheat starch
- 5 g Baking powder

Making the Filling

1. Sieve ingredients together.
2. Mix with the beaten egg mixture from Stage 1.

Stage 3: Pumpkin Filling

Ingredients: Pumpkin Filling

- 500 g Mashed pumpkin (red Kuri squash)
- 25 g Flour T -40 (soft pastry flour)

Making the Pumpkin Filling

1. Mix ingredients together.
2. Using a spatula with a handle, incorporate Stage 3 with Stages 1 and 2

Stage 4: Adding the Butter

Add 200 g softened butter to the pumpkin filling mixture.

Stage 5: Baking and Assembly

1. Form the (7) 22 cm round moulds with shortcrust pastry.
2. Spread a layer of orange marmalade over the shortcrust pastry.
3. Put a disk of 16 cm round sponge on top.
4. Add 180 g of pumpkin filling in each circle.
5. Bake for 50 minutes at 180 °C.
6. After baking, dust with icing sugar and burn with a torch.
7. Decorate with a marzipan pumpkin.

John Slattery (United Kingdom)

John Slattery is the owner of Slattery Pâtissier & Chocolatier Ltd., a chocolate shop based on Bury New Road in Whitefield, Manchester. John has always been a little in love with chocolate: eating it, cooking with it, creating with it. For John, chocolate can be used to create a million possibilities. Having worked in baking and confectionery all his life and being part of the family business for over 40 years, spending every day with his favourite ingredient was a natural move. Having trained at college, John has also attended courses in the world's chocolate capitals—Switzerland, Belgium, and Austria—gaining both skills and experience. His passion for chocolate is apparent, as John is a member of the British Confectioners Association, the National Association of Master Bakers, and the International Richemont Club, a centre of excellence for master bakers and confectioners.

Sharing his passion for chocolate, John offers various chocolate, cake decorating, and other confectionery courses on the third floor of the shop, otherwise known as the School of Excellence. John also has taught worldwide, and now shares one of his favourite recipes with you, the Manchester Tart.

John and Jimmy met each other through Richemont Club International when Jimmy was Irish Richemont President. John has also visited Jimmy in Galway over the years, and they recently met in Zagreb, Croatia. Both John and Jimmy enjoy each other's company, and they both agree it's always a pleasure to hang out and talk shop.

Follow John: Facebook, https://www.facebook.com/john.slattery.313

~ John Slattery

51. Manchester Tart with A Chocolate Twist

John's chocolate tart is a twist on the traditional Manchester tart, much beloved in its heyday of the 1970s and 1980s when it was featured on school dinner menus.

With one look at John's Manchester tart, his prowess and mastery of fine chocolate decoration are evident. He manages to turn a strawberry into a piece of chocolate art by dipping it in white chocolate and adding milk chocolate and caramel stripes and then setting off the colours of the underlying chocolate filling with small chocolate dragées of white, milk, and dark chocolate. You can also use your own imagination by adding your own personal touches to this timeless Manchester favourite. This recipe makes 10 individual tarts. You'll need 10 × 9 cm wide tartlet rings and a small amount of fruit jam.

Ingredients: Shortcrust Pastry

500 g	Butter or margarine
200 g	Caster sugar
200 g	Whole eggs (medium)
700 g	Plain flour T-45 (pastry flour low gluten)

Making the Shortcrust Pastry

1. In a stand mixer, cream together the butter and sugar.
2. Add the eggs one at a time.
3. Add the sieved flour and bring to a paste without working it too much.
4. Wrap in plastic and chill/rest in the refrigerator for at least 30 minutes.
5. Using a rolling pin on a lightly floured surface, roll out the pastry.
6. Line small tart cases.
7. Allow them to rest in the refrigerator to avoid shrinkage.
8. Bake blind (i.e., without the filling) at 180 °C for approximately 10 minutes.

Ingredients: Custard Filling

150 g	Whole eggs (medium)
120 g	Caster sugar
10 g	Vanilla paste
40 g	Cornflour
640 g	Milk (full fat)
100 g	70% Chocolate Callets (drops)

Making the Custard Filling

1. Make a custard by whisking together the eggs, sugar, vanilla, and cornflour.
2. Bring the milk to the boil then add to the egg mixture.
3. Return the combined ingredients to the pan and cook for a few minutes, whisking all the time.
4. Remove from the heat.
5. Add the chocolate callets, stirring well until dissolved.

6. Deposit a little fruit jam onto the baked pastry and spread out in a thin layer. (Base fillings can include various fruit jams or spreads.)

7. Pour the chocolate custard over the fruit jam, allowing it to cool completely.

8. Add some chocolate flakes or any other desired chocolate decoration to finish.

Alternative Fillings and Finishes

Try adding fresh fruits to make a variety of these tartlets. Raspberries or blueberries work well, but fresh strawberries are particularly delicious. Bake some fresh strawberries into the tartlet by placing a few strawberry halves over the thin layer of jam before adding the custard. When baked and completely cooled, finish with a fresh strawberry half-dipped in chocolate. Chocolate flakes or other chocolate decorations can be used to garnish the top of the tarts.

Other Pastries

Sergio González (Argentina)

Sergio González is an Argentinian master baker. He's the 3rd generation of baker in his family. Since the age of 13, Sergio began working, without interruption, in his parents' bakery. The Güiraldes bakeries are located in the Villa Lugano and Mataderos neighbourhoods in Argentina.

Sergio began to compete internationally in bakery tournaments in 2003; he is a three time national champion and a finalist at the world cup in Paris, 2008. He's been a member of the Argentinian bakery teams of the Latin American championships four times and was team captain in 2007. Sergio also was an international jury member at the world cup in Paris, 2016, where he was awarded the EBI medal. He was the coach in the final of the Master de la Boulangerie 2018 in France, and since 2015, he's been the Argentine team coach.

In 2008, Sergio met Jimmy as a competitor, and later, as a jury member for the CDM de la Boulangerie in Paris where Jimmy was the president of the jury. Since then, a great friendship has formed, one based on a shared passion and one which they continue to nurture at the different events in which they participate.

Follow Sergio: https://www.instagram.com/sergiogonzalezpana/

~ Sergio González

52. Sweet Childhood Joy

Sergio's colourful Sweet Childhood Joy pastry is a special treat from his bakery. It was designed as a gift for children, but adults have loved them for three generations too! A sweet yeasted dough infused with peanut butter, citrus fruit zests, and chocolate chip cookies, it's a time capsule, capturing sights, colour, and flavour in a pastry. Then pastry, which is finished with icing, sprinkles, and chocolates, is sheer indulgence and childhood memories wrapped up in a very unique and different pastry from Argentina.

Ingredients: Poolish

- 50 g   Strong baker's flour
- 100 g Whole milk
- 10 g   Fresh yeast

Making the Poolish

1. Place the ingredients in a bowl on a stand mixer with a dough hook. Mix them together to form a dough and cover with a lid to prevent skinning.

2. Rest at 26 °C until doubled in volume.

Ingredients: Dough

- 330 g Flour strong bakers
- 100 g Whole milk
- 80 g   Butter (delayed addition)
- 50 g   Whole egg
- 40 g   Sugar
- 2 g   Salt
- 10 g   Fresh yeast
- 20 g   Orange zest
- 40 g   Orange juice

Making the Dough

1. Place the poolish in a stand mixer with a dough hook and add the dough ingredients (leaving out the butter).

2. Knead for 5–8 minutes on 1st speed to develop a windowpane. Then, add the butter and knead for 5 more minutes until the dough is developed and extensible.
3. To finish, mix for another 2 minutes on 2nd speed until the dough is soft and smooth.
4. Allow the dough to ferment, covered, at 26 °C until it doubles in volume, about 45–60 minutes.

Ingredients: Filling

140 g Chocolate chip cookies
180 g Peanut paste

Making the Filling

1. Crush the chocolate chip cookies and then mix them with the peanut paste and make 8 balls of 40 g each. You will insert these cookie/peanut paste balls into the fermented dough balls to make the centre of the treat.
2. Chill well.

Preparing the Pastry Treat

1. After fermentation, divide the dough into 8 equal parts of 80 g each and make ball-shaped buns.
2. Allow to rest for 10 minutes. Flatten the dough into a flat disc large enough to fold over the cookie/peanut paste balls.
3. Place the cold cookie/peanut paste ball into the centre of the flattened dough.

4. Close the dough to cover all the filling and form a ball again.
5. Place the dough balls on a baking tray, spacing them apart so they don't batch.
6. Wash them with egg.
7. Proof the dough at 26 °C until it doubles its volume, about 45–60 minutes.
8. Place the buns in the oven at 200 °C for about 10–15 minutes or until they are golden brown.

9. Removed from the oven and cool completely before topping with the warm chocolate.

Ingredients: Topping and Finishing

300 g	White chocolate
16	Marroc chocolates or (Rolos);
16	Liquorish/jelly sweets red and black
300 g	Multicoloured vermicelli or dragées to coat the outside
8	Small pastry cards for presentation

Finishing the Treat

1. Melt the white chocolate.

2. Cover the buns with white chocolate by pouring it over the buns on a wire tray.

3. Roll them in the multi-coloured dragées or vermicelli.

4. While the chocolate is still warm, add the red and black gumdrops and the Marroc cylinder chocolates or similar decoration.

5. Allow them to set full. Placing them in a fridge for 10–15 minutes will help them set.

Brett Noy (Australia)

Brett is the managing director of Uncle Bob's Bakery and Creative Crusts Baking Company. He's co-founder and president of the not-for-profit organisation Southern Cross Baking Group in Australia. Brett was recently manager and coach of the Australian baking team for the Louis Lesaffre Cup, 2015. Brett was also a finalist in the Bakery Masters in Paris, 2014, where he placed 3rd globally. He's the first Australian baker to ever be invited twice to judge at the world's most prestigious baking competitions, the Louis Lesaffre Cup and the CDM de la Boulangerie.

Based on his extensive international competition experience and training, Brett regularly gives technical advice for bakery product design and development. He's also a keynote speaker and uses his experience in baking competitions to inspire others. However, his greatest passion is to share knowledge and empower others in baking to achieve their goals.

Brett and Jimmy first met at the Louis Lesaffre Cup in Guangzhou, China, in 2011 where Jimmy was on the jury. Brett remarked that Jimmy put everyone at ease, adding that "it was nice to have someone else there who spoke English!" Brett and his team left Jimmy a special present under his hotel room door after the competition. Since that day, both Brett and Jimmy have worked on several international juries together. The most recent time was January 2020 in Paris at the CDM de la Boulangerie, just before the COVID pandemic gripped the world and shut down air travel. Brett's says it's always informative, educational, and extremely funny spending time with Jimmy and that he's always looking forward to the next opportunity they can meet up.

Follow Uncle Bob's: Instagram, https://www.instagram.com/unclebobsbakery/.
Follow Brett: Instagram, https://www.instagram.com/brettnoybaker/

~ Brett Noy

53. Brett's Chocolate Trilogy

Brett's chocolate trilogy is a unique creation of Brett's ingenuity and creativity. Taking several elements from other delicious pastries, Brett has fused three amazing flavours and eating sensations into one magnificent creation. Enjoy a slice with coffee or as a dessert. This pastry will certainly tantalise your taste buds and having you craving more and more! One slice is just never quite enough.

Ingredients: Three Raspberry Fanciers

- 30 g Plain flour
- 50 g Almond meal
- 90 g Castor sugar
- 7 g Freeze-dried raspberries
- 81 g Egg whites
- 75 g Butter, melted
- 8 g Honey

Making the Three Raspberry Fanciers

1. Blend flour, meal, sugar, and raspberries together in a food processor.
2. Whip the egg whites a little, just until separated and liquid.
3. Combine egg whites into flour mixture and mix to a paste.
4. Melt the butter and honey until only just melted. Don't de-crystallise.
5. Blend the mixture until combined and the mixture is nice and shiny.
6. Place 170 g of the mix into the base of a lined medium loaf pan or shape (800 g/2 lb).
7. Refrigerate before placing the brownie mix on top.

Ingredients: USA Brownie

30 g	Pastry flour
44 g	Eggs
97 g	Sugar
3 g	Salt
5 g	Vanilla bean paste
101 g	Butter (melted)
30 g	Cocoa powder
30 g	Pecans (chopped fine)

Making the USA Brownie

1. Whip the eggs and sugar until light. Then, add the salt, vanilla, and butter and mix until combined.
2. Sift together the dry ingredients and fold into wet ingredients until fully incorporated.
3. Place 170 g of the mix into the medium loaf pan on top of the cooled raspberry financier.

Ingredients: Chocolate Brioche Topping

420 g	Strong Flour
7 g	Salt
42 g	Castor sugar
168 g	Egg (cold)
30 g	Yeast (fresh)
8 g	Milk powder
55 g	Water (cold)
63 g	Butter
21 g	Butter
21 g	Cocoa Powder
126 g	Chocolate (melted)

Making the Chocolate Brioche Topping

The DDT is 21 °C.

1. Mix all the ingredients (except for the butter, cocoa powder, and chocolate) for 2 minutes on 1st speed. Then mix for another 8 minutes on 2nd speed until a windowpane is formed.
2. Slowly, add the 63 g of butter in 3 additions and mix until it's evenly distributed.
3. Mix to a smooth developed dough.
4. Add in the remaining ingredients and mix until the dough is fully developed.
5. Mould into a ball and allow 1 hour of bulk fermentation time. Then, refrigerate for 2 hours.
6. Divide the dough into 60 g pieces, and shape them into round dough pieces.
7. Place the round chocolate brioche pieces into groups of 8 on top of the USA brownie layer.
8. Proof until the brioche has doubled in size.
9. Bake at 190 °C in a deck oven for 40 minutes.
10. Cool on a wire tray, eat, and enjoy!

Christophe Debersée, World Champion 2008 (France)

After studying for 5 years for his pastry master's certificate, Christophe worked in bakery for 7 years. After getting his baker's certificate in 1998, he became a pastry and bakery teacher for young students. Christophe shared the title of world champion in 2008 (piece artistic category) with Pierre

Zimmermann (coach), Alexander Lopez (bread category), and Thomas Planchot (Viennese pastry category). Christophe's participation in the World Bakery Cup allowed him to combine his knowledge of two areas which are bakery and pastry. This adventure gave him priceless personal and professional enrichment. Presently, Christophe gives professional training to the industry as a consultant in schools. He shares his tremendous knowledge of artistic piece design in France and teaches it all over the world.

Christophe first met Jimmy during CDM de la Boulangerie 2008, when Jimmy was a jury member, and Christophe was on the French team that won the CDM de la Boulangerie. Since then, Christophe has worked with Jimmy as fellow jury members at Coupe d'Afrique in Casablanca, Morocco 2013, 2015, 2017, and 2019—the two have enjoyed many professional engagements together. In March 2019, Christophe was honoured by being selected as just president for the competition. In January 2020, Christophe came to Technological University Dublin at Jimmy's invitation and was engaged in the national team's bakery training for 3 weeks before the COVID lockdown. Following the training, Christophe and his partner Sophie came to Galway with Jimmy, and they spent several days together touring the beautiful West of Ireland.

Christophe Debersée

502 rue Gambetta 59450 Sin le Noble France

Tel: +33 6 50 01 52 79

e-mail, chrisdebersee@gmail.com; website, http://chrisdebersee.over-blog.com

~ Christophe Debersée

54. Christophe's Savoury Twist

White Sauce

- 200 g Butter
- 200 g Flour
- 750 g Milk
- 500 g Whipped cream
- 170 g Grated cheese

Making the White Sauce

1. Melt the butter and add the flour.
2. Boil the milk.
3. Add the butter-flour mixture to the milk.
4. Thin with whipped cream.
5. Add the grated cheese.
6. Set aside until ready to use.

Ingredients: Savoury Twist

- 350 g Puff pastry (see Erica Roessing Almeida's recipe, #49)
- 1,600 g White sauce
- 500 g Leek
- 500 g Onion

Making the Savoury Twist

1. Lay out a piece of 30 cm × 40 cm puff pastry.
2. Spread the white sauce on half of the pastry.
3. Add the leeks and onions on top of the white sauce.
4. Fold the dough on the ingredients part.
5. Cut into strips of 4 cm.
6. Cut in the centre each band through the top layer of pastry to expose the filling. Twist the bands in opposite directions.
7. Place the twists on trays, spacing them out to allow for expansion.

8. Bake at 220 °C for 12 minutes.

Step 4. Fold the dough

Step 5. Cut the strips

Step 6. Twist the bands

Ludovic Richard, Meilleur Ouvrier De France (France)

Of Breton origin and the son of a baker, Ludovic started his baking career by learning patisserie. He then turned his attention to bakery. With his CAP de Pâtissier in his pocket, the following year he earned his master's certificate in Vannes. Since then, Ludovic has taught bakery with a passion in a

professional school in central Brittany. At the age of 26, he submitted his first application to the European competition, the Coupe D'Europe de la Boulangerie. He won the European Cup in 1997, sharing the podium with Jimmy's Irish team, who placed 3rd. Ludovic finished 2nd in the CDM de la Boulangerie in Paris in 1999, and finally, in 2000, won the most coveted title a baker can achieve in France, the Meilleur Ouvrier de France.

With his excellent technical experience, Ludovic also passes on his know-how in France and many other countries worldwide as a technical consultant. He also has business interests in Japan and travels there regularly. Ludovic met Jimmy when they were both candidates in Coupe d' Europe, 1997, where they shared the podium together there. Ludovic and Jimmy have remained friends ever since, and they regularly meet up at Europain in Paris. Ludovic recently released a fantastic book on baking titled *Passion et Tradition, Boulangères* (2019).

Purchase *Passion et Tradition:* https://ecolebellouetconseil.com/boutique/index.php?id_product=37&controller=product&id_lang=1

Follow Ludovic: Instagram, https://www.instagram.com/ludovic_richardmofboulanger/

~ Ludovic Richard

55. Caprice De Bretagne

Brittany is situated in North Western France. The Breton people are considered Celtic descendants with similar ancient cultures, music, and language as the Scottish, Irish, and Welch people. They're also very creative bakers famed for their many delicious biscuits, cakes, and pastries. Ludovic celebrates his Breton heritage with an amazing tart using a Breton biscuit base and locally sourced apricots, with an exotic touch of the tropics added in the form of grated coconut and rum used effectively for both flavour and texture in this sumptuous tart.

Ingredients: Biscuit Base

520 g	Brown sugar
320 g	Egg yolk
400 g	Sweet butter
6 g	Fleur de sel (salt)
600 g	Flour type 55 (French bread flour)
300 g	Grated coconut
12 g	Baking powder
12 g	Liquid vanilla
15 g	Red rum
6	Apricots
150 g	Brown sugar
5 g	Cinnamon powder

Making the Biscuit Base

1. Blanch the egg yolks and brown sugar very lightly.
2. Add the butter to the blanched mixture. Then, add the vanilla and rum.
3. Add the mixture to the shredded coconut.
4. Sieve the flour and baking powder together 3 times to ensure that it's properly dispersed.
5. Combine the coconut with the flour mixture to make the biscuit dough.
6. Chill the dough in the refrigerator and hold at +4 °C.

Filling and Assembling the Pastry

1. Pinout the biscuit dough to a thickness of 1.2 cm.
2. Cut the shortbread into a circle (35 mm).
3. On top of the shortbread, arrange lumps of the freshly sliced apricots.
4. Mix together the remaining 150 g of brown sugar and the 5 g of cinnamon powder. Then sprinkle the mixture over the apricots.
5. Bake in a fan oven for 25–30 minutes at 160 °C.
6. After cooling, very lightly sprinkle the pastry with icing sugar and decorate with a cinnamon stick and some fresh fruit.

Marios Papadopoulos (Greece)

From his early childhood, Marios remembers the aroma of all the spices his Middle Eastern parents infused in their cooking both at home and in their small pastry shop. He applied his economics studies to organize the family pastry shop and make his love of pastry a success story! He took over the Averof pastry shop in Thessaloniki in 1989. In 1995, he moved to a new and big laboratory. The same year, he also introduced sugar paste in Greece and organized the first seminars for professionals on 3D cakes. In 1997, Marios created and produced fresh, sugar-free products, a first in Greece. With the brand DH Products, Mario organized a hop in shop system for selling the product range throughout Greece. In 2003, he won first prize in cake decoration in the 4th Greek competition. In 2007, he represented Greece in Germany by celebrating the 50th anniversary of the European Economic Community and creating Europe's birthday cake at the event.

In 2011, he was elected as president of the pastry chefs and owners of Thessaloniki, his birth city. It's well known as "the sweet city" because of the variety and the high level of the pastry shops there. With a team of experts, he organizes pastry shops, introducing the production of Greek pastries worldwide in countries such as Panama, the USA, the Balkan States, and Cyprus as well others.

Marios met Jimmy in 2011 in Granada, Spain, at the UIBC International Congress representing Greece and Ireland. Since then, they have met in many international competitions and events representing their professions' highest level. They both recently brought international bakery teams to the annual international Fête du Pain event in Paris, 2017, which took place in the square opposite the Notre Dame Cathedral. Marios says it's always a great honour to co-work with Jimmy, and Marios is delighted to be included in this book.

Contact Marios: https://www.averof.gr/zaxaroplasteio/en/averof-patisserie/?v=f214a7d42e0d

~ Marios Papadopoulos

56. Marios' Kourabiedes

Kourabiedes are a Greek traditional sweet. It used to be made especially for the Christmas period, but now you can find them throughout the year as they characterise Greek pastry products. This recipe produces 46 pieces, scaled at 40 g each.

Ingredients: Dough

900 g	Pastry flour(soft)
500 g	Cow or sheep butter 99 9% fat
220 g	Icing sugar
3 g	Vanilla powder
250 g	White, blanched almonds (semi–roasted)

Ingredients: Finishing

500 g   Icing sugar
15 g   Brandy or rosewater

Making the Pastry

1. Allow the butter to soften at room temperature for 3 hours.
2. Preheat the oven to 160 °C.
3. Using a stand mixer, beat the butter in the mixer for 5 minutes on high speed until it gets white/light and creamy. Then, add the icing sugar and continue mixing for 10 minutes at fast speed.
4. Add the almonds and the vanilla sugar and continue to mix for 1 minute at slow speed.
5. Slowly add the flour and mix with the beater until the dough has a breakable texture that doesn't stick to your hands.
6. Scale at 40 g each and shape into balls, crescents, stars, or other shapes.
7. Place the pastries on a tray with silicone paper or a silicone mat.
8. Bake for 40–45 minutes until they become a golden colour. Don't over bake or they'll become very hard. Ideally, the inside should be like a soft, crunchy cookie.
9. Allow them to cool at room temperature. Be careful when they're hot— because of the high percentage of butter in the recipe, they're both very soft and fragile.
10. When the pastries are cold, spray them with brandy or rosewater and cover/roll them with icing sugar and then, enjoy this Greek delicacy!

Paul Kelly (Ireland)

Paul Kelly is best known for his pastry mastery, having spent 20 years perfecting his culinary industry skills. He started as a commis chef in the Sand House Hotel in Rossnowlagh, County Donegal. Following this, Paul worked in many five-star hotels and top restaurants in Ireland and worldwide. In Ireland, he worked in the Park Hotel in Kenmare, where he found his true calling in the culinary world—pastry. Following his time there, Paul travelled the world. In Johannesburg,

Dubai, Hong Kong, Sydney, and Paris, he worked in many five-star hotels and searched for new ideas and inspirations to satisfy his insatiable curiosity.

Paul later moved back to Dublin to work in l'Ecrivain, as their first full-time pastry chef. He finally found his place as the executive pastry chef at the Merrion Hotel in Dublin, where he worked since the hotel opened in 1997. Paul is a creative risk-taker, which has led him to develop many unique concepts, such as the Merrion Art Afternoon Tea. This is a creative and inspiring new take on classic afternoon tea while incorporating Merrion's extensive art collection. Paul's aim was to bring the incredible Merrion Hotel's art collection to life in food—edible art. Paul never intended his pastries to be a direct and obvious copy of the selected paintings. Instead, Paul wanted to inspire hotel guests to venture into the mind of a pastry chef and his interpretation of the art. When Paul looks at a painting, he's looking for colours to match with food and shapes that he can match to classic pastry items, coupled with flavour and balance.

In addition to spearheading the Merrion Art Afternoon Tea, Paul introduced the making of the hotel's own brand of chocolate, which is very unique in Ireland. He's widely known for his role as a judge on TV3's infamous bakery show, The Great Irish Bake Off. In this ultimate baking battle, passionate amateur bakers compete to be crowned Ireland's Best Amateur Baker. Paul and Jimmy met at Technological University Dublin, where they are both lecturers. Paul and Jimmy have visited each other's bakeries and kitchens. They've had lots of great times working together, including being invited to Stockholm as jury members for the Nordic Bakery and Nordic Pastry Cups, 2017.

Follow Paul: Instagram, https://www.instagram.com/pastrypaul/

~ Paul Kelly

57. Paul Kelly's Afternoon Tea Collection

This is one of Paul's favourite edible art works from his Merrion Art Afternoon Tea collection. He loves it so much because it looks simple, yet, it requires skill and precision to create. For the garnishes, you'll need grey, white, and red chocolate.

Ingredients: Mango Panna Cotta

250 g	Mango purée
250 g	Fresh cream
4 leaves	Gelatine (12 g / 3 g per leaf)
80 g	Sugar

Making the Mango Panna Cotta

1. Soak the gelatine in 200 ml cold water to hydrate (approximately 10 minutes). Ensure the soaked gelatine leaves are soft and fluffy with no hard or dry pieces. Strain off all the water and set aside.

2. Warm the cream, mango purée, and sugar.

3. Add the soaked gelatine to the warmed mango purée mixture. Strain the mango mixture and pour into a selected mould.

4. Set in the freezer for 30 minutes.

Ingredients: Raspberry Jelly

200 g	Raspberry purée
50 g	Sugar
3 leaves	Gelatine (9 g / 3 g per leaf)

Making the Raspberry Jelly

1. Soak the gelatine per previous directions. Set aside.

2. Using a saucepan, warm the raspberry purée and sugar together.

3. Add the soaked gelatine, blend fully, and allow to set slightly.

Ingredients: Pistachio Biscuit Base

300 g   Pistachio nuts crushed
100 g   White chocolate (melted)
 80 g   Butter (melted)

Making the Pistachio Biscuit Base

Mix all the ingredients together and roll to a thin base. Cut to the required shape.

Assembling the Pastry

1. When the mango panna cotta sets, scoop out the centre and fill it with the raspberry jelly.
2. Allow it to set again in the freezer for at least ½ an hour.
3. When it sets, remove it from the mould and place it on a pistachio biscuit.
4. Garnish as required with the different chocolate pieces.

François Wolfisberg, European Gold Medallist (Switzerland)

François owns and operates the very successful Boulangerie Wolfisberg at Carouge, Switzerland.

He also has several shops located in Geneva and Rolle, and each location has wonderful seating and food offerings made daily at his bakery.

A family man with seven children, François is always generous with his friendship, recipes, and time. He's involved in politics in his town and is active as an international jury member on the world bakery circuit. François was jury president for the CDM de la Boulangerie, 2012; former president of Richemont Club International in (2013), and president of the Richemont Club, Switzerland, in 2019. Additionally, he visited the Japan Home Baking School some years ago where he taught Swiss specialities to Japanese students for several weeks over the summer.

François met Jimmy when they were candidates for Coupe d' Europe, 1999 in Nantes, France. Jimmy was on the Swiss team that won the gold medal that year. The two also competed together in the CDM de la Boulangerie, 2002 in Paris. As members of the International Richemont Club, they regularly met at European competitions and at the annual Richemont International congresses held in various countries for nearly a decade. François and Jimmy most recently worked together in Croatia during a trade fair for the bakery solutions company TimZip, in Zagreb, 2017. François finds pleasure in the fact that Jimmy refers to him as "the Cardinal", in recognition of his flamboyant red bakery attire.

Follow François: Instagram, https://www.instagram.com/f_wolfisberg/
Follow the Boulangerie Wolfisberg: Instagram, https://www.instagram.com/boulangeriewolfisberg/

~ François Wolfisberg

58. François's Salée au Sucre

One of the most famous creations from François's award-winning bakery in Switzerland, the Salée au Sucre is also one of François's personal brioche favourites both to make and to eat. Made using a buttery brioche base dough, it's light and refreshing on the palette and creates a longing for more—many more! This recipe makes 19 pastries.

Ingredients: Brioche Dough

600 g	Strong bread flour
300 g	Milk
33 g	Egg
90 g	Sugar
30 g	Fresh yeast
3 g	Citron zest
9 g	Salt
90 g	Unsalted butter (cut into cubes of approximately 1–2 cm)

Making the Brioche Dough

The DDT is 24 °C.

1. Using a stand mixer with a dough hook, mix together for 2 minutes on 1st speed and for 6 minutes on 2nd speed.

2. Check the dough for gluten development by doing the windowpane test.
3. When the dough is well developed, add the butter in 3 increments (33% at a time).

4. Mix the dough well until it clears the bowl after 2–3 minutes on 2nd speed.
5. Ensure the butter is completely incorporated into the dough by mixing it to clear.
6. Ferment the dough for 45 minutes at room temperature.
7. Roll flat to degas, wrap the dough in plastic, and place it in a refrigerator for 30 minutes at 3 °C–4 °C.

Scaling and Processing the Dough

1. Take the dough from the refrigerator and scale 19 units at 60 g each.
2. Mould round and cover for 20 minutes of intermediate proofing. (While the dough is proofing, prepare the filling.)
3. Re-mould and pinout to 10 cm round, flat discs.
4. The final proof time is 60 minutes at 27 °C.

Ingredients: Salée au Sucre Filling

- 300 g Fresh cream
- 160 g Castor sugar
- 66 g   Custard powder
- 30 g   Potato starch

Making the Salée au Sucre Filling

Whisk all the ingredients together using a hand whisk and place the filling in a piping bag.

Handling the Final Dough and Adding the Filling

1. Flatten the proofed dough discs in the centre with a floured ramekin dish 5 cm–6 cm in diameter, leaving a bay or depression in the centre.

2. Pipe 25 g of the filling into each flattened brioche disc.

3. Bake in a deck oven at 180 °C for 8–10 minutes or until golden brown. Do take care with the baking as it's easy to bake this for too long and dry out the brioche.

4. Immediately remove the Salée au Sucre from the hot trays and cool on wire trays.

Filling Alternatives

Try a raspberry or chocolate filling as an exciting alternative to the plain variety.

Raspberry variety: Break up two frozen raspberries and place in the centre depression of the brioche. Top with 20g of the Salée mixture.

Chocolate variety: Place 10 g of chocolate chips in the centre depression of the brioche. Top with 20 g the Salée mixture.

Finishing Tips

When cool, mask the baked brioche with a ramekin dish and dust heavily with icing sugar. The centre remains uncovered in sugar and creates a beautiful contrast in colour.

Salée au Sucre I made in 2019 at the School of Artisan Food in the UK using François's original recipe. I chose the raspberry filling option and finished the pastries with fresh raspberries and mint leaves from the herb garden at the school.

Recipes: Other Pastries

Lulu Lee (Taiwan)

Lulu Lee is a considerate, kind, and inclusive team player who lights up every room she enters. Lulu is Taiwanese but grew up overseas in Paraguay, South America. She's worked in the pastry industry for the past 20 years, and since 2009, has been the coach to the Taiwanese teams for international pastry and bakery contests. Thanks to this precious challenge and experience, Lulu got the chance to attend all the various remarkable events and contest around the world. This is also how she got to meet and work with Jimmy! Lulu describes Jimmy as a professional and talented guy who is always taking care of and entertaining people at competitions as she does in her role of team manageress. She's honoured and grateful to be Jimmy's friend and a part of his book.

Follow Lulu: Facebook, https://www.Facebook.com/lululeepy

~ Lulu Lee

59. Lulu's Green Onion Pancake Roll

Lulu's Green Onion Pancake Roll recipe is special to her because it brings back childhood memories of when her mother used to make the rolls for her for breakfast. Lulu remembers when she went back to Taiwan and found out this type of breakfast food can be found everywhere among Taipei's exciting city street food vendors. She shares the recipe here with you as a gesture of the friendship she shares with Jimmy. This recipe will make 25 portions.

Recipes: Other Pastries

Ingredients: Dough

1000 g	T–55 flour
350 g	Boiling water
pinch	Salt
10 g	Oil

Ingredients: Green Onion Mix

200 g	Chopped green onion
10 g	Salt, add a pinch
30 g	Cooking oil

Ingredients: Egg Mix (Per Roll)

55 g	Whole egg 1
5 g	Green onion mix

Making the Green Onion Pancake Roll

1. Pour the boiling water into the flour and the salt.
2. Pour the oil into a plastic bag and the flour mixture to it. Mix until it becomes a dough.
3. Allow to relax in the refrigerator overnight.
4. The following day, scale the dough into portions of 50 g each, folding 5 g of the green onion mix into each one.
5. Roll out the dough into a round shape about 20 cm in diameter and 2 mm thick. Pan-fry both sides with a small amount of oil.
6. Prepare the egg mix, and then, fry it until the egg is semi-cooked.
7. Place the cooked egg mix on top of the fried dough and roll it up like a Swiss roll.
8. Drizzle with soy sauce if desired. (For smaller portions, you can slice the rolls.)

Kathryn Gordon (United States)

Kathryn Gordon has been a chef-instructor in the professional Pastry & Baking programme at the Institute of Culinary Education (ICE) in NYC since 2003. She's also the co-chair of the Centre for Advanced Pastry Studies (CAPS). She's a co-founder of a consultancy group for bakeries and other food businesses, Food Start-up Help.

Kathryn worked in management consulting after finishing an MBA at NYU Stern and undergraduate degrees at Vassar College but turned her knowledge and interest in cooking into a passionate career. In 2017, Kathryn was honoured by The Dessert Professional as one of the top 10 pastry chefs in America. In her path to pastry chef, Kathryn was privileged to train under renowned pastry chef Jacques Torres, MOF. She earned honours certification from L'Academie de Cuisine in Maryland and trained at two 4-star NYC restaurants, Le Bernardin and Le Cirque. She refined her culinary skills while working in the kitchens of The Rainbow Room and Windows on the World, where she was the pastry chef of Cellar in the Sky. Kathryn was an assistant producer for the Carymax World and National Pastry Championships for 13 years and has appeared on The Food Network. Kathryn is a featured chef in the first American Almond Look Book and a member of Les Dames d'Escoffier, New York chapter.

Kathryn leads an annual culinary course in the western Loire Valley, France, at Le Moulin Brégeon—a hotel owned by friends. Her first cookbook, co-written with Anne E. McBride, was released by Running Press in 2011. The Wall Street Journal described *Les Petits Macarons, Colourful French Confections to Make at Home* as the most "comprehensive and inspiring" book on macarons in any language. It's also now available in Chinese. Their second book, *Les Petits Sweets, Two-Bite Desserts from the French Patisserie*, was released by Running Press in September 2016. Kathryn's third cookbook, *Le Moulin Brégeon, Le Petit Moulin of the Loire Valley* was recently released to commemorate the first 20 years at the hotel and the Loire Valley Cooking program. Kathryn's fourth book, *Food Business Idea to Reality, A Food Entrepreneur's Guide to Launching a Food Product*, co-authored with Jessie Riley and Jeff Yoskowitz of Food Startup Help, is set to be published in 2021.

Kathryn and Jimmy met at ICE in New York in 2015 when he was an assistant teacher with Peter Yuen's Viennoiserie class at the ICE school. In 2016, Kathryn also visited Ireland during her holidays and met up with Jimmy in Galway.

Follow Kathryn: Instagram, https://www.instagram.com/chef_kathryn_gordon/

~ Kathryn Gordon

60. Earl Grey-Lavender Macarons

Recipe adapted from *Les Petits Macarons, Colourful French Confections to Make at Home* (Gordon & Mc Bride, 2011). This recipe makes 80 small (about 2.5 cm / 1") macarons, enough to make 40 sandwiched Earl Grey-Lavender Macarons. Additional resources and a video can be found at https://www.lespetitsmacarons.com/

Ingredients: Macaron Shells

165 g	Almond flour (ground almonds)
165 g	Confectioners' sugar
1 g	Fine sea salt
150 g	Granulated sugar
5 g	Powdered dry egg whites
115 g	Whisked "aged" egg whites (about 4 large)
4 drops	Purple gel food colouring (6 drops if liquid)

Chef tip: To age the egg whites properly, separate them 1 week in advance and refrigerate in a grease-free container.

Making the Macaron Shells

1. Stack/double tin 2 sheet pans on top of one another. Line the top sheet with a Silpat silicone mat.

2. In the bowl of a food processor, pulse together the almond flour, confectioners' sugar, and salt 4 times for 4 seconds each to combine.

3. In an electric mixer bowl, stir together the powdered egg whites and granulated sugar. Add the aged egg whites and whisk on medium-high speed until stiff glossy peaks begin to form (after about 11 minutes).

4. With the paddle attachment, mix the flour/sugar/salt mixture at low speed into the meringue until the batter is smooth and shiny.

5. Add the desired colourings and mix again briefly until slack. To test for readiness, look at the batter while the mixer is mixing on low speed. Stop mixing as soon as it becomes shiny and the mixer doesn't hold any pattern or "ribbon".

6. Halfway fill a pastry bag fitted with a ¼" round tip. Tie the top of the bag with a rubber band.

7. Using very firm pressure, pipe the meringue onto the silicon sheet-lined baking sheet into quarter-size mounds, about 3 cm (1 ½") apart from one another. (You'll want to do a test bake, so only pipe some of the batter at first.)

8. From about 15 cm (6") above the table, slam the baking sheet down firmly 10 times to remove excess air from the shells.

9. If the day is dry, air dry the macarons for 15 minutes until a skin forms, and then bake for 9–11 minutes at 176 °C. If the day is humid, oven-dry the macarons for about 12 minutes until a skin forms and then raise the oven temperature to 179 °C and bake for 9 minutes. The macarons will be baked when (a) they can just come off the silicone sheet when you lift them by wiggling the bottom or "feet" of the macaron and (b) the centres have risen but don't have any dark indentations.

10. Cool the macarons completely before removing them from the tray with an offset spatula. Freeze for 15 minutes for easier removal.

Ingredients: Earl Grey Tea-Lavender Ganache Filling

- 100 g   Bittersweet chocolate, finely chopped
- 120 g   Heavy cream
- 2 g   Loose Earl Grey tea
- 0.25 g   Dried culinary lavender buds
- 13 g   Unsalted butter, softened

Making the Ganache Filling

1. Melt the chocolate over a double boiler.

2. Bring the cream to a boil in a small saucepan over medium-high heat. Remove from the heat, stir in the tea and lavender, and let the mixture steep for 5 minutes.

3. With a fine-mesh sieve, strain the mixture into the chocolate and whisk from the centre to the bowl's edges until the ganache's smooth and homogenous.

4. Whisk in the butter until it's fully incorporated. Allow the filling to set in a shallow pan before piping the filling into the macarons.

Peter Yuen (United States)

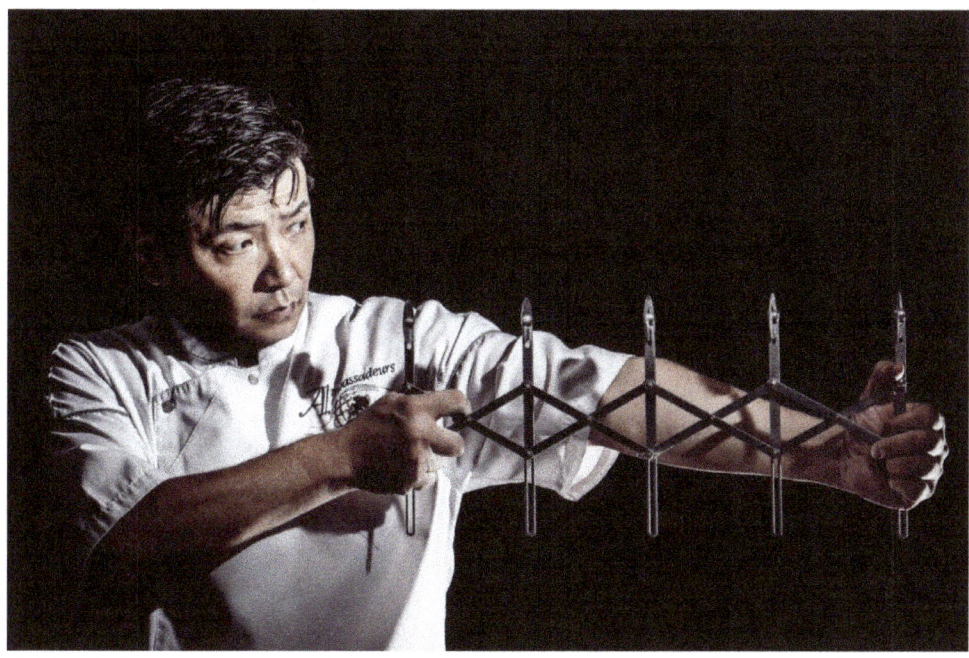

Chef Peter Yuen is an award-winning pastry chef and world-renowned lamination specialist who began his career working part-time at his family's bakery. In 2000, he graduated from the French Pastry School, a world-renowned pastry school located in Chicago. Following his graduation, he worked as a pastry chef at the French Mill Bakery and was later recruited to work at the Four Seasons Hotel in Chicago. With a growing interest in bread making, Peter became head baker of the Sofitel Chicago Water Tower. In 2004, he opened his own up-scale bakery named La Patisserie P.

Peter's impressive achievements and teaching appointments are vast and global. He's earned his title "The Laminator" through his hard work, dedication, amazing creativity, and natural talent. Peter was a member of the Bread Bakers Guild Team USA 2008 which competed in the CDM de la Boulangerie—Peter placed first in the Viennoiserie category. In 2010, Peter was invited to compete as the USA representative at the Viennoiserie category in the first Master's de la Boulangerie—Peter placed second. Peter has been a member of Ambassadeurs du Pain representing the Southeast Asia

Region since 2009 and was voted by his peers as one of the 2011 Top Ten Best Bread Bakers in America. In 2014, he pioneered the Universal Number System for managing lamination. As all nations understand math, it's understood internationally by all languages, and he's taught his system to thousands of people the world over. In 2019, he was featured in Pastry Arts Magazine.

Peter currently travels the world as an international baking/pastry consultant. He's the official viennoiserie trainer for the German National Baking Academy. Peter has taught at the French Pastry School in Chicago; the Bellouet Conseil in Paris; and the Culinary Institute of America in Hyde Park, New York among other numerous pastry and baking institutions in 33 countries all over the world.

Peter met Jimmy in 2008 at the CDM de la Boulangerie. Since then, their interactions have blossomed from a candidate/judge relationship to a friendship of tremendous mutual admiration. In 2015, during a trip to the USA to visit relatives, Jimmy joined Peter in class.

Contact Peter at La Patisserie P.

1050-52 W Argyle St, Chicago, IL 60640, United States

Tel: +1 773-878-3226

Facebook, https://www.Facebook.com/LaPatisserieP/ , https://www.facebook.com/groups/230254614848637 and Instagram, https://www.instagram.com/baker_peter_yuen/?hl=en

~ Peter Yuen

61. Peter's Arowana Pastry

One of Peter's recent creations, the Arowana is a stunning laminated yeasted pastry with a delicious pineapple cake filling. The main flavouring ingredients are coconut, brown butter, and chocolate chips. Beautiful layers of bicolour laminated dough surround a succulent pineapple filling

to give a delicious flavour to this unique pastry designed by the master of lamination himself. The ingenuity and creativity behind this pastry have helped earned Peter respect and recognition as one of the world's foremost authorities on laminated pastry by his legions of admirers. This pastry is best when the dough is made the day before lamination to give it time to develop flavour, aroma, and strength. The Piña Colada cake must be made the day before it's used.

Ingredients: Piña Colada Cake

176 g	Powder sugar
141 g	Desiccated coconut
35 g	Almond flour (ground almonds)
176 g	Bread flour
4 g	Baking powder
44 g	Trimoline
483 g	Egg whites
2 g	Vanilla
264 g	Butter
176 g	Chocolate chips
1	Whole ripe pineapple (chopped)

Making the Piña Colada Cake

1. In a saucepan, caramelize the butter to make brown butter.

2. Stop cooking and add in the almond flour, coconut, vanilla, and powder sugar.

3. Then add in the chopped pineapple.

4. Make sure the mixture is cool before adding the remaining ingredients—if it's warm, the chocolate chips will melt and the baking powder will give up its aeration.

5. Allow the cake batter to mature overnight in the refrigerator at 3 °C.

6. Pipe the mixture into small rectangular silicone moulds about 4 cm × 13 cm. (You can use silicone ice stick moulds available from Amazon.com.)

7. Bake the cake batter in the silicone moulds at 200 °C for about 12 minutes or until golden brown.

8. Allow the bars to cool before removing them from the moulds.

Ingredients: Laminated Dough

959 g	T–55 bread flour/strong bakers' flour
264 g	Water
264 g	Whole, fresh milk
25 g	Milk powder
2 g	Malt powder
21 g	Instant yeast
115 g	Sugar
19 g	Salt
31 g	Butter, diced
500 g	Lamination butter

Making the Laminated Dough

1. Place all the ingredients except the lamination butter in the bowl of a vertical planetary mixer. Manually mix until the ingredients are roughly blended together, approximately 2 minutes.

2. Place a dough hook attachment on the machine and mix at 2nd speed for 5 minutes or until the dough begins to gain strength.

3. The final dough temp should be around 25 °C –26 °C.

4. Place the dough into a container and cover with a lid or plastic wrap.

5. Allow the dough to rest for 1 hour at room temperature. Refrigerate at 3 °C overnight.

6. The following morning, prepare the dough for lamination with the lamination butter.

7. The lamination method is 3-4-4 for both détrempés of identical weight, original and coloured. In this case, one is original while the other is red coloured. If the dough is to be coloured, mix the powder colour with all dry ingredients when mixing it.

Suggestions and Variations

You might consider having another design working that needs the same basic colour scheme so the dough could be shared for each design. Each book of dough will be divided at the last fold then mixed and matched as desired. The lamination options are:

3-4-3 (original) + 1 (coloured) and 3-4-1 (coloured) + 3 (original)
or
3-4-2 (original) + 2 (coloured) and 3-4-2 (coloured) + 2 (original)

When using powdered colour, the intensity varies among different brands. Always use the best non-toxic food grade colour available to you. Natural food colours are also an alternative when available. Use the recommended quantity as advised by the colour manufacturers as a baseline standard and then change according to your personal preferences.

Making the Arowana

1. Prepare the butter block: roll to between 4-5 mm thick and place it in the refrigerator to chill.
2. Roll the dough into a rectangle, the same height and twice the width of the butter and chill in the freezer for 10 minutes.
3. Take the butter block out of the refrigerator and allow the butter block to become flexible, about 9 °C –11 °C. Place it on the dough rectangle.
4. Fold the dough to close or lock in the butter. There are now 3 layers, known as a 3 lock-in.
5. The pastry is then rolled out into a long rectangle approximately 4 mm thick and given the first 4-fold, or book turn.
6. Turn the dough 90 degrees. Roll the pastry a second time to 4 mm thick and give it its 2nd 4-fold. You can decide to mix and match the original and coloured pastry to your liking at this stage.
7. Wrap the pastry in plastic and place it in the freezer at −18 °C for 30 minutes to rest and chill.
8. Roll the pastry to 48 cm wide, turn 90 degrees, and sheet it down to 4 mm.
9. Cut the sheeted pastry into 8 strips. The actual dimensions are not as important as they all are evenly divided.
10. Chill the pastry between ice blankets for 5 minutes and then cut using a lattice cutting tool.
11. Open the pastry to form the lattice pattern. Each strip will yield 3 pieces. The total yield is 24 pieces per book of pastry.
12. Flatten using the palm of your hand in one direction to expose the layers. Make sure the pastry is put neatly back together to expose the lattice pattern evenly.
13. Place the Piña Colada cake at the centre and roll it up as the filling.
14. Place the pieces on a tray in free form or into small loaf tins for perfect symmetry.
15. Proof the pastry at 26 °C–27 °C for 90–120 minutes.

16. Bake in a convection oven at 170 °C for 18 minutes or until lightly golden brown.
17. After baking, remove carefully from tins and cool on wire racks.

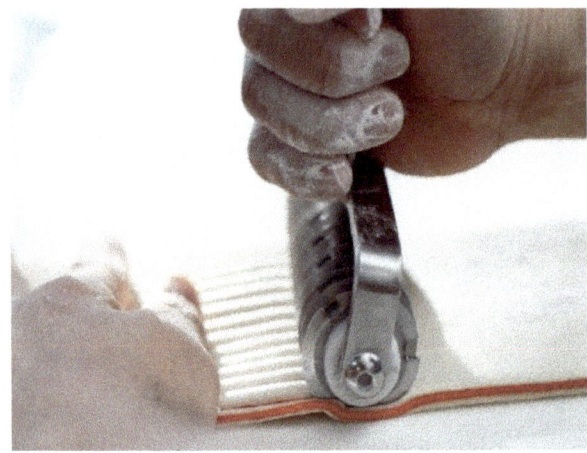

Step 10. Cut dough using lattice tool

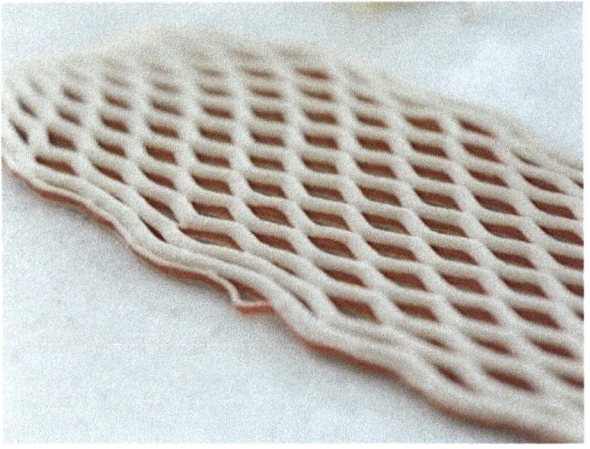

Step 11. Open dough making lattice pattern

Step 13. Roll the dough around the filling

Bibliography

Boland, R. (2014, October 6). Callan calling: A street that acts as a bridge to the past. *The Irish Times*. https://www.irishtimes.com/life-and-style/people/callan-calling-a-street-that-acts-as-a-bridge-to-the-past-1.1949494

Boyd, C. (2017). *From the source: France. Authentic recipes from the people who know them.* Lonely Planet Food.

Bread (Prices) Order, 1951. S.I. No. 123/1951. http://www.irishstatutebook.ie/eli/1951/si/123/made/en/print#

Calvel, R. (2001). *The taste of bread* (J. J. MacGuire, Ed., R. L. Wirtz, Trans.). Springer.

Cauvain, S. P. (2017). *Baking problems solved* (1st ed.). Woodhead Publishing.

Doves Farm. (2020, May 17). *European flour numbering system.* https://www.dovesfarm.co.uk/hints-tips/cheat-sheets/european-flour-numbering-system

Gordon, K., & Mc Bride, A. E. (2011). *Les Petits Macarons, Colourful French Confections to Make at Home.* Running Press.

Haegens, N. (2014). Pastries. In W. Zhou, Y. H. Hui, I. De Leyn, M. A. Pagani, C. M. Rosell, J. D. Selman, & N. Therdthai (Eds.), *Bakery products science and technology* (2nd ed., pp. 603-610). John Wiley & Sons. https://doi.org/10.1002/9781118792001.ch34

Hutkins, R. (2008). *Microbiology and technology of fermented foods.* Blackwell Publishing.

Parkinson, A. (Writer & Director). (2016, April 7). Special: Into the ocean (Season 8, Episode 6) [TV series episode]. In L. B. Lucas (Executive Producer), *River Monsters*. Animal Planet. https://www.youtube.com/watch?v=286lYr-Lxug&list=PLOcWEiL3wAqrlGDRU67fgezwxIVIziebT&index=1

Pastry Arts Magazine. (2019, April 17). *Peter Yuen: World traveler, viennoiserie expert and pursuer of the perfect croissant.* https://pastryartsmag.com/people/peter-yuen-interview/

Whitley, A. (2011). *Bread matters. The state of modern bread and a definite guide to making your own bread.* Andrews McMeel Publishing.

Appendix A: Glossary of Abbreviations

AEHT	European Association of Hotel and Tourism Schools
CAP	certificat d'aptitude professionnelle (baker's certificate)
CDM de la Boulangerie	Coupe du Monde de la Boulangerie (Bakery World Cup)
CDM de la Patisserie	Coupe du Monde de la Patisserie (Pastry World Cup)
CIPAN	Inter-American Confederation of Bakers
DDT	desired dough temperature
DIT	Dublin Institute of Technology
EBI	Elite de la Boulangerie Internationale
EBP	École de Boulangerie et de Pâtisserie de Paris (School of Bakery and Patisserie of Paris)
IBA	world trade fair for the bakery industry
IGBF	Intergalactic Bakers Federation
INBP	Institut National de la Boulangerie Pâtisserie (French National Baking and Pastry Institute)
JHBS	Japan Home Baking School
SME	Subject matter expert
UIBC	International Union of Bakers and Confectioners
UIBC	Union International Bakers and Confectioners

Appendix B: Resources from Jimmy Griffin's YouTube Channel

This is the link to my YouTube channel: https://www.youtube.com/c/JimmyGriffinbaking/. There, you can find all of the videos I suggest here plus many more. The links are generally organized categorically by topic in alphabetical order.

Bicolour Pastry Resources

Croissant bicolour 3-4-4 pastry process https://youtu.be/q-o0cyjane0

Twisted chocolatine bicolour shaping and makeup https://youtu.be/qr_SS3aWSRs

Butter Preparation Resources

Butter block and hand lamination https://youtu.be/KI7VTQQISFw

Making raspberry butter https://www.youtube.com/watch?v=6IRKAD_AfII&t=32s

Making raspberry butter block https://www.youtube.com/watch?v=2QkdR-gyrq0

Croissant Related Resources

Croissant make-up dough video with rolling and a 3 fold https://youtu.be/nhsavshz6c0

Hand rolling a croissant https://www.youtube.com/watch?v=VoeUD3wwRQ0&t=52s

Cross Lamination Resources

Cross lamination time-lapse https://www.youtube.com/watch?v=gonLzVe8sTQ

Hacks/Tips for Ease of Processing

Brød &Taylor home proofer https://brodandtaylor.com/

Chilling laminated dough using frozen vegetables https://youtu.be/-WZ9w0gPjyg

Chocolatine scored using a claw and scored using a knife https://youtu.be/s-aV1bzKnpc

Explaining elastic recoil tension in laminated pastry https://youtu.be/vi90mhc2t_U

Glazing cinnamon buns with fondant icing https://www.youtube.com/watch?v=0P7l3XF_P2Uo

Hand lamination hack using wooden guides https://youtu.be/fyRCB4G4-Qo

How to incorporate trimmings to reduce wastage https://youtu.be/mA22qWphP8E

How to insert frozen crème pâtissière into proofed pastry https://youtu.be/NBm1Ti-YAWU

Making frozen crème pâtissière pieces for viennoiserie https://youtu.be/kwUZEcjtak4

Slicing laminated pastry to relieve elastic recoil https://youtu.be/gscqic8hpxk

The correct procedure for wrapping laminated pastry https://youtu.be/RAb-aVWX6tQ

Lamination Lessons/Resources

3-4-3 Hand ice hockey puck technique https://www.youtube.com/watch?v=Ni3AdxeQm RY&t=133

5-4-3 Hand lamination sourdough croissant pastry https://youtu.be/irmbjlvxls4

Lock-in Resources

The lock-in process of dough and butter in pastry making https://youtu.be/J_j4umea7ow

Other Pastries

Black and white pastry ribbon for advanced viennoiserie https://www.youtube.com/watch?v=uRKfVOb6bGU

Christmas jiggle jiggle https://youtu.be/2ifa63fspqs

Coffee vanilla chocolate time-lapse baking https://www.youtube.com/watch?v=gonLzVe8s TQ

Cruffin™ style Hazelnut Nutella time-lapse https://www.youtube.com/watch?v=s4NF8Pr93 Ow

Cruffin™ style pastries: https://youtu.be/yturuzkkmdc

Cruffin™ style shaping, stack method https://www.youtube.com/watch?v=1QjieiSB7EM&t =6s

Golden delicious apple pastry https://www.youtube.com/watch?v=caiZRKQkCzY

Pear and chocolate basket made with croissant pastry part 1 https://www.youtube.com/ watch?v=-vomajpeUik&t=17s

Kouign Amman preparation final fold https://www.youtube.com/watch?v=gNM22D7jLhY

Pear and chocolate basket part 2 https://www.youtube.com/watch?v=9FPKev88Uic

Raspberry pear marinade, dusting and masking techniques https://youtu.be/qYUHmcZby pU

Rum and Californian raisin almond croissants https://www.youtube.com/watch?v=fulEH-Ewe-c&t=30s

Pain Chocolat/Chocolatine Resources

CDM Chocolatine Toulouse, France 2019 https://youtu.be/HQW4TfDnmvY

Christmas chocolatines https://youtu.be/bxzinvf118e

Chocolate bars for pain au chocolat https://youtu.be/0wMbMnD5ZxY

Double chocolate pastry making https://www.youtube.com/watch?v=kUIibcwg43o&t=52s

Pain chocolate shaping: Three ways https://youtu.be/uheq8fjbffk

Twisted chocolatine shaping using homemade chocolate bars: https://youtu.be/klsvyc1omoo

Other Resources

Seaweed dissertation https://arrow.tudublin.ie/tfschcafdis/1/

Science of time-lapse chocolatine https://www.youtube.com/watch?v=gPuiilgzgxw

Puff Pastry Resources

Butterfly palmier cutting and shaping https://www.youtube.com/watch?v=QqMIMygTaEM

Butterfly palmier baking time-lapse https://www.youtube.com/watch?v=2962NCLkOWU

Christmas sweet mince pies made with butter puff pastry https://youtu.be/qJN_Qbf9ZNM

Appendix C: Characteristics of Wheat Flours

Country	Wheat flour type					
	Extraction rate (%)					
	90–98	85–90	82–85	72–82	65–72	45–55
	Ash content (%)					
	1.40	1.00–1.20	0.75–0.90	0.62–0.75	0.50–0.62	below 0.50
	Protein content (%)					
	~13	~15	~14		~11	~9
Argentina	1/2	0	00		000	0000
Australia	Whole meal flour		Bread flour		Plain flour	Cake/pastry flour
Canada	Whole wheat flour		Bread flour	Bakers patent	All-purpose flour	Pastry/cake flour
Czech Republic & Slovakia	Celozrnná mouka	T1050		T650	Hladká mouka	Hladká mouka výběrová
France	Farine Intègral 150	110	80	65	55	45
Germany	Vollkorn 1600	1050	812		550	405
Holland	Volkorenmeel	Gebuilde bloem	Tarwe bloem		Patent bloem	Zeeuwse bloem
India	Chakki Atta	Atta			Maida / Safed	
Ireland	Whole meal flour	Wheat meal flour	Bakers flour	Strong bakers flour	Soft flour	Pastry/cake/biscuit flour
Italy	Integrale	Tipo 2	Tipo 1		0	00
Poland	Razowa	Sitkowa	Chlebowa		Luksusowa	Tortowa
Portugal & Spain	Harina Integrale 150	110	80	70	55	45
UK	Whole meal flour	Brown flour	Strong bread flour		Plain flour	Patent flour
US	Whole wheat flour	First clear flour	High gluten bread flour		All-purpose flour	Pastry flour
Argentina	1/2	0	00		000	0000

Note. Adapted from Doves Farm, 2020, Flour numbering system. https://www.dovesfarm.co.uk/hints-tips/cheat-sheets/european-flour-numbering-system

Appendix D: Characteristics of Rye Flours

Country	Rye flour type						
	Extraction rate (%)						
		90–98	85–90	82–85	72–82	65–72	45–55
	Ash content (%)						
	2.10–1.7	1.74	1.37	1.18	1.15	1.09–0.997	0.95–0.85	0.815–0.610
	Protein content (%)						
	14–12	10.5–9	10–9	9	9–8	9	~ 8	~ 8–6.5
Austria	R2500, Black rye				R960	R960 light		R500
Germany	T1800, Coarsely ground rye meal	T1740, Pure dark rye	T1370, Dark rye flour	Type 1180	T1150, similar to R500	T997, close to R500	T960	T815–T610
Ireland	Whole grain rye	Dark rye			Medium rye		Light rye	White rye
Russia	Oboynaya whole meal		Obdirnaya medium					Seyanaya
UK	Whole grain rye, Chopped rye grain	Dark rye	Medium rye				Light rye	White rye
US	Dark rye	Whole grain	Medium rye			Light rye		White rye

Note. Adapted from Panasonic, 2010, Types of flour: Naming conventions in different countries. https://experience-fresh.panasonic.eu/how_to/types-of-flour-naming-conventions-in-different-countries/

Index

A

ABC company, 175
ABST (Alliance for Bakery Students and Trainees), 92
Academie, 222
ACE Bakery, 36
African Bakery Cup in Casablanca, 45
Akademie Deutsches Bäckerhandwerk, 100
Alans' Chocolate Caramel Sticky Buns, 22, 28
Algae, 88, 114, 116
All-purpose flour, 162, 236
Almond Daycaise, 184
Almond meal, 204
Almond nougat, 183
Almond paste, 185
  softened, 186
Almonds, 213
  blanched, 212
Amazon rainforest in Brazil, 190
Ambassadeurs, 105, 136, 225
American Bread Bakers Guild, 164
American Institute, 164
Amino acids, 55
Aniar Boutique Cookery School, 84
Aniar's Irish Soda Bread, 85
Animal Planet, 231
Anna's Russian Taiga Bread, 117
Annual culinary, 222
Antioxidants, 25, 55, 120, 159
Antonio Arias Ordóñez, 110–11
Antonio's Pan, 111
AP, 60, 67
AP flour, 177
Appétit, 181
Apple cores, 152–53
Apple rings, 152
Apricot glaze, 44
  boiled, 45
Apricots, 210–11
  sliced, 211
  sourced, 210
Argentina, 28, 138, 200–201, 236
Argentine team coach, 200
Argentinian master baker, 200
Arowana, 226, 229
Arras, 56–57
Art collection, 214
  incredible Merrion Hotel's, 214
Artisan Bakers, 48, 127, 136, 168
Artisan breads, 17, 36, 190
  authentic, 36
Artistic Design category, 155
Artistic pieces, 22
Arturo Blanco, 133–34
Ash content, 7–8, 10, 236–37

Asian creativity, 144
Asian influence, strong, 122
Asian World Cup qualification, 76
Asia selections, 40
Assembling, 31, 148, 162, 192, 211, 216
Assembly chambers, permanent, 52
August Zang's Viennese, 1
Aurillac, 40, 62
Australia, 93, 98, 203, 236
Australian baker, first, 203
Australian baking team, 203
Austria, 187, 196, 237
Authentic Irish Baking, 164
Autolyse, 14 24, 26, 39, 97, 126, 142
Avignon, 48
Awards
  honorary, 100
  prestigious, 40
Award-winning Spanish restaurant Cava Bodega, 84

B

Babassu flour, 24–25
Baggenstos, Jacob, 155
Bagnat bread, 64
Baguettes, 15–18, 22, 37, 42, 53, 176, 178
  small, 115–16
Bake Jimmy, 68
Baker Christian Vabret, 63
Bakers and pastry chefs, 11
Baker's CAP, 56
Baker's Federation of Loire-Atlantique profession, 52
Bakers flour, 50–51, 236
Bakers flour/strong flour/AP flour, 137, 173
Bakers Guild Team, 168
Bakers of Spain, 133
Bakery and Pastry Arts, 4
Bakery competitions, vi, 59
  international, 134
Bakery Cup in Morocco, 45
Bakery education, 164
Bakery excellence, 136
Bakery exhibitions, global, 103
Bakery Masters, 117, 203
Bakery/pastry, 56, 182
Bakery products science and technology, 231
Bakery Schools, 81, 138, 171
Bakery team, 56, 105
  national, 149
Bakery tournaments, 200
Bakery trade, 76, 181
Bakery World Cup, 120, 139, 232
Bakery worlds, 133, 163
Baking Akademie in Weinheim, 68
Baking and Pastry Arts Programme, 27

Baking excellence, 48
Baking experts, 100
Baking flour, strong, 107
Baking hearth bread, 19
Baking industry, 5, 7
Baking institutions, 226
Baking journeys, 1, 49
　personal, 127
Baking paper, 27, 126, 192
Baking students, 92
Baking studio, 98
Baking Team Canada, 27–28
Baking Team Ireland, 81
Baking workshops, 132
Baking world, 3
Bakr, 178
Banh Mi, 176
Barley, 7, 79–80
Barley malt powder, 107
Barley Recipes, 79
Barm brack, 101
Basil, fresh, 50
Baskets, 17–18, 27, 75
　wicker, 17
Bassinage, 57–58, 97
Batards, 15–17
Batard shape, 58
　sharp, 131
Batch, 15, 35, 118, 202
Batching, 62, 154
Batter, 43, 110, 146, 223–24
Bedu, David, 48–49
Bee pollen, 163
Beer Bread Dough, 65–67
Beer mixture, 65–67
Beer mixture topping, 66
Beesham Soogrim, 141
Beesham's Seeded Nutrition Bread, 142
Bejkr, 168
Belgian speciality, 188
Belgian Sweet Rhubarb Tart, 188
Benny Swinnen, 187, 188
Berlin, 68, 75
Bernardin, 222
Bernd, 75–76
Bertarini, Dario, 103
Bienefelt, Peter, 114
Biggest Birthday Cake, 122
Biscuit Base, 210–11
Biscuits, 9, 43
　pistachio, 216
Bite
　conger eel, 91
　meaty, 23, 79
Black and white pastry ribbon for advanced viennoiserie
　　https, 234
Black dough, 41–42, 115–16
Black gumdrops, 203

Black pepper, 35, 161
　cracked, 83
Black pepper aids, 159
Black rye, 237
Blanco, Arturo, 133
Blankets, ice, 229
Blueberries, 172–74
　marinated, 175
　sun-ripened, 172
Blueberries work, 199
Blue ginger, 125
Boba tapioca pearls, 148
Bogna, 92–93
Boiled Barley Ingredients, 79
Boiled flour, 118
　saccharified, 119
Boiled Flour and Rye Sourdough, 118
Boiled sugar-water mixture, 183
Bolo bread, 148
Bottom heat, 74, 178
Bottom sweating, 116
Boudin Bakery, 164
Boulangerie Coupe, 232
Boulangerie Europe, 144
Boulangerie-hofmann.ch, 194
Boulangerie International, 33, 40, 179
Boulangerie jury, 172
Boulangerie Wolfisberg, 216–17
Bran, 7–10
Brazil, 4, 22–23, 25–26, 171–72, 182, 190
Brazilian communities, 25
Brazil's flavours, 23
Brea Bakery, 164
　traditional Russian, 117
Bread bakers, best, 71, 226
Bread Bakers Guild, 157, 164, 225
Bread dough, 14, 24, 26, 69
Bread Ingredients, 77
Bread Making, 13
Bread preparations, standard, 106
Bread quality standards, 133
Bread recipes, 14
Breads & Buns, 21–178
Bread samples, 164
Bread sommeliers, 68
Bread travagghiatu, 105
Breton biscuit base, 210
Brett's Chocolate Trilogy, 204
Brett's ingenuity, 204
Brewer's yeast, 106–7
Brioche, 9, 11, 41–43, 60–62, 160, 162, 219
　assembled, 44
Brownie, 99, 205
Bruiel, Nathalie, vi
Brush, 51, 64, 67, 133, 155
Bundesakademie, 68
Bun glaze, 103, 154–55
　super sticky, 151

Buns, 28, 31, 33–35, 137, 150–52, 154–55, 162, 202–3
Burst, magnificent, 128
Butter, 41–44, 60–61, 102, 112, 146–47, 160–62, 174–75, 183–85, 192, 201–2, 204–6, 213, 227–29
  brown, 226–27
  chilled, 162
  cold, 153, 192
  peanut, 201
Butter additions, 160
Butterfly Stencil, 139
Buttermilk, 47, 76–77, 85
Butter Preparation Resources, 233
Button, 6, 19
B-vitamins, 120

C

Caddy, Wayne, 150–51
Caffe Pralet, 122
Calcium, 55
Calculating DDT, 12
California, 157, 168
Californian raisin almond croissants https, 234
Californian Sourdough, 166
Callebaut ambassador, 78
Calvel, 231
  Raymond, 14
Camp Bread, 164
Canada, 27, 33–34, 36–37, 138, 164, 236
Cancer, v
Cancer Care West, v
Candidate/judge relationship, 226
Caprice De Bretagne, 210
CAPS (Centre for Advanced Pastry Studies), 221
Caramel/ganache mixtures, 32
Cardamom pods, 153
Cardboard, thin, 139
Card paper, hard, 124
Carouge, 216
Casablanca, 45, 49, 207
Cases, small tart, 198
Casserole, 184–85
Caster sugar, 102, 153, 198
Caster sugar/white sugar, 191
Cast-iron pot, 132
Catchy shamrock shape, 82
Cauvain, 231
Cayenne pepper, 79–80
CDM, vi, 1, 3, 23, 37, 45, 64–65, 117, 120, 155, 157–58, 203–4, 207
CDM Chocolatine, 56–57
  world silver medallist, 4
CDM Chocolatine Toulouse, 234
CEBP, 181
Centre for Advanced Pastry Studies (CAPS), 221
Ceop-pan, 133
Champagne mousse, 183–84, 186
Championship, 103, 138
  global professional, 22
  international, 138
  national baking, 179
Characteristics of Rye Flours, 237
Cheesecake, 181
Cheese cloth, 166
Chef-baker, 48, 117
Chef Fernando de Oliveria, 23
Chef Peter Yuen, 225
Cherries, 101
Chicago, 60, 64, 120, 168, 225–26
Chile, 62, 138
Chill, 12, 61, 110, 145–46, 202, 211, 229
Chilli Crab Filling, 125–27
China, 4, 40, 94, 182, 204
Chinese Bakery & Confectionery Association, 175
Chinese flour, 41
Chocolate, 22–23, 31, 196–97, 199, 201, 203, 206, 219, 225
  couverture, 31
  dark, 31, 61, 197
  red, 215
  warm, 203
Chocolate bars for pain, 234
Chocolate crosses, 155
Chocolate custard, 199
Chocolate decorations, 197, 199
  desired, 199
Chocolate flakes, 199
Chocolate ganache, 28, 31–32
Chocolate Twist, 197
Chocolatine, 233
Chopped green onion, 221
Chopped pineapple, 227
Christian Vabret, vi, 49, 62–63, 172
Christian Vabret MOF, 95
Christophe, 206–7
Christophe's participation, 207
Christophe's Savoury Twist, 208
Ciabatta, 15, 155, 157
Cinnamon, 38, 189
Cinnamon sticks, 153, 191–92, 211
Citron zest, 217
Citrus fruit zests, 201
Claude, Jean, 52
Club Elite, 176
Club Richemont España, 136
Coals, warm, 133
Coating, 148
Cold Fermentation, 81
Cold proof, 104
Colomer, 136
  Fernando, 136
Colonial period, 176
Colourful French Confections, 222–23, 231
Colourful Sweet Childhood Joy pastry, 201
Competition training, 82
Competition years, 82, 194
Confectioners' sugar, 161, 223
Confederation of Bakers of Spain, 133

Conger eels, 68, 94, 165
Conger loaf, 94, 98
   world-famous, 4
Consumption, durum wheat, 134
Convection oven, 35, 43, 51, 163, 230
Cook-caterer David Bedu, 48
Cookie coating, 148
Cookie dough, 108–10, 144–48
Cookie/peanut paste ball, cold, 202
Cookie straws, rolled, 148
Cooled raspberry financier, 205
Cornmeal, 173–74
   cooked, 172
Cornmeal porridge, 173–74
   warm, 174
Couche cloths, 17, 27, 39, 116, 135
Coupe Louis Lesaffre, 37 94, 117
COVID, 108, 128
COVID pandemic, 204
Crab meat chunks, 125
Cracked einkorn, 169
Creative Culinaire School, 122
Cremai exhibition, 49
Crème fraîche, 65
Crystal salt, 69
Culinary Institute, 226
Curcuminoids, 159
Currants, 116
Curry powder, 80
Custard, 145, 147, 198–99
Custard powder, 181, 218

D
Dakar, 120
Dame Cathedral, 95
Daníel Kjartan Ármannsson, 78
Daniel's Fiery Icelandic Sourdough, 79
Daniel's Icelandic Dough, 80
Dario, 103
Darío's Pan Tramvai, 104
Darjeeling tea powder, 145–46
Dark beer, 65–66
Dark cocoa powder, 42
Darker bran, 7–8
Dark rye, 237
Date financier, 43
Date paste, 46–47
Daughters Janice, v
David's Flowerpot Tomato Bread, 49
DDT, 12–13, 39, 41, 47, 50, 57, 73–74, 76, 135, 137
   desired, 149
Debail, Nadine, vi
Debersée, Christophe, 206–7
Déborah Ott-Libs, 59–60, 65
Déborah's Chocolate Raspberry Brioche22, 60
Decorative stencils, 139, 141
Degrees Celsius, 5
Degrees Fahrenheit, 5

Delayed salt technique, 96
Delicious cheesecake, 180
Derek O Brien, 4, 88–90, 100–101
Derek's Barm Brack, 101
Desiccated coconut, 227
Desired Dough Temperature, 11–12, 232
Digital scales, 6, 15
Dillon, 98–99
Dinkel, 8
   label, 10
Diploma programme, 100
Distribution network, large, 68
Dough, 8–12, 14–19, 23–27, 41–44, 46–47, 57–64, 75–77, 96–98, 115–16, 121–26, 130–31, 145–50, 227–30

Dough balls, 77, 140, 202
Dough-butter-dough, 192
Dough conditioners, 4
Dough consistency, 58
Dough development, 41, 112
Dough ferments, 102, 119
Dough hook, 24, 26, 39, 41–42, 44, 77, 119, 121, 156, 201
Dough ingredients, 119, 121, 201
Dough mass centre, 14
Dough mixer, 67
Dough mixer/stand mixer, 13
Dough overnight, 61, 143
Dough Preparing, 50
Dough temp, 12
Dough temperature, 131, 174
   final, 104, 107
   ideal, 6
Doves Farm, 231, 236
Dragées, multi-coloured, 203
Drain, 27, 33, 39, 58, 64, 98, 104
Dried culinary lavender buds, 224
Dried oregano, 50
Dried sweetened cherries, 38
Dried yeast, 102, 126, 176–77
Drizzle, 130, 221
Dry moringa, 120
Dry pine shoots, 118
Dry yeast, 11, 37–39, 188
   active, 11
Dumonceaux, Alan, 27
Durum wheat flour, 134–35
Dusted flower, 55
Dutch Boulangerie, 114
Dutch ovens, 19

E
Ear, 91
Earl Grey-Lavender Macarons, 223
Earl Grey Tea-Lavender Ganache Filling, 224
EBI, 63, 111, 120, 232
Ecole Artisanale, 127
École Christian Vabret, 63
Ècole Gastronomique Bellouet Conseil, 22

Eel attack, conger, 86, 94
Egg Mixture Ingredients, 195
Eggs, 29, 60, 101–2, 109–10, 112–13, 125, 146, 184–85, 194–95, 198, 201–2, 205–6, 221
Eggs and sugar, 194, 205
Egg whites, 184, 186, 189, 204–5, 223, 227
Egg yolk mixture, 161, 184
Egilsstaðir, 78
Egypt, 45, 48
Egyptian artisan baker/pastry chef, 45
Egyptian tablet bread, 46
Egyptian team, 45
Einkorn Bread, 169–70
Elaboration, 134
Ellen's Tapioca Tea Bread, 144
Ellis, Ricky, 131
Endosperm, 7, 9
  lighter, 7–8
  wheat berry's, 7
ENIAP bakery school, 103
Equipment, advanced bakery, 132
Erica Roessing Almeida, 190, 208
Erica's Ultimate Portuguese Custard Tart, 191
Espigas, 134
Esther, 190
Europain, 22, 127, 138, 172, 179, 210
European flour numbering system, 231
European Gold Medallist, 193, 216
European Prize, 75
Europe's birthday cake, 211
Euro Skills competitions, 79
Euro-Toques Ireland, 84
European Association, 232
Exner, Tobias, 67
Exotic touch, 210
Expansion, 110, 123, 208
Expose, 208, 229
Extensibility, 9, 96
Extraction process, 7
Extraction rates and ash and protein content, 8

F
Facal, Hector, 171–72
Fan oven, 62, 211
Fans, 23, 193
Fantastic, 72, 92
Fantastic book, 210
Farmers, 84, 106, 158, 169
Farmers' markets, 158
Fat Freddie's Pizzeria, 84
Father, 62, 68, 71, 110, 181, 187, 190
Favourite combinations, 108
Favourite fillings, 63
Fermentation, 8, 12, 14, 118, 166, 170, 173
Fermentation process, 11
Fermented bean paste, 125
Fermented foods, 231
Fermented rye malt, 118

Fermenting, 97, 102, 125, 166
Fermenting dough, 17
  preshaped, 16
Ferment overnight, 96, 107, 118, 145
Fernando's Babassu Bread, 23
Fernando's Genipapo Bread, 18, 26
Feuilletine crunch mix, 183
Fiery Icelandic Sourdough Ingredients, 79–81
Final Rye Sourdough, 74
Fingers, 113, 140
Finish, 83, 113, 116, 181, 184, 186, 199, 202
Finishing, 44, 181, 186, 189, 203, 213, 222
Finish twisting, 59
Finland, 138
First clear flour, 236
Flammekueche, 65
Flatbreads, 9
Flatten, 51, 54, 58, 97, 126, 219, 229
Flavoursome, 156
Flemish Brabant, 188
Floral shape, 54
Florence, 49
Florida Bakery Ltd, 144
Flour
  almond, 223, 227
  biscuit, 109, 177
  cake, 43, 177
  dry, 192
  flour/AP, 96, 149
  ground, 7
  manioc, 26
  meal, 74, 85, 123, 236
  milling, 7–8, 10
  naming, 9
  patent, 9, 236
  potato, 17
  refined, 10
  seed, 24
  semolina, 106
  sieved, 198
  soft, 109, 236
  strong, 8, 66–67, 80, 96, 145–46, 174, 177
  unbleached, 123
  un-hydrated, 24, 26
  white, 9, 38, 85
Flour T-55, 121
Flour T-65, 53, 63
Flour T-80, 137
Flour T-1370, 118
Flour temperature, 12
Flour type, 9, 210
Flour/water slurry, 166
Flower, 54
Flowerpots, 49–50
Flue, 19
Folding/Degassing First, 14
Followers, 141
Food processor, 125, 205, 223

Food Product, 222
Food product development, 3, 36, 132
Foods, Weston, 36
Forest Fruits Compote, 185
Forgiveness, 46
Form, free, 229
Formal relationship, 158
Formula, 12, 72, 163
Formulas, late-night, 158
Fortin, Mario, 33–34
Foundation, 124, 158
Founder Christian Vabret, 40
Fournette bakery, 60, 64
Fournil Christian Vabret, 62
Fragilete, 185
François's Salée, 217
François Wolfisberg, 216
Freeze, 33, 183–84, 186, 224
Freeze-dried raspberries, 204
Freezer, 42, 61, 162, 186, 215–16, 229
French Pastry School, 225–26
French Patisserie, 222
French recipe, 176
French teams, 52, 59, 207
French term, 57
Fresh chillies, 125
Fresh compressed yeast, 152
Fresh cream, 215, 218
Fresh cream cheese, 181
Fresh garlic, 50
Fresh mint, 60, 62
Fresh mint sprigs, 181
Fresh onion, 35
Fresh pumpkin, 129
Fresh rhubarb, 189
Fresh yeast, 11, 24, 26, 47, 60, 66–67, 76–77, 82–83, 104, 201
Friendship, 49, 52, 63, 72, 216, 220, 226

G

Galway, 52, 60, 68, 71–72, 84, 90–92, 197
Galway Food, 84
Ganache, 32, 60–62, 225
Ganache Filling, 225
Garden sprayer, 19
Garlic, 50, 125
Garnish, 44–45, 62, 152, 162–63, 180, 199, 215–16
Gas, 10, 14–15
Gastronomy, 111, 173
Generations, 3, 33, 56, 71, 98–99, 191, 200–201
Geneva, 216
Genipap Blue Milk, 26–27
Genipapo, 26
German Bakers Confederation, 100
German bakery school in Weinheim, 138
German Bakery Trade in Weinheim, 75
German Baking, 4, 100
German Streusel, 162

German strong rye bread, 72
German term Dinkelvollkorn, 10
Ghee, 46–47
Ghoush's Forgiveness Tablet Bread, 46
Glass jar overnight, 170
Glaze, 30, 32–33, 152, 175
   sticky pan, 28, 30–31
Gluten development, 13, 130, 218
   constant, 160
Gluten flour, 166
   high, 165–66
   unbleached high, 165
Glutenin, 8
Gluten matrix, elastic, 8
Gluten structure time, 16
Golden Bread Cup in Italy, 138
Golden corn syrup, 30
Gold medal, 40, 59, 114, 193, 194, 217
González, Sergio, 200
Good Bread, 105
Gordon, 223, 231
Gordon, Kathryn, 221, 223
Grain rye, 237
Great Irish Bake off, 214
Greece, 211
Green algae, 116
Green genipap, 27
Green Onion Pancake Roll, 221
Grey, Earl, 156
Gribanova, Anna, 117
Griffin, Jimmy, 3–4, 78, 86, 95, 100, 108, 164–65
Griffin's Bakery, 84, 93–94, 96
Ground, 7, 27, 50, 155, 161
Ground almonds, 43, 184, 223, 227
Guangzhou, 94, 182, 204
Guédille, 34
Guests, 60, 117, 121, 159
Guinness, 66
Gülten, 148–49
Gülten's Recipe Suggestion, 150
Gülten's Simit, 149
Gülten Yağmur, 148–49
Günther, 176, 181–82
Günther Koerffer, 176, 181
Günther's Royal Princess Cake, 182

H

Hacks/Tips, 233
Haif Hakim, 120
Haif's Moringa Bread, 121
Hannover, 68
Hard wheat, 8
Hard wheat flour, 34
Hazan, Jack, 179
Health benefits, 55, 121, 128
Heart, 62, 72, 158, 190
Hearth breads, 17–18
Hector's bakery, 172

Hector's Corn Bread, 172
Height, 42, 145, 193, 229
Heinz, 72
Heinz Rye Sourdough, 72
High gluten bread flour, 236
High protein flour, 41
Hofmann, Olivier, 193–94
Hofmann's Bakery-Pastry-Confectionery, 193
Holland, 138, 141, 236
Honey, 103–4, 106–7, 118–19, 151, 153–54, 156, 174, 177, 204–5
  camu camu, 22
Honorary Professorship of Bakery and Pastry Arts, 4
Honours certification, 222
Hoops, round baking, 102
Huerta Bread, 136
Hummus Yeast Preparation, 46
Humphries, Robert, 18, 81–82, 95
Hungary, 82

I

IBA, 4, 81, 182, 232
IBA Cup, 81, 117
IBA European Cup, 59
ICE (Institute of Culinary Education), 221, 223
Iceland, 78–79
Icelandic baking team, 79
ICE school, 223
Icing sugar, 42–45, 146, 155, 180, 184, 211–13, 219
IGBF (Intergalactic Bakers Federation), 65, 120, 232
INBP, 22, 40, 52, 232
Incident, 86, 93
Increments, 30, 218
Indian fruit, 26
Indian nuts, 26
Indulgence, 101
  sheer, 201
Industry, 22, 36, 52, 75, 81, 144, 207
Infuse, 37, 53
Instagram, 65, 68, 105, 108, 204, 214, 217, 223, 226
Instant yeast, 29, 130, 156, 228
Institute of Culinary Education (ICE), 221, 223
Intergalactic Bakers Federation. *See* IGBF
International Baking Championships, 81
International Bread Convention in Mexico, 172
International Federation, 175
International Food Technologist, 164
International instructors, 108
International Richemont Club, 196, 217
International top-class specialist bakers, 1
International Union, 232
Irish Bakers, 63, 81, 100
Irish bakery team in Nantes, 114
Irish baking team members, 194
Irish Food Writers Guild, 100
Irish National Baking Teams, 100
Irish Richemont President, 197
Iron, 25, 55, 120

cast, 19
Israel, 138, 141, 179
Israeli Bakers & Pastry Association, 179
Israeli baking champion, 179
Italian bread flour, 104
Italian flour Type, 49–51, 107
Italy, 23, 103, 105, 138–39, 141, 171, 173
Ivana Orlovic, 94

J

Jack's Israeli Fancy Cheesecake, 180
Jacob's Earl Grey Ciabatta, 155
Japan, 4, 34, 108, 188, 209
Japanese flour/strong bakers flour/AP flour, 126
Japanese students, 216
Japan Home Baking School (JHBS), 33, 108, 188, 216, 232
Japan Home Baking School's Melon Pan, 108
Jarlath Conneeley, 93
Jean Claude Choquet, 52–53
Jeffrey's Osmotolerant Starter, 159
Jeffrey's Turmeric Bee Pollen Brioche Feuilletee, 159
JHBS. *See* Japan Home Baking School
Jimmy Griffin's YouTube Channel, 233
Jimmy's Conger Loaf, 96
Johannesburg, 131, 213
John's chocolate tart, 197
Josep Pascual, 138–39
Joy, 36, 111
JP McMahon Recipes, 84
Judges, 78, 92, 122, 139, 203, 214
  guest bakery, 92
Judy, 122–24
Judy Koh's Turmeric Chilli Crab Bread, 139
Judy's Turmeric Chilli Crab Bread, 124
Jury president, 78, 117, 141, 149, 168, 216

K

Kamal Rahal Essoulami, 49
Kamut, 142
Kao Sieu Luc, 175–76
Kao's Vietnamese Baguette, 176
Kelly, Paul, 213
Khorasan, 142
Killary Fjord, 86
Kneading time, 74
Knife
  pallet, 32
  sharp, 42, 98, 167
Knights of Good Bread and Élite, 105
Knowledge, 3, 22, 71–72, 99, 114, 204, 207
  exchanging, 172
  sharing, 122
Koerffer, 2
Koh, Judy, 53, 57, 69, 73, 118, 122–23, 126
Koh's starter, 96
Kranjc, 87
Krasnoyarsk, 117
Kugel, Max, 71–72

Kütscher, Bernd, 75–76

L
Laboratory, 56, 211
amination, 57, 123, 192, 227–28
Lamination butter, 160, 228
The Laminator, 225
Languages, 3, 210, 222, 226
Lattice pattern, 229
Lava rocks, 19
Leaf/petal shape, 54
Leak, 124, 147
Lecturers, 3, 68, 81, 100, 214
   guest, 151
Legions, 23, 227
Lemon peel, 191–92
   fresh, 191
Lemon zest, 78, 184
   grated, 154, 184
Lesaffre, 40, 148
   Corinne, vi
   Louis, 149
Lesaffre Gold, 160
Lesaffre Group, vi
Lesaffre Yeast Corporation, 11
Letter, 8, 192
Levain Preferment Starter, 107
Licuri, 26
Licuri nuts, 26
Lifetime Achievement Award, 176
Light rye, 237
   grain Medium rye, 237
Linen cloths, 17, 83
Liquid leaven, 53
Liquid levain sourdough, 170
Liquid vanilla, Vanilla Bean, 210
Lockdown, 98–99
Loire Atlantique, 48, 52
Loire-Atlantique Baker's Federation, 52
Loire Valley Cooking program, 222
Lonely Planet, 231
Loose Earl Grey, 224
Los Angeles, 157, 164
Los Espigas, 133
Louis Lesaffre competition, 37
Louis Lesaffre Cup, 22, 28, 33, 40, 65, 111, 203–4
Louis Lesaffre Cup world quarterfinals, 182
Low protein flour, 42–43
Low protein flour/cake flour/biscuit flour, 44
Ludovic Richard, 209–10
Lulu Lee, 220
Lulu's Green Onion Pancake Roll, 220

M
Macarons, 22–23, 222–25
Macaron Shells, 223
Madeleine, Marie, 52
Madrid congress, 171

Maestro Giorilli, 105
Mafalda, 106
Mafalda Sicilian Bread, 105
Magnesium, 55, 120
Maize grits, 83
Making Jeffrey's Osmotolerant Starter, 159
Making sourdough bread, 124
Malt, 104, 106, 118, 160
Malted barley flour, 38
Manchester Tart , 196–97
Mango Panna Cotta, 215–16
Manipulation, 16
Maple Leaf Pastry Competition in Canada, 164
Maple syrup, 38
Marais, 62
Marc, 183–84
Marcus's Maple Cherry Nut Loaf, 18, 37
Mariathas, Marcus, 36–37
Mario Fortin, 33–34, 211–12
Mario's Hot, 34
Mario's influence, 33
Marios' Kourabiedes, 212
Marios Papadopoulos, 211–12
Marmalade, orange, 194–96
Marroc cylinder chocolates, 203
Mascarpone, 183–84
Mash, 72–73
Mash Ingredients, 73
Masters Boulangerie, 172
Master's certificate, 120, 209
Max, 71–73
Max's father, 72
Max's Heinz Rye Sourdough, 72
McBride, Anne E., 222
Meats, 139, 142
Medium rye, 118, 237
Meilleur Ouvrier de France (MOF), 52, 62, 209, 222
Melon essence, 108–10
Melt, 43, 152, 203, 205, 208, 225, 227
Melted butter, 50, 113, 180–81
Memories, 12, 84
   childhood, 85, 201, 220
Meringue, 184, 186, 189, 223–24
   stiff, 184
Merrion Art Afternoon Tea collection, 214–15
Mexican sweet bread, 111
México, 110, 138
Michelin-starred Aniar Restaurant, 84
Middle East, 148–49, 211
Mike's Einkorn Bread, 169
Mike Zakowski Recipes, 168
Milk chocolate, 183
Milk powder, 101–2, 109, 112, 206, 228
Milk Sponge Preferment, 152
Millers, 7, 9
Minerals, 9–10, 25, 159
Minh City, 176
Mint springs, 181

Minus, 12–13
Minutes of intermediate proofing, 58, 112, 175, 218
Mix, brownie, 205
Mixed ginger, 195
Mixed spice, 151, 154
Mixer, 24, 26, 30, 41–42, 47, 77, 107, 145–46, 160, 180–81, 188–89, 201, 213
Mixer bowl, electric, 223
Mix hummus, 46
Mixing, 24, 28, 57, 60, 112, 115, 213, 224, 228
Mixing bowl, 42, 64, 70, 112, 130, 161–62, 166–67
Mixing process, 14, 57
Mixture
  butter-flour, 208
  flour/sugar/salt, 223
  mango, 215
Moisten, 47, 113
Moisture, 19, 148
Mondial, 23, 193
Montenegro, 94
Montevideo, 171–72
Moringa, 120–21
Moringa Bread, 121
Moringa oleifera tree, 120
Moringa Paste, 121
Moringa powder, 120–21
Morocco, 45, 48–49, 207
Mother, 110, 187, 220
Mother Dough Ingredients, 166
Movie, action, 4
Muerto, 111
Muffin tins, 32
Multicoloured vermicelli, 203
Munich, 81

N

Naegel pastry shop and café, 65
Namibia, 11–12
Naming conventions, 237
Nantes, 52, 103, 114, 136, 138, 187, 193
National Bakery School, 3–4, 81
Negrete, Alan, 163, 165
Netherlands, 114, 141
New York, 164, 222–23, 226
New York City, 171
Nightmares, 92–93
Nordic Bakery, 141
Nordic Bakery and Nordic Pastry Cups, 214
Nordic Bakery Cup, 79
Nordic Pastry Cups, 214
North America, 36
Northern Alberta Institute, 27
North Western France, 210
Noy, Brett, 203
NYC, 221

O

Oats, 7, 130
  rolled, 129–30
Oat Sourdough Ingredients, 129
O'Brien, Derek, 100
Occasion, 23, 65
O'Keefe, 90–91
  David, 90
Oliveira, 22–23
Olives, 83, 115
  green, 115
Olivier's Pumpkin Tart, 194
Olympic Baking Seminar in Japan, 34
Onion mix, green, 221
Open crumb structure, 17
Open dough, 230
Orange paste, 195
Orange zest, 112, 201
Organic bee pollen, 159
Organic bread flour, 152
Organic bread flour Stage, 154
Osaka, 108, 188
Osmotolerant, 11
Osmotolerant yeast, 11
Oven damper/door, 171
Oven heat, 70, 143
Oven peel, 18, 119
Oven setters, 75
Oven stone, 119
Oven temperature, 67, 83, 116, 178, 181, 224

P

Padraig Regan, 91–92
Pain biologique, 168
Pain Surprise, 63
Palmerstown Village, 100
Panettone, 103, 105
Panificadora La Panera, 110
Panificatore Italiano, 49
Pank, 49
Panko breadcrumbs, 116
Pan Tramvai, 104
Paraguay, 220
Parchment paper, 18, 33, 39, 47, 67, 119, 129
Parents, 56, 71, 187, 200
Participants, 117, 139
Participation, 37
Partners, 52, 124
Pastries, 2–3, 8–9, 48–49, 120, 122–23, 157–59, 163, 180, 189–90, 192–93, 200–231, 234
Pastry Arts Magazine, 226, 231
Pastry bag, 224
Pastry baking culture, 187
Pastry Base, 180, 189
Pastry chefs, vi, 48, 56, 212, 214, 222, 225
  award-winning, 225
Pastry flour, 29, 109, 146, 198, 205, 212, 236
  soft, 180, 195
  white soft, 194
Pastry innovation, 179

Pastry master's certificate, 206
Pastry products, 4, 138
Pastry Revolution, 138
Pastry World Cup, 232
Patisserie, 23, 120, 225–26, 232
Pâtissier, 209
Paul Kelly's Afternoon Tea Collection, 215
Paulo, 22, 171
Peel, mixed, 101
Pekmez, 149–50
Peter's Arowana Pastry, 226
Peter's World Master, 114
Peter Yuen's Viennoiserie, 223
Petits Macarons, 222–23, 231
Petits Sweets, 222
Pettit Versailles, 62
Piergiorgio Giorilli, 105
Pierre's Alsace Beer Bread, 65
Pizzas, 17–18, 84, 106
Pizza stones, 17, 19
Place apple rings, 152
Plain flour, 153, 204, 236
Plain flour T-45, 198
Plaits, 42, 173
   4-string, 173
   5-string, 173
   five-string, 172
Plane, 68, 72
Plight, 89
Podium, 209–10
Poilâne Bakery, 164
Poland, 52, 92, 236
Poolish, 28–29, 37–39, 49–50, 72–73, 173–74, 176–77, 201
Portions, 30, 32, 137, 147, 162, 167, 220–21
Porto, 190
Porto Alegre, 172
Portugal, 9, 138, 190–91
Portugal & Spain, 236
Portuguese, 191
Pot, 19, 43, 50, 133
   cast iron, 133
   terracotta, 49
Potato, 27, 83
   mashed, 83
Potato flakes, 67
Potato starch, 218
Potbrood, 132
Potbrood Dough, 132–33
Powder sugar, 227
Pre-Dough Ingredients, 76
Preferment, 96–97, 106, 142, 144–46, 152, 156, 159
   tea levain, 156
Pre-fermented Dough Ingredients, 66
Preferment Ingredients, 142
Preferment levain, 107
Preheat, 19, 70, 129, 193, 213
Preshape, 24, 26, 34, 39, 50
Princess of Sweden, 2

Prize, 138
Process, lock-in, 234
Profession, 22, 52, 62, 71, 111, 155, 194
Professional engagements, 207
Professionals, 134, 211
   baking conditions, 19
Programme, 40, 94, 100, 164
   professional Pastry & Baking, 221
Proofer, 17, 39, 102, 107
Proofing basket, well-floured, 70
Proofing process, 51
Provençal surprise bread, 63
Pumpkin, 128–30, 196
Pumpkin Purée, 129
Pumpkin seeds, 85, 130
   toasted, 130
Pumpkin tarts, 194
Punch, 66, 86
Purée, 61, 130
Purified filtered water, 165–66
Purified seawater, 114–15

Q
Quills, decorative, 112

R
Radio interviews, 93
Raisins, 104, 109–10
Raspberries, 44–45, 181, 199, 205, 219
Raspberry Fanciers, 204–5
Raspberry jelly, 215–16
Raspberry pear marinade, 234
Rectangles, 61, 97, 121, 180, 192, 229
Rectangular cheesecakes, 180
Red Date Financier, 43
Red dates, 43
Red rum, 210
Refrigerate overnight, 82, 112
Regulator, 87–88
Remould, 109, 121
Representing bones, 111
Representing Team Canada, 33
Restaurants, 4-star NYC, 222
Resting period, 14, 66
Rhubarb, 188–89
Rhubarb Filling, 189
Richard, Ludovic, 209–10
Richemont Club International, 105, 197, 216
Richemont Club Italia, 103, 105
Richemont Ireland, 100
Ricky, 131–32
Ricky's Potbrood, 132
Rimini, 23, 105, 138–39
Rings, 152
Rinse, 25
River Monsters, 94, 231
Robert, 81–82
Robert's Potato and Dill Shamrock Bread, 82

Rosa, 171
Rosewater, 213
Rouen, 22, 56
Royal confectioner Günther, 181
Royal Wedding Cake Assembly, 186
Russia, 4, 52, 117, 138, 237
Russian Taiga Bread, 118
Rye, 7–8, 10, 17, 27
Rye Dough, 70
Rye flour, 10, 50–51, 58, 66–67, 69–70, 75, 119, 123
   dark, 10, 237
   meal, 73–74

S

SABA (South Africa Bakers Association), 131
Salée mixture, 219
Sandwiched Earl Grey-Lavender Macarons, 223
San Francisco Baking Institute, 164
Sauce
   pomelo, 43
   white, 208
Savoury Twist, 208
Score, 19, 27, 54, 110, 131, 167, 171
Scully, Ciaran, 93
Seam, 17, 25, 44, 128, 147, 170
Sea salt, 85, 154, 160, 223
Sébastien Lagrue, 56–57
Seedless dates, 46
Segments, 127, 162
Selection, 4, 139, 190
Senegal team in pastry and bakery, 120
Sequence, 175
Serbotel Fair, 52
Sergio, 200–201
Sesame seeds, 46–47, 106–7, 169
   toasted, 150, 169
Setter, 96, 98, 157
Shanghai Young Bakers' School, 40
Shaping, final, 15–16, 67
Sheeter, 51, 162
Sieve, 17, 25, 54, 61, 119, 153, 192
Sift, 110, 126, 205
SIGEP Bread Cup, 23, 111, 138
Silicone moulds, 43, 227
Silicone paper, 77, 186, 213
Silver medal, 48
Simit Dough, 149
Singapore, 122–23, 127, 141
Slattery, John, 196–97
Slicing, 35, 234
Slide, 18, 157
Soaker, 169
Social media platforms, 49, 127
Soft butter, 35, 49
Son Dillon, v, 92, 98
Sophie, v, 56–57, 86, 92, 99
Sourdough, 14–15, 17–18, 72–74, 78, 80, 94, 96, 118–19, 123–24, 139–40

Sourdough & Craft Bakers, 131
Sourdough bread, 16, 78, 94, 98
Sourdough flavour, 167
Sourdough preferment, 69
Sourdough Starter Ingredients, 165
South Africa Bakers Association (SABA), 131
South America, 23, 93, 220
Spanish baking team, 133
Spanish confectionery magazine, 23
Spanish national team, 138
Spanish national team captain, 138
Spelled jenipapo, 26
Spiral mixer, 50, 57, 73, 82–83, 126, 154, 160
Spirals, 106, 140
Spoon, 33, 35, 153
Spray, 19, 124, 126, 162, 167, 186, 213
Sprinkle, 29–30, 32, 64, 107, 155, 201, 211
Sprouted Wheat/Lentils, 24–25
Squash, red Kuri, 195
Squeeze, 185
Stavropol Russia, 4
Steam, 19, 27, 54, 58, 75, 77–78, 81, 116, 131, 141, 143, 171, 178
Stencils, 124, 139, 171
   crab, 124, 126
Step, 16, 19, 54–55, 58–59, 62, 66, 81, 113, 230
Sticky Bun Glaze, 153
Strawberries, 184, 197
   fresh, 199
Strawberry Fruits Compote, 185
Strength, 16, 59, 112, 140, 166, 227–28
Stretch, 58, 92, 97, 104, 126, 157, 170
Stretch and fold, 24, 26, 77, 80, 83, 140, 143, 157
Streusel, 153
   baked, 151, 155
String plaits, 62, 175
Strings, 61, 126, 166
Strong baker's flour, 67, 201
Strong baker's flour/AP/flour/T-55, 112
Strong bread flour, 82–83, 101, 104, 107, 217, 236
Students, 37, 52, 82, 99–100, 108
Subject matter expert, 232
Sugar syrup, 191
Sugar Wash, 103
Sultanas, 101, 151, 154
Superstar baker, 23
Supplies, 145, 182
Svet Ronjenja, 87
Sweat, 93, 105
Sweden, 2, 78, 138, 141, 181–82
Sweden's wedding cake, 182
Sweet, 22, 38, 151, 157, 190, 201, 203
Swell, 69–70, 74
Swelling stage, 74
Swinnen, Benny, 187
Swiss Master Baker, 193
Swiss World Champion, 193
Switzerland, 193, 196, 216

T

T-55, 60, 67, 109
T-55 bread flour, 156
T-55 bread flour/strong bakers, 228
T-85 flour, 156
T-85 Yecroa Flour, 156
T-1370 flour, 118
T-1800, 69
Table, 10, 104, 119, 121, 167, 175, 224
Taipei Bakery Association, 144
Taipei International Bake Show (TIBS), 176
Tamarind, 53, 55–56
Tamarind Juice syrup, 53
Tamarind's healing properties, 55
Tapioca pearls, 144, 147–48
   black, 145
Tapioca Tea Bread, 148
Tartare Café &Wine Bar, 84
Tartlets, 194, 199
Tarts, 2, 187–99, 210
   traditional Manchester, 197
Taste, 1, 37, 48, 108, 128, 231
Taste buds, 128, 204
Team Canada, 37
Team China, 40
Team coach, 3, 105
Team Ireland, 95
Team member Solveig Tofte, 65
Tea powder, 146
   black, 156
Teaspoons, 33, 43, 85
Tea towels, 17, 102, 117
Technological Institute, 171
Technological University, 81
Technological University Dublin, 3, 207, 214
Technology, 3, 27, 231–32
Temperature, 5, 11–13, 31, 44, 70, 74, 81
   ambient, 166, 175
Tension, 131, 167
   elastic recoil, 233
Thessaloniki, 211–12
Third European championship, 136
Thumbs, 12, 107, 140
TIBS (Taipei International Bake Show), 176
TIBS Cup, 111
Tie, 126, 150, 166, 224
Time baking, 78, 158
Tobias, 67–69
Tobias Exner Recipes, 68
Toby's Windmill Rye Bread, 69
Tomato, 134, 150, 174
Tomato pulp, 49
Tomato sauce, 125
Tonka beans, 78
Torch, 186, 196
Toronto, 36
Torsadé, 57
Toulouse, 56

Train, 104, 222
Training, 52, 57, 68, 71, 75–76, 114, 120, 204, 207
Trimoline, 43, 61, 160, 227
Turkish simit, 149
Turmeric, 159, 161, 163
Turmeric Bee Pollen Brioche Feuilletee, 159
Turmeric Pastry Cream, 161
Turmeric powder, 126

U

UCHG (University College Hospital Galway), 90–91
UIB, 171
UIBC International Congress, 212
Uncle Bob's Bakery, 203
Union International Bakers and Confectioners, 232
United Kingdom, 150, 196
United States, 155, 157, 163, 168, 221, 225–26
University, 4, 36, 82, 144
Unsalted butter, 29–30, 126, 146, 153, 160, 217, 224
Unsalted room temperature butter, 30
Uruguay, 171–72
US Dark rye, 237

V

Valencia, 136
Valencian bread, 136
Vanilla, 195, 198, 205, 211, 227
Vanilla pods, 153
Verona, 144, 171–72
Vicente Sancho Colomer, 136
Viennoiserie, 28, 41, 44, 59, 187
Viennoiserie candidate, 28, 117
Viennoiserie category, 157, 225
Viennoiserie Ingredients, 43–44
Viennoiserie specialist, 45, 151
Vietnam, 175–76
Vietnamese French, 176
Vincente, 136
Vitamins, 120, 159
Vitamins B1, 55

W

Wang Li, 40
Wang Li's Red Date & Pomelo Brioche, 41
Warm place, 17, 46, 69–70, 102, 118–19, 123, 159
Wash, 101, 103, 129, 202
Water temperature, 12, 29
Wayne's Spiced Apple Streusel Buns, 150–51
Weinheim, 4, 68, 71, 75–76, 100, 138
Wheat, 7–10, 23–25, 130, 132
   red, 9
   soft, 8–9
   sprouted, 23–24
   toasted, 128–29
Wheat flour, 8–9, 25–26, 51, 80, 98, 128–29, 236
   soft, 85, 189
Wheat grains, 7–9, 25, 142

Wheat sprouts, 25
Wheat starch, 195
Whip, 183, 189, 205
Whisking, 198
White chocolate, 151–52, 197, 203, 216
White rye, 237
Whole-wheat flour, 129
Wife, 52, 89, 92–93, 171
Wild Strawberry Curd, 184
Windowpane, 41, 112, 146, 160, 167, 202, 206
Winner, 23, 64, 120, 164
Winning podium placement, 105
Woo, William, 127–28
Workshops, 56, 141, 190
World Bakery Competition, 149
World Bakery Cup, 49, 207
World Bakery Masters, 155, 176
World Bakery Master's Competition, 28
World Baking Masters' Competitions, 3
World Champion, 59, 64, 81, 114, 206
World Champion Chocolatine, 56
World Championships, 82, 117, 138
World Champion Viennoiserie, 59
World Chocolate Masters in Brazil, 22
World Guinness Book, 122
World silver medal, 168
World Silver Medallist Chocolatine, 86

Y

Yeast, 11, 13, 29, 49–51, 96–97, 104, 107, 132–33, 145–46, 160
YouTube channel, 5, 233
Yuen, Peter, 57, 225–26, 231

Z

Zacwas, 170
Zagreb, 197, 217
Zakowski, Mike, 168
Zimmermann, 207
　Pierre, 60, 64–65
Zinc, 55, 120

Notes

www.ingramcontent.com/pod-product-compliance
Lightning Source LLC
Chambersburg PA
CBHW042359280426
43661CB00096B/1167